T0199112

JESUS
THE CARCASS
AND THE
WICKED GOD

PATRICK WANGUI

JESUS THE CARCASS AND THE WICKED GOD

iUniverse books may be ordered through booksellers or by contacting:

iUniverse
1663 Liberty Drive
Bloomington, IN 47403
www.iuniverse.com
1-800-Authors (1-800-288-4677)

ISBN: 978-1-5320-5989-6 (sc)
ISBN: 978-1-5320-5990-2 (e)

Print information available on the last page.

iUniverse rev. date: 10/05/2018

CONTENTS

DEDICATION

I DEDICATE THIS WORK TO ALL OPEN-MINDED PEOPLE IN THE whole universe, as well as Diana Ingado.

ACKNOWLEDGEMENT

I want to acknowledge the Vice Chancellor, Professor Teresa Akeng'a- University of Eldoret- for her great support and effort in transforming my life; had it not been for her kindness, my life would have remained a wreck up-to-date. My family members: Mother Velonica Wangui, brother Isaak Ndung'u, Uncles: Stephen Kinyanjui, Joseph Ndung'u, Nelson Gacheru and Paul Ng'ang'a, for their unwavering support in my life's journey. My role-models: H.E. Daniel Toroitich Arap Moi, H.E. Vladimir Vladimirovich Putin, H.E. Emilio Mwai Kibaki, H.E. Yoweri Kaguta Museveni, Dr Otieno Argwings, Dr Ayubu Anapapa, for inspiring me to be a greater person in this world. My friends: Chirchir Kiplimo Emmanuel, Ishaili Cylus Etiang, Simon Nga'ng'a Macharia, Paul Waithaka Mukunya, Abraham Kariuki Gakuo and David Gaciri for their support, encouragement and inspiration. The Palm-House Foundation-Kenya- for enabling me to cross the secondary school's bridge for the sake of transforming my life, my family, my society, my nation and the world at large. The Higher Education Loans Board (HELB Kenya) for giving me the financial power to go beyond secondary school's education.

ABSTRACT

THE BOOK HAS SEVERAL SHORT NARRATIVES EACH WITH A different heading. It is titled *"Jesus The Carcass and The Wicked God"* which are the titles to two of the stories inside. The story, *Jesus The Carcass* reveals how the religion is used to loot the pockets of the poor. It gives us an insight on how those who understand the Bible use it to enrich themselves at the expense of the congregation and the wickedness they practice in pretence. *The Wicked God* is about the life of a young girl whose life was fully promising but took a U-turn after receiving what was and is termed as 'Good News'. Everything changed and she ended up leading one of the most terrible lives on earth. Her family lost its glory and name. It's as if she had found Satan rather than her Saviour. She found herself in shackles of doom, her life entangled in what seemed mysterious, aborted her dreams, her great visions became blurred and found herself and her family in a dark cocoon of confusion. The gods of luck and blessings departed from her life, leaving gods and spirits of misfortunes, poverty, bad luck and curses behind. She lost meaning even to herself. She eventually died a very painful and heart-breaking death. The story captures the picture of the majority of the people who become miserable and losers in the name of seeking God. It is a very sad, demoralizing and heart-breaking experience.

There are other stories inside which capture the scenario of the societies we live in as human beings in this world. For example: *The Madness* is a story that shows the doubts that exist in mind and the war between science and religion. *An Illusion or a Dream* is another one that shows the right picture of modern day African states, especially those that are facing grave leadership problems and the eventual liberation of such nations.

Judas Iscariot the Saviour is a story that represents the current leadership in Africa that cannot be discerned by the common eye. It reveals how such leadership is used to impoverish citizens and how the leaders are never in power to solve problems that are facing the general population. It is meant for common people to see the real picture in plain language. It also reveals a general weakness among citizens which is the actual cause of all their troubles and challenges as well as poverty. Traits such as selfishness and shocking greed are manifested among the leaders. *The Infamous Sacrifice* is meant to give us a warning on taking short-cuts in life. It guides us through some sacrifices that are really disgusting and the eventual outcome is the shocking death and disappearance of those involved. It sheds some light to those who value short-cuts, luck, goodies from nowhere, and to those who disregard thinking twice whenever a deal is 'too good'.

AN ILLUSION OR A DREAM?

THE BOY AND HIS SISTER, OYUDA AND AYUDA RESPECTIVELY, were not well blessed on the side of academics. They were twins and spent each second, minute, hour and day together. They had been chased out of school for failure to make any progress in nursery school. They could not pass any test in school to help them proceed to class one from nursery school. They stayed with their parents at home; the parents had no idea where to take them, apart from school, where "they were unfit". Though that was the situation, they never got ashamed of their children but loved them with passion. They knew that even though they were rejected in school, they must have something else to offer to the world. That something else was unknown to them at that time.

They were nicknamed Dreamer and Visionary respectively, by their friends at their village. They used to tell their friends so much each day about what they had dreamt every night. They could tell them how they dreamt about heavy rains, visitors to their village, drought, pests attacking crops, thugs invading their village, among other calamities and good news. Each time they narrated these things to them, they were really astounded at their accuracy and details in happening. They could sometimes get scared when they forecasted the death of a villager or a grisly road accident. For example, they could mention the names of individuals who were to be involved in a road accident and those who could be lucky to survive as well as those who could not make it. They could name individuals who were to be attacked by thugs and what would be stolen. They could inform you in advance when you were to receive visitors, as well as the good rains that would fall on land and the corresponding harvest. These things could happen in accurate details as the two had forecasted. People built their trust in these two kids long before they were even ten years old.

Their parents took keenness in what the two used to narrate as dreams. They could discuss their children's gift almost daily. Their father told his wife often that it must be that that was their talent; dreaming and forecasting, and not books. They had actually realized one secret about their children; the two dreamt one dream concurrently. Each could narrate to them, in the absence of the other, how they dreamt and finally end up giving the same details. If Oyuda said he dreamt immediately after getting into bed, then Ayuda could say she did so immediately after retiring to bed. If Ayuda said she saw a well decorated coffin of Mr so and so, Oyuda said he saw a well decorated casket of Mr so and so. This amazed the parents so much that they decided never to share such a secret with outsiders. They knew that the ability to dream each dream simultaneously was a confirmation of its truth and such a dream was bound to happen. People used to march continuously to their compound each day trying to consult these kids of any help in case of major troubles in the village. They were lucky as they never went home without a feedback. They decided to be contributing something to the children as a way of appreciating their work; be it food stuffs, agricultural produce, money, clothes, furniture, home appliances and such likes. This way, the two and their parents were assured of their daily bread and progress in life. They became rich and the parents were happy as they actually confirmed that the children's talent and gift was in their ability to tell what people could not see with the naked eyes; and was never in school and books.

The trend of foreseeing became well established until they were pros in that field at the age of fifteen years. It was in their sixteenth year that they narrated to their parents a dream that brought confusion. Dreamer narrated his dream to his father while Visionary told hers to her mother. When the two compared the narratives, they saw it was one and the same thing. "My father, yesterday I had a dream just before dawn, before the cock crowed. No sooner had my dream ended than when the rooster crowed." "What was the dream, my son", the father asked his child. "You want me to narrate it to you at this time?" "Yes. If you can recall it, then you may say it. I am ready to hear what you have." "Of course dad, I can recall every detail as usual. I haven't forgotten anything and I think it's hard to forget it. It was peculiar and never before have I had such things in a dream. It is the only dream so far that informed me what shall happen beyond our village. All the other dreams are about our village but this one is about the country. It is very unique." "If you narrate it to me, then I shall be glad to hear it and see how unique it is. What could it be about if it covers the whole country? Could it be that you have become the nation's seer? May I hear it please? Take your breakfast and find me under that tree yonder. I am eager to hear it. Take the breakfast at your pace and then come, I will be waiting. Leave your sister with your mother in the kitchen."

"Father, I also had a dream this morning. May I narrate it to you?" His daughter exclaimed. "Ayuda, let me come and hear your dream later. At the moment, you may take your breakfast and start narrating it to your mother." "Ok dad. I will tell it to my mum." "Thank you for understanding. See you later." He then left them in the house and went to rest under a tree they used to shelter themselves from the daily scorching sun. He started thinking more about what his son had told him; about the unique dream. His mind was lost in thoughts as he wondered why his son could have a dream concerning the whole nation. Later on, Oyuda joined him; he was very excited and seemed to have enjoyed his breakfast. "Father, I want to tell you my dream, are you afraid, you look gloomy? Are you still interested?" "Yes, my son. I am very interested and ready to hear from you. I have been waiting for you. Sit down, relax and tell me what you saw in your dream." "Ok, let me take some seconds to regain my breath, I came running and almost sweat. Did you take your breakfast?" "Yes, I have taken mine; I woke up earlier than you and your sister did." "Wow, I thought you came here on an empty stomach. Did you enjoy the meal? My mother prepared us some sausages and toasts. I have enjoyed the meal so much that I would like her to do it more often. She has never prepared us sausages but it's like this was our day." "Hahahaaaa, I told her to give you a special breakfast so that you may also see that God can provide us with anything we want in life, and that everything is possible with Him. I instructed her to prepare a special lunch too so that you are able to appreciate what we do in order to give you the best life possible. But do not expect a special supper. Special breakfast and lunch are enough though. Is it alright with you?" "Yes, everything is alright with me. I look forward to that lunch and the normal supper too. May I tell you what I have?" "Yes, do it."

"In my dream, I saw a boy. The boy was born in a cave. This cave was in a forest, covered with cobwebs at the entrance and hardly did people see it. To the few who saw it, it made no sense as they could not imagine anybody living in it. They thought it was meant for wild animals and not a single human being could dare get into it for a peep. The cave had extremely poor conditions for life; there was no enough food, very cold, ever dark, hardly did he get water, wrapped himself in tattered clothes, diseases attacked him frequently and was extremely weak. Days could pass without food and he had no hope of surviving at all. Conditions were harsh to him but he found himself still alive. People did not know that such a boy existed. At a very tender age, he had suffered beyond measure and knew very well what it meant by hard life. His parents lived in the same cave as they had no place to call their home. They could walk around the forest trying to gather fruits for their meals. But it was not a guarantee that they got something every time they went out. Most of the times, they came back empty-handed. Life was terrible but could not give up as long as they were still alive."

"This boy attained the age of an adult according to our laws. He moved out of the cave for the first time and left the parents there. Outside the cave, he saw the sky and the environment; trees, animals, land and a seasonal-river that flowed near the cave as it was on a rainy season. The sun rays were very 'sweet to his body' and he could see the moon in the middle of the sky. He then exclaimed, "Wow, what a beautiful scene! What are these? It's so amazing. The whole thing is fascinating and breath-taking. What a wonderful place to live in. I want to live here forever." "Immediately the boy altered those words, Heaven opened and he saw what was in there. He was very afraid but a voice from therein said to him, "Do not fear, we are with you. You shall do as we wish and powers shall be given to you. You shall rule over my people with justice, integrity and wisdom. Let us give you a guide from this place who shall be informing you on what to do and what not to do." Then, a huge ball of fire dropped and hit the ground, near his feet. A hole was created and Hell was opened too."

"A voice came from Hell saying to him, "As Heaven has found it wise to anoint and consecrate you, so has the Hell found it. You shall execute justice among His people, small and great, rich and poor, weak and strong, same and different and all that. People have suffered and are crying for justice, equality and good life. Be strong for you shall make it, simply because He is with you. Your enemies shall not be able to defeat you. Be blessed as He has chosen you among all." At that moment, a large eagle descended from Heaven and landed on his left hand side. It spoke like a human being. "You have been chosen and brought up in this very cave for the sake of God's purpose; to deliver His people. You have been trained the hard way so that you can be a qualified leader and ruler. One who can understand when people are poor, ill, and crying for justice; one who can see the sufferings of the people. You shall see the pain of tribalism, nepotism, corruption, filthy courts, fruitless commissions, rotten police force, sectors that are under rogues, elections that are meaningless, evil generation, lawlessness among the people, dead church, useless constitutions, wickedness in the name of democracy and rights, devil's governments, economy that is in chains, among other abominations. His people are really in snares and cannot disentangle themselves without His hand. You shall clean the nation and do away with what is wrong. You have been given powers to loot out what God has not planted and plant what God shall give you; justice, equity, order, wisdom, true democracy, and the right independence. Look at me and take this." The boy looked at the eagle and saw it lean towards his right hand side. At that point, a drop of unknown liquid sprang from its right eye and got into his left eye. He quickly moved his hand to rub it but it had dissolved into his eye, not to be felt again."

"From that moment, the boy got the spirit of leadership and loathed evil. He could no longer stand the pain of the evils that were in his nation. The eagle then took the boy by its wings and flew him to another place in the city. They rested on one of the main streets and watched what was happening. There he saw all that the eagle had explained. People were killing each other (thugs and thieves), conmen were enjoying their work, innocent people were losing their pieces of land in an unimaginable ways (land grabbing was order of the day), the government was never there for the common citizen (in fact, laws, regulations and rules were being made in parliament to guard the government and big companies against the common citizens; the citizens were treated like animals and enemies of the government and big companies), judges always perverted justices and never considered the poor and less privileged (acquitting the guilty simply because of money and other wicked reasons), the police forces were more like criminal gangs and were greedy for bribes; never helped any citizen and were only there for the rich, mighty and strong. The government was busy looting the resources of the country (killing the elites and patriots, allowing massive corruption, defending the rich and mighty, neglecting the poor majority, barring development, practicing poor politics that's only meant to hurt the people, practicing tribalism and nepotism to unbearable levels, using commissions as another political parties to drive their agendas home, using courts and other independent bodies as their machine tools to enforce wickedness and filth in the land, were striving to turn anyone good into an evil man, among others. In fact, the government was like a workshop for turning anything good into evil). The doctors were busy silently killing the patients rather than improving their health, were really determined to make money and increasing their wealth and riches, leaving the citizens to die."

"The church was a corpse, a business centre and a thugs' hiding place. It was full of abominations, unholy, wicked, and a home for evil spirits and demons; Satan had a say in that church. It was impossible to keep on looking inside the church that was meant for holy works. There was no one to be trusted in the whole land. Each person was on their own way. The right track was full of grass, bushes, trees and cobwebs. The wrong path was well demarcated and clearly visible to all, as all travelled therein. There was a big lamp and a bundle of candles but all had been extinguished, leaving utter darkness covering the land. He also saw drug barons and was greatly surprised to see that all the barons were big people, bigwigs, politicians, government officials, police, rich business people, judges and lawyers, heads of different commissions, doctors and teachers. He could not stand what his eyes were seeing. He turned to the eagle and wept bitterly, saying, "You mean God is so gracious that He has even let these people live? No, you don't mean all this. People cannot be living in such a nation. How did God allow it? Why not wipe all these people out of this land? My heart fails me when I turn my face to see this. I cannot stand it anymore. Please take me away from this place; take me away whether I am alive or dead." Tears went down his cheeks till the eyes were dry. He knelt down and said, "I have a headache and need some rest, please allow me to sleep a little bit.""

"The eagle replied, "I have brought you here to see what God's country has been turned into. Take courage and see more. You must see all this so that when you hear us say that God is just, gracious and merciful, then you shall understand it with ease. You must feel the pain in your heart and mind so that when you start cleansing the land, you shall never turn back to regret it, you shall be delighted in seeing the nation holy and full of justice. Your tears that you have shed today shall never go in vain, shall never be shed in vain and shall be greatly rewarded and wiped out of your face. You shall be glad to see a clean nation that God can call His. Lift yourself up and see more." He supported himself with its wings and stood on his feet. He saw the general population lost; everyone was busy hurting their neighbour, they were busy practicing adultery, promiscuity, beastly, fornication and prostitution. He saw naked ladies, women and girls lying on the streets in darkness and males were busy working on them. Some went ahead to do it with animals; naked girls and young ladies were surrounded by dogs in corners of the streets, men were busy on domesticated animals; cows, goats, donkeys, chicken and other animals were groaning under the bellies of men, some ladies were using objects like bananas, sticks etc while some men were masturbating, and the whole thing was eye-torturing. The streets were full of rotted odour. He fainted at the sight but one of the eagle's wings touched him and gave him strength to remain alert and watching."

"He turned his face to the eagle and whispered, due to lack of enough energy to help raise his voice, "I better die, and there is no need of living. There is no benefit to those who live on such a land. Where is the Lord? Tell Him to inter the whole nation, to perish out of His sight. How can He tolerate such people? His grace and love should cease on man from this day onwards. Please, let me rest in peace, in pieces or in beans, for I don't imagine living with such images in my mind and heart." "Live, for you have been chosen to turn it into God's lovable nation. You must see it all so that you can do His work to completion." He saw families that were languishing in pain; dad was sacrificing his children for the sake of money and wealth, children were killing their parents to inherit what they had, sons were raping their parents and grandparents, there was witchcraft being practiced in families, betrayal was a common thing and there was no peace. It was dangerous to walk on the land because everyone was a menace to each of the citizens. Diseases had engulfed the population and land in general; crops were attacked by unknown pests and diseases, animals could not be treated and people were experiencing new diseases and infections each day. Diseases were complicated beyond their knowledge and wisdom. The land was under a curse and no blessing remained therein."

"He was shown more than he could retain in his mind but was promised to be helped in remembering all. He saw a parliament that looked like a standard one class; small boys and girls were fighting, boxing each other, slapping their friends, throwing chairs, tables, books, sand and stones at each other, walking on tables and chairs, shouting at each other and insulting one another. The place was full of deafening noise and ululations. Some were even tearing each other's clothes. Some were carrying toy-guns, others had pen-caps for whistling, some were rolling on the floor while others had cans full of water. The boy turned to the eagle again and asked, "Isn't this a parliament? Who are those playing such dirty games in such an honourable place? Who took kids into such a house? Why don't you talk to them and chase them out? Chase them, scold and reprimand them so that they can clear out of that place because honourable members might come any time and find the place untidy and filth." The eagle laughed sarcastically and responded, "Those are the men and women in charge of my Lord's country. They are the honourable members. They rule and make laws. That is how rotten they are; it's is impossible to differentiate them from any kid and they are as corrupt as garbage. But don't worry; you are the Lord's servant to clear the mess out of the land. Come and see this." He turned to the far corner of the city and was surprised to see two books. "What are these books for? One is very tidy but covered in blood and iniquity and some black money beside it while the other one is very dusty, surrounded by more papers that are smelling like dead rats and seems useless and meaningless; it is as if it was left here thousands of years ago. What do the two contain?""

"The eagle delayed to respond for some time. "That tidy book but full of blood is the Bible, the Lord's Holy Book. It was given to men by God, to guide them, to make them know Him well and to have the right knowledge about what He likes and loathes. Those in charge (pastors, priests, and many servants) turned it into an abomination. They hold it with hands that have shed blood of fellow humans, they use it to gather riches and it has been turned into a tool for robbing the poor. The men who hold it are likened to tombs that are full of anything that is disgusting; they are the wickedest creatures on the land. The second book is the constitution or the laws of man; meant to govern the land. It was full of dust because it is just a bunch of papers that were collected together and kept aside; it was so because since it was prepared, no one has tried to open it to implement sentence after sentence, word by word and comma by comma; it's only accumulating dust in offices. It was meant for ghosts and dust to read, study and implement; and not human beings who wrote it. The many papers you saw are the laws made after the constitution; laws made by the kids you saw fighting and all that. These laws are not actually for the sake of improving the life of citizens. Let us open some papers and see what is inside." The eagle perused the papers and a cloud of dust rose from the book, almost choking them to death. It took some papers at random and read to the boy. "You see, this one is talking about lowering the age at which children should be engaged in sex. It is indicated that the age should be reduced to allow them enjoy their rights. This one talks about children accessing the family planning drugs; that children have the right to plan themselves without being questioned. They can use these drugs at the "right age" according to them. That is what we have in these papers. Look! This paper is all about the rights of kids in school; that they should never be canned for whatever reason. It talks about the rights of the kids, whether they are rotten or not; they should go caught free. Come and see this one.""

"He looked closely to see what the paper had. "This one has the "honourable members' remuneration". It is about sending the retired honourable members with plenty of money as a reward for serving the nation in the right way. In fact, all these other papers I am holding are about the money these honourable members should receive after any term they serve the nation. There is no need of seeing other papers because you might faint again or have a heart attack." The boy turned away from the eagle and wept bitterly, "You mean they only concentrate on such laws when the citizens are dying of hunger, drought and diseases? With such poverty hovering among the citizens, how can the city have such laws that have nothing to do with improving their lives and living standards? I don't understand the kind of nation you are showing me. Why don't you kill me and chose another man? There are so many men on this land who can do your work." "No, you cannot escape it; it is your task to make things straight and right. God has prepared you for the task and for a long time. He has taken care of you, fed you and kept you alive for the sake of His nation. Let us now go to another corner of the city." The two focussed on other corners of the city and discussed every aspect in details."

"Then, the two sat down on a branch of a tree and the eagle informed the boy a lot. "The first part is over. There are two parts, one is over and the other one is coming. Just take a break and rest for some time before I show you the second part. The third part is not necessary for you to be shown because you shall have achieved the mission by that time. That third part is only about the final state of the nation after you have cleansed it. Just relax for some time and have your energy rejuvenated." The boy fell asleep while the eagle watched over him. In fact, the eagle stretched its wings and covered him, giving him the right warmth. The eagle did not close or blink its eyes for the entire period the boy was sound asleep. Later, the boy woke up and said in confusion, "Mum, where is my food?" The eagle responded, "Take this and eat for the sake of the second part of today's work." It gave him a fruit that refreshed his body and mind. Then it said, "Let me inform you what you shall see. Many shall try to bring you down but in vain. You have been anointed and none can revoke that. Come and see this field." The boy found himself in a field that was full of corpses, bones, blood and a heavy stench of decaying materials. Rivers of blood were flowing from the field into the forest. Fowls were all over; vultures and other meat-eating ones. Hyenas and wolves, jackals, pigs and hounds were also hovering in the field. There was no wind to refresh the air but hot air was covering and rising from the field."

"There were also men who looked like animals in the field. They were holding knives, axes, hoes, swords, bolos, needles, poisonous chemicals, ropes, nails and hammers, spears, bows and arrows, iron rods, sharp sticks, metals that had hooks, guns and pistols, grenades, metal-sheets that were sharper than knives, heavy chains and shackles and other weapons. These well-armed men were feeding on the corpses, bones and drank the thick blood from those rivers. Then, the eagle gave the boy a wire wound into a whip, a pen and a paper that had some writings. "Take all that and get into the field. That field is the nation. Those men with all forms of weapons are the leaders and the wicked ones on the land; you are to wipe such people out of the nation. The carcasses you have seen are the work of their hands for the time they have gone out of the way. They are feeding on their own iniquity as food. You shall wipe all of them out, clear the trash, and refresh the air. Then shall God live there with the citizens. You cannot die for He is with you and in you. You are doing His work and are out on His mission. You shall not rest or slumber until the work is over. Get into the field and fight like a well-trained soldier." The eagle pushed him a little into the field and the boy found himself in the middle of the men."

"All the men started attacking him and he positioned himself strategically for war. Each time he swung the whip, some men fell to the ground, bleeding profusely and succumbed to death. The whip was more of a sword than a normal whip. It was cutting deep into the body and could drop one's head with a single swing. Men were determined to kill him but not a single weapon fell on him. The closer you got to him, the faster the whip caught you and sent you to the ground dead. Some men realized what was happening; they dropped their weapons and ran away, they went beyond the field, just to save their lives. Some chained themselves with the shackles and chains they had. Some slept amongst the corpses and pretended to be dead while some begged for forgiveness. Each time the boy killed some men, the pen cancelled some writings on the paper. Each time some men chained themselves, the pen cancelled some other writings. Each time some men pleaded for mercy, the pen cancelled some other writings. He took those chained and those who were forgiven and forced them to dig a deep and wide grave. They did it and buried every corpse, bone and destroyed the source of the river that had blood. They also filled the river with sand and the field was clean. Then, a heavy wind blew from the forest and cleared the dirty air. There was fresh air and tidy ground. Immediately the place got clean and tidy, the pen finished cancelling all the writings on the paper. The eagle called heavy rains to descend from Heaven and watered the place. Grass grew and blossomed, making the field green and beautiful; a nice place to rest. "Where did that grass come from yet the field was bare after I cleaned it?" "That grass was there, it was hindered from growing by those dead bodies that were lying on it." The eagle congratulated the boy and said to him, "All that you have seen is what you shall do practically. The field is your country and you have been chosen to clear the filth. When you saw the grass growing, that means that your country is rich and full of resources but cannot develop because the wickedness has barred it from happening. Your nation can change to another and better level but the men therein are sabotaging every aspect of development. When you are twenty years old, that is the work you shall start. Go back to the cave and wait for two more years, as you are now eighteen.""

"The boy sweat and whispered, "But I am lucky because I have never seen schools, I am unknown to people, I am not talented whatsoever, I am not rich and not from rich family, my family has no roots in the government, those people in charge of the nation are stronger than me and I am not attractive to anyone's eyes. So, God will excuse me and choose another man. I am not trained as a leader or as a soldier. Please leave me alone because such works and tasks or missions require experts and I am not among them. God requires the best man to do His work, I am not the best, and I am the least among those living." "God doesn't require you to be like those men who are experts because all the evil men you have seen are experts in all fields but have failed the nation." The eagle took the boy back to the entrance of the cave and left; flying back to Heaven. Voices were heard in Heaven and Hell. Claps and shouts were heard in both places, saying in unison, "You have made it, with the help of our Lord. Great is the Lord who has seen it wise to make the land holy once again." Then the openings to Heaven and Hell closed and the boy was left thinking hard about what he had witnessed."

"Dad, that was my dream and I saw it unique. Do you find it peculiar too?" His dad was confused and lost in thoughts. "What kind of dream is that? What boy is that? Where shall he come from? Which tribe and how shall we know when he comes? Which generation shall that be? The dream is for sure amazing and different from the others you usually narrate to us. It is even longer by far than all the others you dreamt before. Who is this boy again? That means God has seen the state of our land and has plans to change it. I told you my son, God can do anything and it's possible for Him to raise His own man to save the rest. I know you are extremely tired and need to rest, let's go back to the house and see what your mum is doing."

They left for house. When the mother told their father what Ayuda had narrated, the two got shocked at what their children had revealed. The parents could not understand it as it seemed more of an illusion than a reality and a dream. They could not imagine such a scenario at all. They cast doubts on it but still new that what the two dreamt could happen as none of their dreams went in vain. "My dear wife, what do you think about that dream? Is it really a dream or an illusion? Could our children be out of their minds? What can you say?" "I also got confused. Could it be an illusion? No, it's a dream and shall happen. They always dream and every dream happens as they narrate. Oh, it's an illusion because such a dream is very detailed and hard to happen; the nation cannot be changed into a good place. Oh, no, no, no, it's a dream bound to happen. God can do it. But what is it by the way? Only God knows. Leave it to God my dear husband."

The two could not tell whether their children were narrating a dream or an illusion. They left the table-room; their mother went to the kitchen to prepare the special lunch while their dad went to rest in bed. Oyuda and Ayuda were left at the table-room discussing their dream.

THE INFAMOUS SACRIFICES

———◆•◆•◆———

THE PEOPLE WOKE UP EARLY THAT DAY AS USUAL. EACH WENT ON their daily chores. Mr Kamau was also up and ready to face the new day. In his house, passers-by could hear some voices from inside but it was the voices of the family members who were discussing the activities of the day. The village centre was not far from the Kamau's homestead. He got out of the house to have a general view of the new day. As if he saw something extraordinary in the far distance, he stood slightly far from the door-step and remained there- stiff like a statue. His eyes were firmly fixed into the horizon that encircled the distant land. But it was not something visible with the naked and physical eye that he was staring at, it was something he saw with his mental eyes.

Mr Kamau was a well-known man in the whole village and beyond. Many knew him through other villagers. Majority used to describe him as a giant because of his huge body-size. His muscles and height were astonishing. In first sight, one could describe him as a remnant of the ancient giants narrated in the holy books. Some used to say he was a soldier who used to serve in the old governments but left the security forces after he had assured the country of everlasting peace and security. But of course these are people who thought they knew everything when they knew nothing. His family was poor and there were also tales that tried to explain the situation.

A close neighbour to the Kamau's was once heard informing other villagers how Mr Kamau was conned all of his treasure by a young lady. The lady met Kamau in a bar one evening and the smile on her face left Kamau breathless. That night, Kamau didn't report to his family but came home at dawn. Although the wife didn't question his unusual arrival that day, it was evident that Mr Kamau started expressing melancholies in his voice whenever he addressed his wife. The lady that tricked Kamau that night had disappeared into the night's darkness, never to be seen again in that village. She was well known too, just like Kamau was. She had amassed a lot of wealth to herself and her family but it was not clear where her riches came from. Many thought she got it from her great grandfather as an inheritance. But this was refuted by those who knew her well. They had known the entire family, from her family to those of her great grandfathers and beyond. The anthem of the whole family was poverty and nothing less; the kind of poverty that was handed over from generation to generation. Maybe, they confused poverty- inheritance with wealth- inheritance.

Another village woman had her own version of the story. Her name was Mugie. She was heard narrating her point of view to her husband. She talked about the source of the lady's wealth as connected to demons. That lady had given some of the wealth to Mr Kamau who would be making love with her in return; which he violated and found himself poor when the demons came and swept everything out of his hands. The demons were her great grandfather's God and were believed to be merciful to the family. The great grandfather had handed over the demons' symbol and a small red book of instructions on how to worship them to the lady. No one had seen the symbol or the book they talked about. The lady followed the instructions, in the red book, in venerating the demons and they decided to bless her abundantly; with wealth, riches, good health and admirable family. But she added something that shocked her husband. The lady had to make love with the demons each mid-night to show her commitment to serve them forever. All this was to happen in a graveyard where many of her family's generations slept. In return, they would offer their unwavering support in and out of season to the lady. They would also protect her from witches' powers and keep at bay everything that would hurt her or cause misfortunes. So, she used to wake up in the middle of the night and head straight to the graves naked in a bid to please the 'mighty, merciful, loving, protecting, providing and well-blessing God'.

The husband could hardly believe what her wife was talking about but had no grounds to help express his disbelief. He almost fainted when she mentioned the lady's sacrifices to her God. The lady had been instructed to offer her husband to the demons in order to help strengthen the bonds between herself and her God. The story explained how she hoaxed the husband to go with her in the mountains of holies. When they got there, they found unidentified flying beings waiting for them. The faces of these beings were likened to those of owls, had tails like snakes and black hooks at the end of the tails, several mouths on their heads, grotesque talons on their toes and fingers, protruding teeth that looked like fangs and body sizes and shapes like wild beasts. Their hooves were split into six parts and the tongues had hooks and scales. Their eyes were red as blood and black rays of light came out of the eyes after several seconds in an alternating pattern. The noses looked like those of dogs but had long hair like horses. The ears were covered with quills like those of porcupines and were green as leaves. Their necks could not be fully described because it was not clear what they were like. They had no wings but flew in a confusing manner-they could jump into the air and plates could spread from their hands mysteriously to help the beings float in air and fly. They vomited fire through their mouths and beams of yellow air and light streamed out of noses when they breathed out.

The beings ordered the two to lift their hands up and immediately their clothes vanished. They were left in their natural brown suits with black blood flowing out of the husband's private parts. The intestines followed the blood in a long chain that scared the lady but could not attempt to show it to the beings. After this drama, his head was struck into two equal pieces by unknown force and the brain was exposed. A heavy pink smoke arose from the brain and a strong stench ensued from the smoke. The smoke left the surrounding stuffy and sent the lady lying flat on the ground, facing the sky, mouth wide open, flames of black fire streaming out of her nostrils, a thick black water gushing from the ears and the eyes turned white like milk. She turned into a gorilla with a dragon's mouth and quickly jumped to the husband's brain. She ate it greedily and chewed the skull into a powder that escaped her mouth and was received into the eyes of the beings, which were surrounding the miserable family. The beings let out a thud that was like a signal to more beings and to their king, to appear for a feast.

At that moment, the lady turned back to the normal human being but looked younger and virgin, still naked. She was more beautiful than any other creature in the land. The king of the beings issued some commands in unknown language and all the other beings ran into darkness in the far parts of the forest. The king was left with the lady and the two made love for some hours. After this, the lady could not wake from the ground. She was unconscious but the king held her by the bossom and she regained her strength. She stood up confused and shivering. The king shouted into the darkness and the beings returned with deafening sounds, carrying black bags. They opened the bags in front of the king and out of one of the bags came out a heavy red smoke that covered the lady. She was strengthened and could talk to the king and his beings in their foreign language. They all discussed and laughed. Then, they burnt the husband's body and made a feast. After the party, the king handed over a black purse to the lady and sent her away.

In the middle of her journey from the mountains, her clothes appeared, covering her body but were wet with black blood. The purse had changed colour and was now red. She then saw, at a distance, her husband's full carcass hanging on a tree. She almost lost her memory but tried to remain stable. She went closer to the body but a numerous number of vultures and vampires flew at a neck-breaking speed from a nearby cave to the body. The vampires tore the body into pieces. At that time, a strong wind blew, swept the pieces into the far end of the forest and heaped them into a huge mountain of meat. The lady dropped the purse she held in hands but the bang that went into the air, when it came into contact with the ground, was like a bomb blast. She fainted. A huge dragon came from a nearby cave and stood by her side ready to gulp her in one bite. A ball of brown fire went out of the dragon's nostrils and covered the lady. Out of the ball of fire came out a huge vampire that went and devoured the huge mountain of meat. All the other vampires and vultures screamed in a deafening voice that woke the lady from her unconsciousness.

She found herself surrounded by a myriad number of bats that had beaks like those of hawks. She swung her elbow to bar them from coming closer but this almost put her into more danger. The dragon was lifted up by one of the vampires into the air and came down and rested on her shoulders. She was to collapse but didn't. She let out a scream that brought all the beings she had left behind into the place of drama. All of them, together with the vampires and vultures, danced in merry as if they were celebrating and cheering their hero, dragon. The lady's hair turned green when the dragon coughed, and the eyebrows turned into thorns. One of the vampires covered her nostrils such that, she could no longer breath. This caused her eyes turn white and popped out of their sockets due to lack of air. She was now heading for a journey of no return, and she died. Another vampire broke her hip bones into two pieces ready to feed on them. The dragon started licking her whole body, which brought her back to life. The pain from her broken hip was unbearable. She pleaded with the dragon for mercy and the dragon was merciful. It restored the hip and the pain disappeared immediately. She was alright at that moment.

Snakes started crawling out of her mouth and nostrils. Some were so long that she almost got choked to death. These snakes were black and some had red spots on their heads. She screamed at the top of her voice at their sight. They all turned back to her and the biggest of them coiled itself on her neck. It was so heavy that she could not stand its weight. She collapsed. The snake rolled out its long tongue and directed it straight into the lady's nostrils. It drained a large amount of liquid out of her nose into its stomach such that, she became deflated like a balloon. At that moment, an extraordinary vampire that had hair on its tongue flew from the far end of the forest and landed on the lady's head. It had a beak at the end of its tail. It used its beak to break the lady's skull into several parts. Then it dipped its hairy tongue into the brain and started to lick the fluids. A vulture that had a fish's mouth and tongue drew a stream of thick and foul-smelling blood out of the lady's eyes. The whole of the lady's body became rotten and all of the creatures left for their caves. Several days passed by with the lady's body lying in the forest in those mountains.

When Mugie narrated the story up to that point, she was exhausted and her husband collapsed to the ground and lost his memory. It seemed he could not hold anymore of the imaginations of the pains and torture the lady was going through. He could not hold anymore of the memories of the lady's husband's death in that same forest. Even the description of the beings, vampires and vultures and snakes made his body cold. Mugie screamed for help from her neighbours in an attempt to help revive the husband, Mr Munii as was known. It was at night and everybody in the village was already in deep sleep. She was also narrating the story in whispers for fear that someone could hear them as sound is clearly heard at night due to the silence that covers the land. It was extremely dark that night and the only sounds that broke the night's silence was that of cockroaches moving on the dirty utensils. Even Mr Munii's breath was not disturbing the silence. She made another scream but it turned into an extremely loud echo which almost deafened her ears. It was as if the scream was magnified by unseen forces from unknown sources. Her body turned cold, she shivered and started sweating profusely. The hands were shaking in such a way that, she could not hold anything firmly.

She let out one last scream but in vain. No sound came out of her scream. She suspected that there were strange things happening in her room. A strong wind blew from under her bed and the lamp went off. The wind continued for some minutes and because of heavy darkness, she could only hear it without seeing what was happening. She could hear stones and papers flying in the air from the bed to the corners of her room. The husband was still on the ground. She could not believe that these things were usual because she had no papers in her bed and no stones were in that room. Then, she heard the sound of knives and hacksaws cutting metal at the table-room. Some sound of water flowing in the kitchen was also heard. Her heart melted with fear. The sweat was now flowing on her body like water and she got shocked to hear her own sweat making sound as it moved down the cheeks. A strong stench like that of rotten eggs filled the room. She was now sure that things were turning pepper. Her mind was racing like a horse trying to figure out what could be causing all this but it could not reach to a conclusion. Then, she felt a very cold hand land on her back. It was so cold that, though she had warm clothing for the night and a scarf on the neck, she felt like she was naked. Indeed, at the touch from that hand, the clothes left her. She was naked for sure. She remembered the lady and her husband in the mountains and went unconscious.

She fell on her husband and both lay on the floor like a heap of cadavers. They were lying in a pool of yellow blood. Out of the yellow blood came out countless gigantic worms that had horns on their heads. They invaded the bodies, licking their noses as if sucking some juices out of them. Under the bed came out balls of blue fire that came into contact with the worms and produced more worms. The balls of fire illuminated the whole room and a gorilla stood by the bodies. Another strong wind blew out of nowhere. The roof of the whole house was swept out of its place. The starry sky was now visible. The gorilla tore the stomachs of the two open and ate the fluids from their intestines. After eating them, it started vomiting wasps that also had horns. Their tails had arrows like those used by hunters in their work. The wasps used their tails to drag the two bodies out of the bed-room through the table-room. At the table room, they found several dead and decaying humans in black masks who were cutting metals with long and wide knives. Two of them stopped their job and lifted their faces to see the bodies being dragged out.

They had flames of fire in their eyes but they had died long time ago. Out of their mouths came out huge teeth that flew and pierced the chests of the two bodies. The two were brought back to life and one of the corpses told them to watch what would happen to them. Another one told them that they would learn the hard way. Then, the gorilla added that they would never share the story with another living being, save with dead people and demons. Then, with a loud voice it said, "You shall never share the secrets of the demons with humans, lest you join your ancestors in serving us in the world of no return. Graves shall not hesitate to crawl into your rooms for your carcasses." Then Mugie remembered the instructions she had received from the woman who informed her about the lady's misfortunes. She broke into tears and pleaded with the gorilla to forgive them. The husband also made his pleas with a sorrowful voice that could touch the inner most nerves of any human being but made no sense to the gorilla. The two were pushed out of table room to the kitchen. There was dim light from the kitchen and nothing could be seen clearly. A heavy smoke that could choke the two arose from one of the spoons and filled the room. Double-edged knives placed themselves in the air pointing to their necks. They were so sharp that one could see their edges shining like gold. Voices came out of the knives asking the gorilla, "Shall we feed on their necks or wait for our due time?" The gorilla answered with a horrifying voice, "At the right time shalt thou have what is due to thee." The knives went back and placed themselves in a plastic cup that had green blood boiling in it. The two were flying to the ground due to excess fear, but one of the worms held them upright. A bright beam of light shone into the room from sky and everything was clearly visible.

The two thought it was the God they used to hear in their churches, who had come to save them, but they were mistaken. They lifted their eyes into the sky to see the God saving them but they were in for another disappointment. They saw a big snake that had a shining body that radiated bright light into the rooms. The snake was floating in the air and had three legs with claws like they had never seen before. The claws were burning but were not being consumed. The sound that Mugie had heard before, like water flowing in the kitchen, was a pipe of fermented mixer of blood and milk flowing out of the kitchen to the garden. The source was unknown. The smell out of the mixer was stinking like a dead person's rotting carcass. The snake dropped into the kitchen and used its fangs to cut Mugie's right hand. It swallowed it as if it had not eaten for several days. She screamed in pain but when she opened her mouth, a worm and a wasp got into her mouth and went straight into her stomach. Sounds could be heard out of her stomach as if the two were slicing firewood inside the stomach.

The husband could not contain himself anymore. He broke into tears after seeing his wife's tragedy. The gorilla slapped him with a slap that sent him flying into one of the cooking pots. The pot got covered with an iron sheet and placed itself on fire. Before he could get boiled, Mugie let out one last cry, pleading for mercy. One of the wasps pulled him out of the pot and dragged the two out of the kitchen. Outside the kitchen, there were numerous silhouettes that resembled those of lions. They could be seen making slow movements towards the two. All waited in absolute silence to see their fate. As the silhouettes came closer and closer to the two, a walking grave was visible. The grave was following the lion- like-shadows. The silhouettes vanished and the grave moved closer to the two until it was in contact with their toes. A blue snake, with eight legs, crawled out of the grave and coiled itself on their necks. Then it bounded into the grave forcing the two inside. Then the grave walked away into the utter darkness, the two holding each other and the snake almost choking them to death. No one knows where the grave took them to since they were never seen anymore.

Mr Kamau was actually seeing how he became poor all of a sudden yet he had assured his wife that she would never taste poverty in her life time, from the time he was proposing to her about their marriage. Some bitterness was choking him and was almost to shed tears. He saw as if the sky was black rather than the normal blue colour. His wife stood at the door and watched her husband in heavy thoughts. She didn't like disturbing him when in such thoughts but had to because the breakfast was ready and she was almost to leave the house for work in the garden down the valley. She got the guts to interrupt the thoughts. She called out, "Kamau, Kamau!" He turned back to the wife like someone who had been awakened from deep sleep. "Yea, yea, here I am my dear. How may I help you please?" He asked. "Please, come in for breakfast, the time is far much spent and we need to prepare the land for the rains have come.", she said. Both went into the house and devoured the breakfast as a family. Then, the two left the room with the necessary paraphernalia for the land, after issuing the normal instructions to the children.

As they walked down the valley, she could see her husband still sticking to the thoughts. She asked politely, "Kamau my dear, what is it that you are going through since you woke up?" He did not want to disclose his thoughts but said, "Nothing dear, I was thinking on how we can prepare the land in two days instead of the four days we usually take." She laughed sarcastically at the husband's response but kept quiet for several minutes. By this time, the two were almost to their place of work. She asked the husband what he wanted to do within the two days they would secure from the normal land's preparation. To her surprise, the husband said he had nothing to do in the span of the two days. He added that he just wanted some more time to relax his mind and body but the wife could not believe what he was saying. After working in the field for about half of an hour, she said in a soft voice like a child, "Dear, you didn't keep your promise. You promised to keep me clothed in riches till I die. Do you remember promising me so at the time you 'tricked me into your box'?"

Mr Kamau could hardly breathe. His eyes were popping out of their sockets and his heart throbbing within the chest like a hammer does on a nail. He remembered his promises and how he had failed to keep them. He replied, "Dear, don't worry about that, soon I will take you there. I mean what I say and say what I mean. Whether I be poor at this time or not, or not or whether, whichever comes first, I will take you there in few days from today. I will show you how great I am and that I can do anything for your sake. I am ready to auction my country just to keep my promise to you.", he said with finality. The wife was shocked and thought her husband was still dreaming in bed while in field or was out of his mind. "But you had a lot of wealth just the other day, what happened to all of your property including money? You left home one evening for a bottle of beer only to come back in the morning which was not usual with you. You changed and do not address me like your wife. Your voice is full of bitterness and you shout at me even when you are supposed to whisper. I no longer understand you. When you try to address me, I cannot tell whether you are addressing or undressing me. How do you expect to make the family rich again in the few days you are talking about? Where did the previous wealth go to in one night?"

A smile came on his face but faded as soon as it appeared. A stream of sweat ran down his cheeks but not the usual sweat that comes due to excess heat or from strenuous activities. It was a sweat due to a shock, something that was devouring his inner being. He was shocked that his wife was enquiring about a secret he was not ready to disclose to anybody. But, because of the tone that was used in asking the questions, he was sure he couldn't hide secrets anymore. It was that day or never. The wife dropped her tools down and looked straight into his eyes to try and understand the sweat more and in details. When he saw how the wife was glaring at him, his eyes turned white and face became pale. The skin tightened and mouth opened wide. He wanted to utter words in a bid to explain something to the wife but words could not come out clearly. He started to stammer, something he had never done before. Before he could finish the first word after countless attempts, he fainted. The wife failed to understand all this drama and was left in confusion.

After what seemed to be a long silence, she grabbed his right hand in disbelief that her husband was unconscious. She turned around to see if there was anybody to help but she was met by a shocking atmosphere. The whole piece of land they had prepared was covered by a yellow and black carpet, with horns glowing out of the ground. The red horns resembled those of buffalos and the blue ones like those of rhinos. On the horns were huge-sized, black-horned and snake-like chameleons. The chameleons had long hair on their tails and each had thirteen legs. The legs had pink claws like those of lions and the tips of their tails were hooves, split like those of pigs. They were walking on the horns that grew out of the ground, and thick, yellow blood mixed with fermented milk with brown worms came out of the horns each time their claws came into contact with them. It was such a terrible site. The whole situation was enigma. Mrs Kamau opened her mouth wide in an attempt to scream for help but at a lightning speed, one of the chameleons fixed its hoof into her mouth, leaving her breathless. After some seconds, she fell on the ground due to lack of enough strength. The hoof had some green teeth that helped the chameleon cut the wife's tongue into two.

Things were turning pepper. The pain was too much to bear. She let out a scream that sent her husband on his feet. She then fell on the ground. When he saw the blood oozing out of her mouth, he shouted at the chameleon in an unfamiliar language. The chameleon talked back and Mr Kamau coughed out purple mucus and the wife's tongue was restored. He asked the chameleon to spare his wife for she didn't know anything yet about their secrets. A loud laugh came out of the hooves and all of their teeth were exposed. The wife was woken up by the laugh and witnessed the hooves' teeth. The sight of the teeth made her hair turn blue. When the husband saw the blue hair, he pleaded again with the chameleons to spare her the wrath. At that time, an enormous mamba came out of one of the horns and declared forgiveness to the wife. At that instant, the hairs' colour was restored. What almost made her loose her mind, was the mamba's mouth that spoke the forgiveness. It was a black mouth with iron lips, blue-black tongue with an eye at its centre and wooden teeth with plastic tips.

One of the horns started walking towards the wife and spoke to her saying, "You shall never crave to know your husband's secret, nor shall you pressure him to keep his promises to you at any time, in any day of the years you live. We are the ones who took the wealth away from your husband in an attempt to have him in our hands once more for some oaths he didn't fulfil. He promised us something precious once we gave him the wealth, riches and money he wanted to help keep you happy, but he has not kept his promise to us. In case we find or discover your motives to understand your husband's ways, we shall do 'good' to you that you shall never forget. It is good you have a general view of what shall happen to you. Just watch what will happen to your husband."

The horn developed a thick, black arm on its forehead. The arm was full of scales and a big quill on the tip. It pointed towards the husband signalling the wife to watch keenly. The husband's body turned red in colour, porcupines quills grew all over the body, eyes turned black, the hair became grey and teeth protruded out of the mouth like snake's fangs. Long hair came out of his ears and two huge horns grew out of his nostrils. The forehead became shinning as gold and a heavy green smoke came out the mouth. The smoke filled the air with an odour like that of a dead and rotting animal. It was choking but she stood strong out of fear. A big earthworm, with a yellow horn on its backbone, arose from the husband's left eye and crawled towards her. She screamed out of fear for help but a small horn on the ground warned her from any movement or scream. The earthworm had a mouth like a crocodile and fifteen legs. It went and climbed on her body, coiling itself on her neck. It stretched its tongue into her nostrils and sucked a lot of blood, swallowing it and producing hot vapour through its tail's tip. Then it uncoiled itself from her neck and went into one of the horns through the horn's mouth.

Out of the rotten husband's body came out a large snail. The snail had three legs and snake's fangs in place of its upper tentacles, with blue eyes at the tips. It came out of his body through the bottom and made its way into his head through the ears. A loud sound came out as the husband's skull broke open into three parts. The wife almost collapsed out of the shocking sight but she feared further consequences. A dense choking smoke came out of the skull with the brain being exposed. The brain was full of worms like those found in latrines and countless maggots. They were writhing in anguish and pain due to the extreme heat that was being generated out of the skull. As they struggled to move out of the skull, blood flowed out of the husband's body though all the openings. The wife could see the brain of her husband boiling like a very viscous acid in the skull and many organisms trying to manoeuvre their way out of the skull. The organisms included different kinds of worms, wasps, termites, flies, scorpions and small snakes. Then the skull closed up and locked every organism inside. Then the body came back to life without the rotting smell and regained the usual colour. He then laughed with a thud that shook the land and vomited many snakes through the mouth and nose for about five minutes. The vomited snakes made their way into a hole on the ground and the hole was covered by a black horn.

She was now sweating profusely and all her body veins were visible. Then the husband said through the ears, "Never pressure me to show you my secrets. From today we are going to be rich but I have to give a holy sacrifice like a certain lady did to her husband on a certain mountain in a forest. But the sacrifice can be made later after we have enjoyed the wealth, riches and lots of money. It's you whom I shall offer as a holy sacrifice to the holies you have seen today." After the statement from the husband, the ears laughed and the eyes began to eat a roasted snake. The eyes had teeth like those of a rat. After eating the snake, the husband's belly bulged like a fully inflated balloon. At the naval, a small hole was created and many green crocodiles, locusts, lizards and snails came out of his belly for several minutes until the belly regained its normal size. The small hole closed up and no more creatures came out of it.

Then, a great vampire flew down a nearby tree and had a tail that was speaking in several peculiar voices and languages simultaneously. It said, "We all live in this world but though we let you live therein, it doesn't mean you belong to our family. We only have mercy on you. No one shall talk of our secrets unless we permit such to do so. Next time, you woman, you desire to know your husband's secrets, you shall not like it. It shall be the beginning of your end. What you have seen happening to your husband is just a hint, but we are capable of doing more terrible things. Nothing has authority over us but we have dominion over anything visible and invisible, great and small, living and non-living and so on. Be careful and watch because we are everywhere, inside and outside anything. You may go home and wait for the wealth I am going to let you have."

"The lady people hear about who conned your husband is one of us because we made her so. She is here with us because we converted her into one of the dragons after she failed to keep our secrets. Wait and see her appear. Maybe you won't like it and that will be a sure way of forcing you to keep secrets and conform to our will. We are stronger than anything and we are proud of ourselves and our might. We come from the uttermost parts and from horizon-less space where we only cover ourselves with nothing. We made whatever you see and cannot see and rule over anything. We can cause anything to happen, calling anything out of nothing, destroying everything we wish and walking invisibly to all places, both on land and in air, water is our carpet while air is our bed. In general, you can only understand us slightly if you could understand the statements we speak to both living and non-living things while in vacuum "We walk in the air, sleep on water and live through the wire". We make wireless wires out of wood, convert air into food while creating life out of papers. We are we. Lightning and thunderstorms are our videos; the sun is our table, any other star is our seat while other planets are our handkerchiefs. Moons are coins to us and we use comets as our torches. Dragons are our insects, snakes are our necklaces, scorpions are tea to us, lions are our pillows, crocodiles are our house-maids, water can be our breath-out vapour, stones and rocks are our cigarettes while soil is breakfast."

"All of you live because we live. Out of us lives nothing. We do whatever pleases us and fear nothing because there is nothing beside us. We want you to watch closely on what the lady became after defying our orders." At that moment, a huge dragon appeared from nowhere and stood in-front of the wife and husband. Red worms and wasps were flowing out of its nostrils and mouth. Small blue snakes were crawling out of its ears. The eyes were rotten and smelling like dead dogs. Its bones were visible from outside like as if its body was transparent. Even intestines, heart, blood-vessels, liver and brain were all visible to the naked eye from outside the body. It was such a terrible sight to the two after seeing a mixture of dead flies, frogs, fish, worms, small snakes, scorpions and centipedes flowing in blood-vessels instead of normal blood. The wife wet herself after seeing the astonishing situation of the lady. The husband was only sweating black sweat but tried to remain strong. After some minutes of silence, a loud thunder broke the silence followed by a blinding lightning. A heavy rain followed for only three seconds and flooded the place. When that unique dragon got wet from the rain, the amazing body changed into the normal lady with normal structure.

The lady was shivering and pleading with Mr Kamau not to reveal any secret without the approval from the Great Creatures. Then the great vampire shouted at the lady, "Go back to your state, for we do not forgive when unnecessary. In your state shall you remain forever. You will always preach to others about our might." With those words, the lady turned into the amazing dragon and a heavy wind blew her out of vicinity. Then the great vampire ordered all of the surrounding creatures and horns to return to their work. All obeyed without arguments and the whole sight was restored to normalcy. Only the great vampire and the two were left on the piece of land. The two gained some strength and the husband was the first to speak to the great vampire. He said in low tone, "Master the great, please show us the way. We believe in you and we know that no one can defy your orders. We live to serve you whether we be alive or dead. We respect you and fear you because you are so. 'Hail the great one, hail the great one.' You are our master forever." The wife also got some courage to speak before the great and mighty vampire, saying, "Hail master, live forever. Thank you for sparing my life and having mercy on me a sinner. We sin whenever we think otherwise from your will. Your will is our food and breath. Live forever, to be praised by everything that is living. Please, show us your ways and will. We are here to serve you."

After the vampire heard this praise, it got excited and greatly pleased. It announced blessings and forgiveness to the two saying, "I am fully pleased and satisfied by your praise, why should I not bless you abundantly! I must help you now and not tomorrow. You are my creatures and have offered the best praise than any other living or non-living being. Now, I give you wealth, riches and money as your wife desired, or as you promised her. I forgive you not to offer any sacrifice to me as we had demanded from you. The sacrifice of praise you have offered to me at this moment is better than anything else you could offer. I grant you good health and many years to live in this world; you shall never be sick but shall live until you ask us to let you leave the world. Nothing shall be against you whatsoever. Go and enjoy this life and I shall give you rest after you have left this world. I am always with you, never fear, and call upon me whenever you want to know more or for whatever reason. I have made you peculiar people to me and to us. The two bags that I am going to give to you, make sure you do as I tell you so that you may reap the full benefits of my blessings this day. But in case you forget to follow instructions, I will still be with you to help you. I want you to have the joy that flows from my greatness."

At that time, the vampire stretched out wings from its tongue and two big and green bags fell from the wings. One bag went straight to the hands of Mr Kamau while the other to the hands of the wife. The bags were very heavy but they could manage to stand their weight. The vampire said, "Look into the bags and see." Inside the bags, they found shining papers from colourless books and the papers were blank. The vampire whispered to them, "When you go home, I will be with you to direct you. You will find imaginary writings on the papers and a small book will appear on your bed. You will only be imagining whatever you want and that which is imagined will write it-self on the papers. Then it shall be done as you wish. Then you will be going through the small book on your bed to help you understand more about me. The writings in that book will be changing each time you read a single page. That will be a proof of how complex we and our ways can be to anything that exists and that which does not exist. Remember that we bless and curse with everlasting impact. The book is going to reveal a lot to you. Just be happy and enjoy your-selves. Many extra-ordinary things will be happening in your presence and absence but it is because we are always with you; in you and outside you. Go now and carry those bags with you because from this moment on, they mean everything to you; your lives, your families and your future. I bless you."

With those words, the great vampire disappeared and left Mr Kamau and his wife alone in the field. Their working tools had changed into pieces of gold and silver. They were amazed but tears of joy were flowing down their cheeks for finding such a great favour from the great vampire. They embraced each other and danced in exceedingly great joy while singing praises to the vampire. It took them about one hour in the joyous mood and still in the field. After that, they decided to go back home because they felt they were also hungry. On their way home, they were discussing the bags they were carrying and how their life would be bright, how they had found favour and blessings mixed with mercy in the great vampire, how they would always praise and sing to the great vampire for the rest of their lives, how their tools were now gold and how they would keep them safe and secure from all alarms. They arrived home and found the children playing in the neighbouring compound. They called them and after exchanging the normal greetings with them, they took their lunch though it was late. Suddenly after the lunch, a wolf appeared in the table-room.

The two were no longer afraid but welcomed the wolf saying in unison, "Welcome and feel at home. How do we help you please? Let us know how you would like us to serve you, your highness. We are your servant and you may do whatever pleases you." The wolf smiled and talked to Mr Kamau saying, "Mr Kamau, inform your wife how you came to know about us. Let her get the information from you and do not be afraid because we have permitted you to do so. We are with you, live happily with your family, help as many people as you can because your wealth shall never decrease.

We are always delighted in helping and saving mankind. We live and have fun in delivering human beings from any form of calamity, diseases, poverty, fear, ignorance, lack of peace, hard labour, early deaths, accidents, enemies and many others that cannot be enumerated; they are myriad. You shall live to be a witness because you have found favour in our sight. We have mercy and compassion on whosoever we choose, those who find us are never confounded, calling upon us will never go unanswered, seeking us means finding us, asking anything from us has benefits and blessings will never be exchanged with curses." The two were listening keenly and with smiles and respect to the wolf.

The wolf continued, "So many times do we try to make ourselves known to humans but we find resistance, hence men end up suffering for no reason. They make their hearts harder than diamond when they are supposed to soften them and allow us into their hearts. They avoid us to the point of being afraid of us when they are supposed to allow us into their lives. This causes their lives to be fruitless and meaningless, full of unnecessary struggles and sufferings, yet we are always available to help. Though they have been against us for so long, we never give up and have never cursed them or caused their sufferings to increase. Instead, we protect them hoping that they may realize these things and turn to us. Be close to us and you shall never know the poor side of life. You shall enjoy the blessings from us in this life and in life to come because we must reward the best way possible after this life. I am gone but remember that we are always with you and around you and in you. Have fun!"

After the wolf had said these words, it disappeared mysteriously and the two were left seated with smiles on their faces. They kissed each other and left for rest in bed-room. There in bed, Mr Kamau started informing his wife how he came to know about the mysterious beings. "I was only walking to our small piece of land early morning", he started. The wife was not breathing. She was full of curiosity and eagerly listened. He continued, "Then I said to myself, 'If and only if I would discover the meaning of my life, I would be grateful. Life seems to have no meaning; it's full of struggles and sufferings, full of mysteries and unexpected and uncertainties. It's like we walk in darkness because we have never known our future in advance. If only we could know what our future has, we would either kill ourselves if it has no good tidings in store or we would live without worries if it has good news for us.' Then, no sooner had I finished my thoughts than when I saw something like lightening from the sky and from the ground at an interval of two seconds."

"I could not believe my eyes but that was the reality. I sat in the middle of the path for some minutes trying to figure out what it could be and its meaning but could not comprehend anything. I later continued with my walk to the field and started the normal duties in the field but my mind was clouded by thoughts. At around 2 pm, I rested under a shade and continued with my thoughts. Suddenly, I heard movements nearby but could not see what was making them. Then I heard a voice saying, "Don't be afraid, I have seen that the people in this world believe in lies and that is what they accept. I am always afraid to help them because they neither accept me nor seek me. I do not like to mislead them but they force me to stay away from them. As for you, I must help you and be with you because I do not have pleasure in keeping my blessings with me. I have heard your concerns from within your heart this morning and must give you all of your desires. You shall be great, no one shall be able to stand before you and everyone shall fear and respect you. I have filled you with wisdom to help you in this life and in life to come. You shall use it to have dominion over many and I shall give you rest in both lives. You are a peculiar person from this moment. Always know that there is none to save, bless, protect, give, answer, defend or do anything to help you except me. This is because there is none beside me. Live to the maximum." After this voice had spoken, I heard the movement of the being walking away and disappeared. I was overcome with joy but didn't want many to know it until the promises from the voice were fulfilled."

"After that, I only rested for few minutes and left the field. As I was heading back home, I came across a small chameleon along the path. The chameleon said to me, "Greatly blessed man, have courage. Do not be afraid of anything in this world or in the world to come. When you get home, a stranger will visit you and give you a small bag full of money. Enjoy life with your family and that will be the beginning of many good tidings in your life." Then, the chameleon disappeared and I continued with my journey back home. As soon as I arrived in the house, an unfamiliar man knocked on my door carrying a small bag. The man said in a soft voice, "Hail Mr Kamau, be blessed as it has been decided. I won't take long because I have to travel back and the journey is long and tiresome. Take this bag and change your life to the brightest life ever. Thank you and live long." With those words, the man left after placing the bag on the table. It was full of money. I used the money to change our lives. I have come from far and I am going far. Let us be showered with blessings because that is the desire of every man that comes into this world."

After the narration of the truth by Mr Kamau to his wife, a male child appeared in the bed room and said, "Excellent! You have narrated it perfectly and we love you." Then, a female child appeared carrying a huge bag and said, "This is a gift to you for obeying the command and narrating the truth to your wife. This bag is very heavy because it is full of gold, diamond and cash money. Do not be afraid to spend because you shall never taste poverty any other day. The papers you were given are meant to help you get whatever you want and to give you your desires to the fullest. Take and enjoy but do not forget to help as many as possible because your wealth shall never diminish. Be a source of blessings to many and we know some shall praise us through you. Enjoy your time and life." Immediately after these words, there was an earthquake and a lightning followed by a thunder. A strong wind also blew against the house and some rain fell within two minutes. After that incidence, the boy said, "That is the confirmation of your blessings. As you cannot call back the earthquake, thunder, lightning, rain and wind, so shall we not revoke the blessings. They have been declared forever. Good bye and enjoy dear family." With those words, the two children left the room through the walls and a long silence dominated in the next one hour.

Later, Mr Kamau talked to his wife and told her, "Let us sleep because we have had a great day that requires to be honoured with a deep rest. We have our eternity taken care of. Our work is to enjoy as all the beings insisted to us. Good night dear." The two fell into deep sleep being assured of the best life in this world. Everything had changed. They did not have to work to earn anything for a living, everything was provided as they had been assured. Several days passed and Kamau's brothers noticed that he was not working and his wealth was increasing. His lifestyle had changed and his wife was becoming bigger each day. They wanted know what was happening with their brother and this forced them to summon him for a meeting. He appeared in the best suit in fashion and his walking style was different. After some hours of lengthy discussion, they just decided to offer him some advice as a beloved brother. They informed him that no one was to live in this world without sweating for his daily food. Other short-cuts are deep-cuts in the end and that there is no short-cut in life. The short-cut shall remain as hard work and sweat for life. They warned him not to involve his life with some powers that entice you into their traps with goodies and later leave you miserable, if not in grave. They later dissolved the meeting and left for other activities.

Not long before Kamau's health started to deteriorate at an alarming rate. He was taken to the nearest hospital but the doctors could not do much to help. He was complaining of headache, eyes not seeing properly, the whole body becoming weak, nose-bleeds, malaria and diarrhoea, lack of appetite and other funny complexions. No drug in the hospital was of any use to him. He remained in hospital for three days without speaking. In the fourth day, his brothers visited him to see his progress. They were shocked to see his thin body yet he was like a boss during their meeting. The change was unbelievable. "What happened to our brother? Who bewitched him since last meeting with him? Are gods against him? Is the devil after his life?" The eldest brother asked but no one answered him. His questions went like rhetoric questions simply because he was asking the right questions to the wrong people. After some silence, Mr Kamau started vomiting. It became severe and it turned out to be a vomit of blood, pieces of glasses mixed with pieces of uncooked meat, sand particles embedded on wooden cubes and many worms that were followed by nails, pins and razors.

They wanted to run away from that room but did not want to leave their brother in trouble. They held him by the back to assist him sit down. The vomiting continued and finally, a big snake came out of his mouth, followed by scorpions through the nostrils. One of the scorpions plucked his eyes out of their sockets and swallowed the others. The brothers jumped out of the room through the windows screaming for help. The doctor arrived immediately only to find the snake and the scorpions disappearing into the ground through a crack under the table. Kamau had no eyes and blood was all over the floor. He did not understand what was happening but Kamau was dead. He called those brothers back. They discussed about those strange things that had happened to Kamau. The doctor instructed some nurses to help take the body to the mortuary. He then called the brothers into a private room for further discussions. In that room, the doctor interrogated them keenly as if he wanted to extract a secret they were not willing to disclose. He found they had nothing to offer as far as his questions were concerned. They later informed him how they had noticed that his life was becoming better without working for it but had warned him.

When the doctor heard that, his face became pale. He seemed restless from that moment on. They asked him to explain what he could have discovered and he responded by saying, "My dear sons, that is very dangerous. I have learnt that he had involved himself with the ancient powers. Anyone who does so is an automatic loser of his life. Those are killers who delight themselves in malicious acts. They lure you with money, wealth, riches and many miracles that are hard to understand. But once you get into their snare that is the beginning of your end. You must end up in grave, whether you like it or not. They even warn you against informing anyone about your 'luck'. They do funny things in your presence to scare you and later, they leave you with something that can work out endless and countless diverse miracles. Once you take that something with you, they are able to track you wherever you go and in whatever you are doing. Never go there my friends." They became cold and afraid. After some silence, the eldest asked, "What do you mean by ancient powers? We have never heard of such a term since we were born."

The doctor shook his head and said in soft voice, "By that term, we mean those powers that live in graves, darkness and forests. They were there since many years ago. According to a renowned witch, they call upon these powers for help when performing their witchcraft. All witches have a bond with them. You give your life to them and they serve you forever. When you die, you join them and become part of these beings. They change into anything and can do anything in this world. They are all-powerful and have many good and bad traits. For example, they can raise somebody from the dead and they can destroy life. They do not eat yet they live, they are everywhere and all-knowing. They do not accept non-sense from any human-being; you must obey what they say." The brothers listened carefully as the doctor explained all this to them. After some more discussions, the doctor left as he had to attend to another patient. The brothers left for home after clearing the bill. When they went home, they discussed further among themselves, wondering how their brother could have come into terms with the ancient powers in the first place. They had many questions without a single answer but life had to continue.

After a week of burial preparation, it was agreed on the day to bury Kamau. Mortuary fee was raised by the family members and when the day came, they went to the mortuary to collect the body. After paying the required fee, they were led to the room where the body was. They could not belief; the body had turned into that of a cat. "What a surprise and a miracle! Where could a cat come from? Was it really a cat or something else?" They asked but the mortuary-attendant could not explain. They decided to lift up and examine it more. Though it was dead, when they touched it, there were meows everywhere in that room and the lights went off. There was total darkness in the room. This sent a cold chill in their bodies and hardly could they breathe. They did not know what would happen next. They were really afraid and wanted to scream but had no strength to do so. The meows grew more and louder and closer to their ears. The attendant decided to walk to the switches and try to put the lights on. He lifted his leg to move but stepped on something extremely cold. It was so cold that, the cold penetrated through the shoes to his body. He withdrew his leg at a lightning speed. Then, he felt a hand, as cold as snow, touch his cheeks and he fainted. When the rest heard him fall with a thud, they let out a scream that left the room silent and with lights on. They had already wet their clothes but unharmed. The cat was no longer there but a child's body that resembled that of Mr Kamau.

They took the attendant with them and left the room. When outside, one of them said, "We cannot tell what we are dealing with. He was vomiting unusual filth, then, he turned into a cat and now a child. We need not try to take such a thing to bury. Let us do first aid on the attendant and leave this place." After some minutes, the attendant recovered and vowed never to work in a morgue any other day of his life. He resigned and kissed everyone good-bye. That is how this man's career came to an end. The brothers went home empty-handed and delivered the shocking news. They gathered all the mourners together and explained in details, everything that had happened. The mourners got confused as they had not heard such a thing before. In the evening, each left for their homes.

Rumours spread all-over the village; that Mr Kamau's worshipped demons, devils, evils spirits and Satan. Each person had their own version of the story. The next day, the family levelled the grave and planted a wattle tree as was the custom of their tribe.

Few weeks later, Mrs Kamau went to the field for a nature walk. As she was returning home, she was astonished to find her husband alive and reclining on a rock, along her path to the house. She melted with fear but decided to greet him. As soon she shook his hand, a huge dragon slid from the rock and asked her to leave immediately for her time was limited. It said, "Please, for your sake, leave immediately and go back to your house. Your time is almost up; soon you will join your husband and our fraternity at large. You need to see your children for the last time as a human being." She left in a hurry without turning back. She could not believe what was happening as she had only enjoyed 'good life' for a very short time. At the compound, she found black grass everywhere. She had no time to think what that meant as her mind was racing like a wild-beast in danger. She found her children taking tea together and wept bitterly as she remembered the dragon's words that she needed to see them for the last time. The children did not know what that meant but went and embraced her. She then asked them to take tea and after supper they should sleep for early waking up.

She then went out of the kitchen and found that the darkness was too much outside. She remembered the black grass and fear multiplied in her. She gathered some courage and got into the table-room. That is where she met her fate. The dragon was there on the table and Kamau was holding a very sharp, double-edged knife in his left hand. He had no eyes and his tongue was hanging out of his mouth, full of blood and worms. On his neck was a hole through which a snake's tail was visible but its head was inside the throat. His ears were cut and were on the table, next to the dragon. He had a bushy tail on the chest and his forehead was full of tattoos resembling vampires and snakes. The right hand was a foot while the left leg was a hand. The teeth were pink, protruding out of mouth and with hooks at the ends. The feet had hooves like those of a cow while the nose had no openings. It was a terrible sight to her but she did not show much fear as she knew that she was to join him soon. Lights went off and she trembled. She felt herself naked and a cold object touched her belly. It was the knife she had seen her husband holding.

It was so cold that she became numb almost everywhere. The knife went through her belly and came out through the backbone. She felt no pain as the bigger part of her was numb. She later felt something cold too touch her thighs. The legs became as cold as snow. Blood froze in vessels and she became unconscious. She became like a statue, fixed on the ground, though almost dead. The lights switched themselves on and a voice came out of the knife saying, "You must sacrifice yourself as soon as you fall into out trap. You will join us tonight and help us in carrying out our daily plans. Wake up and see." As soon as the voice said so, she became conscious and found her husband holding knife that was dripping blood on the table. There was a knife's hole on her belly and the backbone was broken into pieces though no pain. The dragon dragged its tail on her bossom and her body became warm. The numb was gone and she could hear, feel and see well. Kamau dropped the knife which turned unto a scorpion that walked out of the room. The blood on the floor turned into sand and the snake's tail on his neck became a small maize-plant. Then he dropped to the floor and became a big spider. The spider formed a web on her belly which sealed the hole that the knife had left. Then it flew out of the room through the window.

The dragon stood on the table by its tail that had few hooks. It developed several hands on its body and a mouth like that of a man. Then woman-like hair appeared on its head and the face turned to that of a young lady. Then it spoke and said in a very attractive voice, "Hi my dear? Do you want to make love with me before you join our colleagues? Remember that you should be making love with me every now and then but I have always spared you." Then it kissed her forehead and continued, "Please dear, talk to me. You must die tonight and be part of us, which is inevitable. There is nothing you can give in exchange for your life." She broke into tears and said, "Just kill me, I no longer need pleasures of life. Kill me quick, what are you waiting for?" The dragon became furious and slapped her, a slap that sent her flying on the wall. Her teeth were misplaced and blood was oozing out of her mouth. It lifted her with one hand and bellowed, "What the hell do you think you are saying? Are you greater than me? You dare answer me like your husband? I am to be feared by all, even after one is dead. I do not accept anything that lowers my ego!"

Darkness covered the whole room though the lights were on. The dragon coughed and out of its cough came out wasps, scorpions and centipedes. All of these creatures entered into her body through the nose and ears. They started eating her up from inside. The pain of their bites made her scream to the top of her voice but no one could hear her beyond that room. "This is the sacrifice we want from you that you go through pain before you join our team. I do not even want to sleep with you; I am no longer interested in that. I am now concerned with the sacrifice, nothing else." The dragon said in anger as the woman continued to scream. Then, it clapped its teeth like hands and a foul smell like that of a corpse came out of the sound. It chocked her almost to death. It sneezed and few chameleons came out of the nose and mouth. They went straight to her and plucked her eyes. They ate them and started sucking her breasts. They drained her blood and water through the breasts before they bit them and shared among themselves. She gave out one last scream that shook the room and she gave up her ghost. The dragon left her on the floor and buried itself into the ground in that room.

The children came into the room after supper for sleep and found their mother in a way they could not easily recognize her. They ran out and screamed for help from everybody. The neighbours came and were restless after finding the corpse. They didn't know what had happened and no one could explain the mystery behind all that mess. After she had been taken from the floor, all the villagers agreed not to keep her long but to bury her in the next day. Early in the morning, all the people gathered and a coffin was made. They placed the body inside and sealed it. It was placed under a tree outside the house for a short church service and last respect. In the middle of the ceremony, when the children were giving their speeches, there came a big bang out of the coffin; like that of a gunshot. They all melt with fear, unable to move. Then the coffin opened and a voice came out of it saying, "Let no one deceive you that there is anything free in this world; that you can sit down and say you found luck that assured you of a better life, full of joy and painless. You shall work to earn a living, you shall struggle for all the days of your life; that way, you shall enjoy the fruits of your labour. My family has perished in the name of luck. They appeared to us and enticed us with good words, not knowing that they were beckoning us towards early grave. Always remember that when the deal is too good, you should think twice. We are now paying for our folly. We wish we had not listened to their voices." Then she lifted her head out of the coffin and gave out one last, loud breath and said, "Don't be deceived that I am alive, no, I am dead. Just bury me and forget about me."

The coffin locked itself and it was seen no more. People rose from the ground, full of fear and breathless. They all witnessed the whole drama and could not believe what they were seeing. They had come for burial for the second time but in vain. They carried out the usual ritual of planting a wattle tree on the grave and left for their homes, having known the biggest secret ever. Such cases have not been heard again since that day.

JESUS THE CARCASS

———◆•◆•◆———

THE MAN OF GOD, PASTOR, MR MUNGAI, WAS NOT FEELING WELL after the several days spent in cold with his family. The former church, Jesus' Power Church, had decided to chase him out of their premises after he raised his voice against the sharing of offerings. It was in July and the cold weather and rain was not friendly to his health. His wife was not affected that much but had some flu which was normal to everyone during such season. She was also stronger in terms of her body size, stature, strength and so on; which made her less prone to the harsh environment. The children were well fed and clothed which helped secure their health throughout. Spending one week in cold was like a punishment he had never received since he was born. Church members did not want to see him or offer any help to him. They loathed him for going against the other pastors' decisions and it was not his first time to do it. He had received several warnings and admonitions before about his decision to oppose the fellow pastors' plans on sharing the church offerings. The discrepancies arose when Mungai decided to oppose equal sharing of the offerings among the four ordained church- pastors; Mr Muturi, Mr Waithani, Mr Kibe and himself being the top ranked pastor. He actually wanted the offerings shared according to their ranks and not equally among them. He also wanted the most senior pastor to be left with the task of deciding how to share the tithes with the rest of his fellows. His thoughts and stand were not making much sense to his colleagues and since it was not his first time to do it, this time they decided to evict him out of the church premises and to ban him from taking part in any church function; be it normal mass, preaching, organizing and implementation of programs among other activities.

The wife saw his husband's health was deteriorating and decided to take a quick move before it was too late. She visited her friend on the other side of town and explained to her about the misfortunes that were surrounding her family. This friend was not part of her church members but just a friend whom they met when she was in secondary school, but lost strong bonds of their friendship after school. This friend, Wangeci, felt sorry for her family and offered to support the entire family in the meantime. Mrs Mungai was very grateful and went back to pick her family to Wangeci's place. They settled there and Mungai's health was restored after few days of treatment and good care. The children were doing well and were happy each day, just like when they were residing in the church premises. Wangeci was happy too to see how Mungai's health improved. She was actually providing everything to all members and was always encouraging Mungai to keep his psyche alive. Mungai was greatly pleased with this young lady for such hospitality to his family yet he personally did not know her before. Wangeci was the kind of people who delighted in helping friends whenever they called upon her to save a situation.

After three weeks in Wangeci's home, Mrs Mungai started hustling for menial jobs in that side of the town. At the beginning, it was difficult to secure any as many people were not familiar with her. But after seeing her for several days, most residents started trusting her and seeing her as not being a stranger to them. They offered her jobs here and there and she was able to earn some little money. As Wangeci was providing all the basic needs to the entire family, Mrs Mungai decided to save the little she was getting with an aim of starting a small grocery in town. She knew that a journey of thousands of miles starts with a single step; which made her more determined and focussed. She knew she would make it in life and finally secure a home for her family. She had seen many who were set back in life but were resilient in both mind and body; they had recovered and made it far in life than before. Wangeci was one of her role-models as she had a lot of property and meeting her basic needs was not a big deal to her. She was not married as she was still searching for the 'right man'. She had met several men but these were not the right ones. Some were thugs and conmen, others were hypocrites and were after her wealth, while the rest were the 'wrong men'. She had no family to support as her parents were living abroad and richer than most villagers. Therefore, she had everything in plenty and fully comfortable with her life. She had invested wisely in big businesses and real-estate. She had shares in many companies and did not struggle to earn money. Her parents were also sending her some amount each month as her upkeep. She was really enjoying life, living stress-free life.

On the other hand, Mungai was not fully decided on what to do as he was still trying to fully absorb the shock he got after the incidence in his former church. He was spending a whole day and night thinking hard on what direction to take in life. He was thinking between employment and self-employment, between being a pastor still and becoming part of congregation. His mind was not stable and he required some time to finally make decision. One thing he was sure in his mind was that he would have made up his mind before three months were over. The thought that crossed on his mind most of the time was that of continuing with stewardship; pastorship. That idea never left him and he had several reasons for being a pastor for the rest of his life. He was always thinking, "First, you don't have to toil but only to study your Bible hard and have your followers. Secondly, it is very lucrative in terms of offerings and tithes plus other gifts that congregation offers to church leaders, mostly pastor. Thirdly, when you are a pastor, you live closely to other people as they usually call upon you to visit them in homes for prayers while others visit your office and home to bring their supplications to your attention. In every way, you are with them daily and you never feel lonely and you never lack something in return. In fact, you live like a king or queen. Again, most people always trust you and respect you so much that you feel exalted above them. Some who are not careful end up revering you like their God. You always feel good and life becomes more comfortable each day. Young ladies are always close to you and stand by your side each time you need them; they even give you comfort in a "special way that your wife cannot afford". They see you off after the church service and they sometimes pay you a visit in private. In fact, they used to brighten my days in church, especially when they needed special prayers in solitude. I long for those days. And the cost of all this is just a Bible and a good tongue. All that you need is your Bible and a place of worship."

He stood firm with the idea and finally made up his mind that he was to continue being a pastor. But the issue was on how to acquire a piece of land and erect a structure for worshipping therein. Wangeci remembered how long Mungai, the man of God, had lived in her house and had not suggested anything to her, just anything. In her heart, Mungai was extremely handsome. She decided to say something to him, but indirectly. She had hoped that he would have suggested something to her but time was fleeting and was not on their side. She thought in her mind and heart, "If this man was wise, he would have said something long time ago. We are mostly alone in the house but I have not seen any sign of luring me to his side. It is long since his wife gave him happy moments and he is still not bothering with me. He has to open his eyes or I force him to. We cannot suffer here all along yet we can help each other. Maybe his wife is not interested in 'good times' at this period because of much stress, but it does not mean that I am not suffering. It is very difficult to approach him and it is much more difficult for me to lure him to fall victim of my trap. But does he know how much I long for him? Why does God not touch his heart and reveal to him what I want, and even soften him to surrender to me? A man well brought up, well created and nourished yet I cannot access his heart. But I must win him at whatever cost, or else, they leave this house."

One afternoon, Wangeci approached him with a suggestion. "Mr Mungai, why don't you take it upon yourself to be conducting a short service each day before we retire to bed? I thought it wise and right to have someone guiding us towards seeking the face of the Lord. We should never forget our Lord because of the countless blessings He has bestowed on us for free. The Lord is not to be ignored in any way; we need to be closer to Him each day and never turn our ways out of His vicinity. Suppose that we ignore Him and He also ignores us? What do you think would happen? My friend, we would perish out of this earth, never to be seen again. Everything would be catastrophic and terrible, beyond explanations. Is that what you want? You want us to be wiped off the face of the earth? No my friend. We need to be seeking our Lord always, day and night. When God said in Romans 10:13, "For whosoever shall call upon the name of the Lord shall be saved", He was intending to pressure us to seek His face every time. I thought you are a man enough to have that mind too. Come on my brother in Christ, come on! We cannot hide ourselves from His face. Imagine all those blessings He has crowned on us since we were born! See the food we have, the housing and clothing, the cars that I have, the wife and children you have, the handsomeness you possess, the breath of life, the rain and sunshine each time we need them, good health and others. He has indeed laurelled our lives. Blessings are countless my brother in Christ, you cannot exhaust them my dear in Christ. You want us to ignore His great works on us? I thought that is what you have been thinking about since you recovered your health."

He smiled and thought for some seconds before he aired his views. "Thank you my sister in Christ. In fact, that is what I have been thinking about for so long but I was wondering what your position on it would be. I feared you would have rejected the offer in anger and probably sent me away from your place. You know I am only a sojourner in this house and therefore must have some fear and doubts. I wanted to suggest the same to you tomorrow but it seems I was taking too long and God saw it good in His wisdom to put the same idea in your mind for the sake of achieving the same goal and make our lives better. God is really wise and has countless ways of achieving the same gaol. Indeed we have to give Him first priority; we must put Him first in whatever we are doing. We have to show our gratitude for the many things He has given us, the many blessings He has shed on us and the many ways He has used to enable us escape dangers and snares of the devil. If we come together, we become stronger and stronger. In fact, He has said in His Holy book, the Bible, that where two or more come together in His name, He is there with then and among them. Therefore, if you allow us to use your table room and all of us come together each day in His name, we can be greatly and abundantly blessed. Our enemies would fear us and call us 'Blessed' rather than calling us by our names."

"Jesus Christ came and opened our way to access our Father in Heaven without restrictions, at any time and the way we are. We need to use that chance to seek His face when He can be found; as He has said in the book of Isaiah. In fact, His servant Paul is asking us in the book of Hebrew to approach our Father boldly so that we may find mercy and grace to help in times of need. There are times we really need our Father for help, there are times when we long for our Saviour to guide us, and the right time to seek Him is when we see we do not have needs; when we are comfortable with life. It is like a farmer who stores some food during plenty for the sake of the times of scarcity. I thank our Lord for opening your heart so that we may grow together spiritually and in other ways." "Ok, thank you so much my Lord for giving me such a wonderful man in life that we may grow together in your grace. Thank you Jesus for opening his heart and my heart too; that we may approach you as one for the sake of worshipping you because you are worthy." After all this, She said in low tone, "But I would even prefer having some prayers in the morning before we break to face the day, then in the evening, you should give us a short preaching and a prayer, that is: before we retire to bed. You need to ensure that we are as close to God as possible. I cannot imagine a life without Christ. We need to involve Jesus our Saviour in whatever we do and at all time. Maybe, if you get time, I would prefer you preach to me over lunch time for like five minutes. It won't interfere so much with your program because it can be for up to five minutes or less. I always consider you as the man of God and the most blessed in this world. I don't even blink my eyes when you are preaching; it's like the Spirit of the Lord Jesus hovers around whenever you preach, just to ensure that we understand whatever your tongue offers to us. You are chosen by God to be His servant, and I don't have any doubt that Jesus has anointed you for our sake. I cannot miss to be with Jesus in His kingdom yet I am at the feet of His servant this day. It would be shameful and disgracing if He comes back to take His elects and I am left behind. I want you to draw me closer to Christ's bosom using all the means possible. I want to see our Father, His servants like Abraham, David, Paul and many others, including you. If God has blessed you with His wisdom in drawing sheep closer to Him, why not take that advantage? Come on my brother in Christ Jesus!"

"It's ok my sister in Christ Jesus, I am going to do as you wish. I know this is Jesus speaking through you and I must obey His word and calling. He speaks to us through many ways and if we are keen, we are able to recognize His voice; as He has said in the book of John that His sheep hear His voice and He knows them by their names. We are His sheep and must be able to recognize His voice whenever He is speaking to us. Thank you Lord, thank you Jesus, thank you my Father in heaven for choosing my sister in Christ, Wangeci, to speak through her in an attempt to make me see your will. Thank you once again and may your name be glorified in all generations. I love the way you manifest your wisdom among us with an aim of glorifying yourself forever." After the much speaking and what seemed to be like a short and unplanned sermon, the two sat staring to each other's face. They were only smiling to each other without words. After some minutes of silence and smiles, Mungai decided to raise his concern on acquiring a church of his own.

"My sister in Jesus, I have a concern that has almost eaten up my heart and mind. I don't sleep well like I am supposed to. During the day, I am only thinking hard about it but have found no way out. Maybe if you allow me I can express myself now and share with you. It is not wise to conceal what I have yet I cannot solve it alone. Jesus might decide to use you as a vessel and then I get the way forward." Before he could continue, Wangeci interrupted quickly. "Yes, my dear in Christ. Just speak it out and share the problem. In fact, people say that a problem shared is a problem half-solved. Even Jesus would not be happy to see you keeping problems to yourself yet I am here with you all the time. Feel free and share with me. I am yours in Christ Jesus and you own me and all that I have in Christ Jesus." Mungai sweat and trembled after her words that were spoken in the best intonation possible. She moved closer to him and rested her head on his thighs. Mungai shivered like a feeble twig on a windy day. His face turned from stressed one to a glittering one. Then he composed himself to share his problems with this sister in Christ.

"Since I was kicked out of church by those greedy animals, Jesus has been speaking to me in dreams and visions on how I should recover from the calamity. He has insisted that I must continue with the work I started and must be in charge of His sheep for the rest of my life. I really wanted to start business and seeking for a job but He has insisted that I get a piece of land and position a church for His sheep to use in worshipping Him. He showed me in a vision how His sheep are scattered simply because the shepherd is sitting in this house, just eating, drinking and sleeping. He wants me back to pastorship in the shortest time possible. In that vision, He again took a bottle of Olive oil and anointed my head as a sign of calling me to His kingdom and to herd His sheep till He comes back. In fact, He was angry when He pointed to His lost sheep and I was just resting in a shade like a person who did not know what he wanted. He took several minutes to reprimand me for being ignorant of the sufferings that His sheep were undergoing. I promised Him to take the necessary action and take charge of His sheep. He appeared to me several times and reiterated that message until I was fully convinced of His will. He later appeared to me in a dream and asked me to hurry up."

"My concern is this; that I need a small piece of land and a church placed thereon. Then I should equip myself fully with the Bible and get to work. Now my dear in Christ, I don't know where to get such land nor money to build His church of choice. I am really in a dilemma. If you have any suggestion, please air it out and I shall be glad. In fact, God might give you such an idea for the sake of helping His servant not to have a heavy heart anymore. Think about it and Jesus is going to make a way, that one I am sure of it. He has used you to open my heart and He is still willing to use you not once, not twice but countless times more." "That's point taken, point taken my dear in Christ. My love in Christ, you should never worry over such small issues. As I said that I am yours in Christ Jesus and that everything I have is yours in Jesus, you should have discerned all these. I have a lot and you can use some of it to glorify our Saviour. He died on the cross and rose again because of the love He has for us. He loves us so much that He even counted His life worthless for our sake. Why don't we show the same towards Him? Why don't we use what we have to bring honour to His mighty name? We must be willing to serve Him in whatever way possible and at all times. Just take a walk and see all that I have; there are several pieces of land that I own in this town and you can select the one that pleases the Lord, and then use it to fulfil His wish. He really deserves all of our will, efforts, mind and body. Never keep problems to yourself; I am here to share all of my secrets with you and vice versa is applicable too."

"Thank you my dear in Christ Jesus, thank you so much. May God send a heavy rain of blessings on you, now and forever. Let's offer a short prayer to thank our Lord for His manifold blessings. "Lord God our Father, our Creator and provider, we thank you this morning for your great works. You are the only wise and powerful, possessing everything we see and we don't see. Thank you for my dear Wangeci, you have given her all for the sake of praising and honouring your name. May your Holy Name be blessed, praised and honoured forever. We love you; we adore thee and want to serve you for the rest of our days." Thank you Wangeci and God bless you abundantly. May my Lord Jesus Christ of Nazareth, the very Son of God and David on earth, be with you and protect you forever. May he be your provider and strength now and in all times. I really love you in Christ Jesus my Saviour." "I love you too in Christ my Saviour." They embraced each other for some minutes as a sign of togetherness. Then they stood up and looked at each other like people who had not seen each other before. Then they kissed each other to say goodbye, but the kiss went deep and deeper. They held each other tighter and never felt like letting each other go. Finally, they threw each other aside when they heard a knock on the door. They sat down very fast; Mungai took a magazine that was on the table while Wangeci equipped herself with a cup of water that had been on the table since the previous night. They pretended to be busy as they waited for the visitor. They burst into laughter when it turned out to be one of Mungai's children who wanted to take a toy from his bag. The child got in the bed-room and came out of the house with his toy.

"I thought it was your wife coming back to collect something she had forgotten. She would have devoured us alive, I know she does not entertain non-sense; I was with her in secondary school and I learnt she is a very strict lady. But even if it was a neighbour, we would still be in trouble because such people are out to ruin one's reputation. But thank God we are still safe." "Did you see that I was trembling? My heart was racing like a horse in a competition. If it was my wife, things would have turned pepper instantly. I too fear her; she is very principled and does not go to the extent of allowing the devil into her path. But anyway, we are safe as you have said. I thought you could take me around to see the pieces of land that you have; I need to see them today because time is not on our side and I now don't have a reasonable excuse not to serve my Lord." "Yes my husband in Christ Jesus. Ooops, sorry for calling you 'my husband'. Have I offended you? Please forgive me, I humbly ask for your forgiveness." "No, no, no, no harm at all. I can be anything to you in Jesus Christ. You know, we are all together and one thing in Christ. Whatever we do and do it in Christ, then we are right and God is with us. You are also my wife in Christ, is that a big deal? No, it is not, we are one family and Jesus protects us. Call me whatever you wish and I shall appreciate it. You said you and your possessions are mine in Christ, I too am yours in Christ."

"Thank you my dear in Christ, I love your understanding and being civilized to that extent. You know some guys out there pretend to be civilized when they are not. They think being civilized, disciplined and principled is being strict to their fellows. But I love you because you are different and never like them. Continue like that and you shall reap the benefits of being near Christ our Lord. As I was saying, I want to take you around the town so that you are familiar with the lands that I have and from there you can make your decision. I want you to serve the Lord as He has instructed you to do. Don't omit even an iota of the instructions because He can get angry with you as He did to king Saul who did not kill all the animals after he got victory over his enemies. And do you remember what God said to him through Samuel? That obedience is far much better and acceptable before God our Lord than burnt offering of sacrifices. Therefore, I am concerned too much with you obeying His voice to the end. Get ready we go before we come back and prepare lunch. But for now I can give you a cup of juice and two sausages to cool the pangs of hunger."

She rose from the sofa set and went to the kitchen. She came back with three sausages on a plate and two cups of juice; all placed on a tray. She served him with a cup of juice and two sausages. She took the rest and they started enjoying after the pastor gave thanks to the Lord for being so gracious to them. As they were enjoying the snacks, they were turning to each other countless times and that was speaking more than words. "I want you to have the necessary and enough energy; you have a lot to do one of these days." She said in a whisper as she took the last bite of the sausage. He turned to her and smiled but did not make any comment on the same. After the refreshment, she whispered to his ears, "If you don't mind, let's have one last kiss and then we go. My heart is longing for one and that will energize and rejuvenate my mind and body. It's like petrol to my car. After the kiss, they got into her car and she drove off. While in the car, each was lost in their own ocean of thoughts. There was a lot going on in each ones' mind. Mungai looked far ahead as the car left the compound. He was not interested in mastering the town. "But she is very beautiful. She even reminds me of Mrs Muigua; though I spent only few nights with her and she did all that I wanted. She was 'very sweet'; she was very beautiful, had the body shape and size as I have been admiring. She had dimples like this lady. The two smile like little children which even takes my breath away. The skirt she is wearing is perfect in colour, length and design, such a transparent one. I like such mini-skirts and I wish my wife could adopt such skirts as I advised her long time ago, but she ignored. In fact, she answered me rudely and I vowed never to tell her that again. I remember her words very clearly, "Go and advice prostitutes to wear such skirts, I am not one of them. I must command respect from all those I meet in this world. If you want me to wear mini-skirts, go and tell your parents and my parents too, so that they are all aware that I have become your prostitute." Those words hurt me and I usually feel like we should divorce and I marry a lady like Wangeci. Ladies who will give you what you want; at whatever times you want it."

"Wangeci is the kind of person who can keep you happy for the rest of your life. Her face shines like stars, inside her skirt I can see goodies, her legs so smooth, the hands so soft, hair like that of a horse, body size like I have never seen before, body shape like I have been longing for and the beauty like that of an angel. This girl is damn beautiful. What if I marry her to be my second wife? No, no, no, that is not allowed in church when one is a pastor. My parents would also not allow me to do it too. Or should I divorce my wife and marry Wangeci customary? I will think over it with time. I cannot go on persevering in marriage; I don't enjoy my wife's company at all especially when I see all these beautiful ladies and girls all over, searching for men like me; men whom God has blessed to represent His image on earth. Yes, God is handsome and He has blessed some of us to possess His attribute. I wish this lady said more than a kiss before we left the house. I wish she could have opened her heart and say it all. No man can fail to recognize her beauty. Her teeth are well aligned in the mouth and are as white as snow, contrary to my wife's. I think she can make a good family and have very admirable children. I think Jesus has a reason for not allowing her to get a right man as she thinks. I think I am the right man she has been looking for and if she opens her eyes well, she is going to see that before it's too late. I am willing to welcome her into my life at whatever cost but she has not realized such a great secret. Jesus, open her eyes and touch her heart to accept me."

On her part, Wangeci was used to the roads in the town and hence didn't have to concentrate too much for safe driving. She was thinking hard about this handsome gentleman who was blind to the extent of not seeing her heart's desires yet he had 'the Holy Spirit and was next to God'. "This man is taking too long to say something that can bring life to my soul. I have been waiting for more than two months and he has been like an idiot. How can you live with a lady like me when you are a man and say nothing? Unless you are not normal! I wish God would touch him to see what I am going through for his sake. But I must win him, whether through orthodox means or unorthodox means. I don't care about his wife, but I only need to keep it secret and never to demean her because she is still my friend. After all, she has brought me 'the broth' right into my house. I cannot suffer anymore when this man is around. But why is he not bothering with me even when I walk almost naked in the room? Does he fear me or am I the one supposed to speak first? Maybe he fears his wife, or thinks I might spread the news to his wife through gossips like any other woman. He does not know that I am secretive more than men. I have spent countless nights with countless number of men in town and in my village, yet I have never disclosed such vital information to any lady or man. If he could read my heart and the countless secrets that I have, he would gain courage to approach me, being assured of total secrets. A man ever in suits is very appropriate for me to be walking around with before I throw him out of my life. I cannot retain him as my husband, what for? If I have not retained the other men, who is he? After I use him for some time, I know that the urge and desire to have him will have disappeared and longed for someone else; which would be the perfect time to walk away from him."

"I would hate myself if I would find myself clinging to a man when I don't have feelings towards him. How can you live with a man yet you are bored by him? It's not possible at all. Even when they say we must marry one man and live together forever, I wonder what they mean because that cannot apply to me. What if I am bored? I continue forcing myself to live with him? Never! The right way, I think, is to have a man for some time, once you are bored, you walk out of such a relationship and go looking for better relationships. Men are all over and I wonder why you can be a bastard to live in one place with one man. Furthermore, what about when several men come after you? You disappoint all the others and walk with one? Impossible! You keep all of them as a wise and smart guy. You don't just go choosing one and letting all the others go. But if this man is interested in me, why not say something special when we are alone like today and now in particular? Does he see me like an ugly lady that he cannot want to walk around with? Maybe it's because of fear; let me not judge him wrongly. Maybe he would go mad if I suggested something to him directly without asking for useless kisses that don't 'eliminate this haunting thirst'. But I still have hope, that before this week ends, he would have accepted my priceless offer."

"He thinks I am interested in him preaching to me? If he thinks so, then he is mistaken and wrong. He better change such a belief and think otherwise. But is it good to destroy such an innocent soul? I usually see him innocent and it would be like a curse to infect him with my disease. I would end up regretting for the rest of my life, for destroying the innocent. But is he innocent really? Jesus said, in Mathew chapter seven, verse one onwards, that we should not judge others; therefore, I don't judge this man as innocent. If I judge him innocent, he might judge me guilty and that would make him fear me even more. But how shall he repay the services I have been providing to him and his family? I have provided food, shelter, clothing and now a piece of land for his church. Plus other things I have done to the whole family. Should all these go unpaid? No, no, no, I refuse. He must repay. I have scratched his back and he has no option but to scratch mine. I have lived with this deadly disease for the last five years and have no hope of living for the next five years. My days are numbered and must hand-over my sufferings to as many as I can. I got it from a pastor, a man of God, and I must leave it with a man of God too. So far, I have handed it over to eight senior pastors and that is not yet enough. I must part it with these men of God until I am satisfied. He cannot escape it, whether he likes it or not. But what if he infects his wife too? Won't God persecute me for such wickedness? But I am a lady too, and I was infected, who is she then? Is she important than me? Of course not, I am greater than her, yet I have it. If she succumbs to the same, well and good, it's up to her and upon her; I shall not be answerable to anyone."

"If he is infected, he would have learnt a lesson that he would never forget. I learnt the hard way, from my mistakes and they too should learn it that way. I don't care if we shall all perish. There was a time I heard rumours about his 'dirty ways'. That time, I heard he had been caught with a church member's wife. I heard they were caught in a cave near the forest by a congregation of his own church, who were coming back from a visitation to one of their own who was sick; and he had lied to them that he was could not make it because he was not feeling well too. There was a time I also heard his wife complaining about him luring female church youth members to visit him each at a time in a lodging outskirts of town. That time he denied the allegations and escaped any possible legal action against him. It was only last year when he was caught with a Sunday-school child in his room and both were naked. He slammed the allegations and said it was his enemies who were out to taint his good record in pastorate. He defended himself saying that he was at the table room while the child was taking tea in the kitchen. It was a white lie because both were in the washroom and had no water or towels. Didn't I hear the other day how several ladies went to church and accused him for impregnating them and failing to take care of their children? How many were they? Four of them, yes I recall, carrying their infants and wanted him forced to contribute towards raising up of the kids. That case was 'killed' and we have not heard anything about it since then. I can actually liken him to a leopard in sheep's shed. He is actually an animal."

At that time, Mungai received a call on his phone. The ringing drew their attention from the land of thoughts. He checked the screen to see who it was before he answered. It was Wanjiku, Ciku as they called her in church. He trembled but remembered that Wangeci was waiting for him to answer the call. He answered it reluctantly; fearing that what she was to say would 'spoil the broth'. "Hallo, good morning?" "Good afternoon, it's already afternoon and not morning." "Ooooh, sorry, it's afternoon, my mind was busy the whole morning and that's why I had forgotten. How may I help you please?" "What are you doing right now? I need to discuss something with you. The pregnancy I got is not giving me easy time." He interrupted her very fast, "Please call me later; right now I am on the road and cannot concentrate well. Call me after two hours please." He disconnected the phone call, switched it off and placed it back to the pocket. He kept quiet for the next few minutes waiting for Wangeci to comment on what she heard over the phone. Wangeci went on with her endless thoughts, "This man thinks he is wise? Idiot! Is he trying to make fool out of me? I have heard about pregnancy and he disconnected the phone to make fool out of me. I assure you young man, you cannot escape my snare. I am going to turn your wisdom into folly. Today and tomorrow, you must have fallen victim of my plans. You must carry my disease to the next few people that I cannot reach in the remaining time."

Mungai was also lost in thoughts. "This Ciku would have caused me trouble. If she was near, I would have killed her, with my bare hands, on the spot and thrown her in the place I threw the body of the other child who died when we were in bed. But, gosh, that child was under 'marriage-age' and I didn't know. If I knew, I would have spared her but I regret I did not know in advance. But she told me she was not feeling well and her body was weak. If I listened to her, she would still be alive. I wish that issue shall never surface itself in whatsoever way. If God decides to confound us, He would bring all these deeds to light and that would be my end. Anyway, the child is in grave and I cannot reverse it. This lady is wasting my time; she is supposed to have said something good before we return home." At that point, they arrived to the first plot. "Here we are my hubby in Christ Jesus. Let's park the car under this tree and have a view of the land." She parked the car and they alighted. It was a good piece of land and the size was appropriate too. After some minutes, they drove off as time was not on their side. The second plot was few metres from the first one. It was larger than the previous and well positioned in the heart of the town. The third one was the best positioned for constructing a church. The size was twice as large as the previous two combined together. It was surrounded by many residential houses and no church was around. It was the best place so far for the church as many people would swarm to his church like bees. He even suggested to her that there was no need of seeing the other plots as this was far much better than any other place. "The size is good and can even help us build several residential rooms for further income. Such people that would reside there would be assembling in my church for sure, no doubts; which would help scale up offerings and tithes. Let's go back to the house for lunch, I am hungry." "I wish we could see the rest of the plots because you might decide to make more investments. I said I am yours and anything I have is yours too in Jesus Christ. Therefore, make as many decisions as you can. Let's go and see the rest."

They left and he was shown several other plots. They were big enough for a church but were not strategically positioned for church. Later, they were very tired and needed to have lunch and rest. They started their journey back home and this time round, each was waiting for the other to introduce a 'good topic'. As they approached home, she asked him, "You mean we are going back to the room without you appreciating my work? I have felt that I have done a lot and I need to be appreciated. How do you want to appreciate my work?" He smiled and aired his mind out. "Tell me all that you want and I am going to agree with you. I can appreciate your work in any way possible. Just fell free to suggest anything. I am yours in Christ and you are my wife in Christ. Remember that Jesus has set us free and we are no longer slaves. We are no longer judged according to the Law but we are fully justified through faith in Jesus my Saviour; as He has said in Romans 14:23, "For whatsoever is not of faith is sin". He has liberated my soul and body and I walk by His grace. Do you believe this my wife? If you believe it, then we are free and can enjoy life in Christ. We should strive to enjoy within Him and not outside our Lord."

"In the beginning, God gave us His Law so that we could be justified by the Law. All this can be found in the books of Exodus and Deuteronomy. We could be made right before God our Father. But we all lost our way and no one was found worthy to stand before God; this can be read in the books of Psalms and Romans, that no one is righteous under the sun. Therefore, we were to perish. But God my Father came to realize all this and came up with a new way of saving us from the Hell-fire. This way was through His only begotten Son; who was to lose His life on the cross for the sake of justifying us through faith in His Son, Jesus Christ. This is also reiterated in the book of Acts chapter 4 verses 12, "Neither is there salvation in any other name under heaven given among men, whereby we must be saved." We are no longer sinners in any way. We are holy and righteous; we are God's children and sons. We shall rule with Jesus forever in His kingdom. We cannot be sinners anymore as we have been sanctified in His blood once and for all. We are like God Himself as long as we are in Christ Jesus, our Saviour. I hope you now understand why we cannot be condemned by anyone. Whatever we do, whether, in the eyes of men, it is seen as wrong, unethical, immoral or anything like that, we shall remain holy forever. The Bible has clarified this; it has stated categorically that no more sacrifice shall be offered for us because God Himself has sanctified us forever. These things are clear in the Gospel books and that is why we are always happy and enjoying life in Christ. So, no sin can take you back to the Devil once you are made righteous through faith. Visit again the book of Romans chapter 14 verses 23, "For whatsoever is not of faith is sin". Here, God is telling us that if we do anything and we have faith in Christ, then we are safe. Even if you sin but you are in faith, then you are holy, righteous, sanctified and precious in His eyes. The same book chapter 10 verses 13 have it, "For whosoever shall call upon the name of the Lord shall be saved." In general, He is saying that even if we do filth, evil or abomination in His sight, we are still holy because we have faith in Him and call upon His name. The sin according to the Bible is whatever you do but not in faith. Just practice wickedness and maintain faith, just do evil and mischief but keep faith. Therefore, when you do evil, it is actually not evil but good. You only need to maintain your faith in Him, remain in Him and call upon Him for help. Are we together my wife in Jesus? There is a lot that I can say but I don't want to exhaust your mind; as they say that, too much of something is poisonous."

"Thank you so much my dear and hubby in Christ. I love you so much in Christ. That is why I always say that you are God's chosen pastor, whom Jesus Himself has entrusted with His sheep. You are the custodian of God's people, truth and anything that is holy. You are a gift from heaven. It's very rare to get a person who can understand the Bible and elaborate it to many without concealing anything important. You have the right wisdom from heaven, from Jesus Himself. May I now suggest what I want?" "Yes dear, suggest without fear. Say all that is in your heart. I am ready for anything." She parked the car at the roadside. She put her hands on his shoulders and looked into his eyes. "Now that we are late for lunch, I just want a good kiss; a kiss that will leave me breathless and helpless. I want to lose my mind in the process and I don't want to ever forget this day. Ready? Let's go, do it with all of your heart, mind, soul and spirit." "I am going to do it in Jesus and in faith, even if you want more than a kiss, just say it and we shall do it in faith and in our Lord." After 'doing it', they drove off back to the house.

Few days later, Mungai visited Mr Kibe for some discussions. The two met in his former church. Mr Kibe was his friend for a long time and was against Mungai's kicking out of church, but his voice was not as strong as that of his cohort. They were glad to meet again and were ready to share a lot on matters concerning the church. "I am glad to meet you. We have not talked since I left the church but I hope you are doing well." "Oh, yes,

I am glad to meet you too. How have you been? You left us in a hurry and we have not communicated since then." "I have been doing well, my family is fine and we are healthy. God has protected us and has been our provider all the times. Life has been good and my wife is struggling with simple jobs. Is there any news since I left?" "Oh, yes my friend, indeed God is great; He is caring and has been on our side since time immemorial." He lowered his voice and whispered to his ears, "Ok, since you left us, we have increased in number and consequently, the income has gone up too. We are able to collect almost thrice of the previous offerings, gifts and tithes. In fact, Mr Waithani has been promoted to take your position. He has the best tongue ever to help attract more sheep. He has devised many ways of increasing our income; he has started campaigning for expansion of the church where members contribute 'heavily' if I may say so. He ensures that the three of us escape with more than three-quarters of each day's contribution. You know members cannot discern this craftiness and we try to maximize on that weakness."

"We must be as cunning as hare. But we try our best to have reasons to give, though not genuine, in case one of the members becomes mad and asks for us to account for the money we have so far. Waithani has devised several other ways to make the members contribute. For example, he comes up with many mini-fund-raisers and we gain a lot from these. Without such ways, it is difficult to earn good money in church. Do you know that we have each bought a small plot in this town since you left us? And you know how expensive plots are in town, but we have made it. That gives you a hint on the type and amount of money we get from these members. But one thing we exercise every day is preaching to them every verse that talks about tithes and offerings, gifts, giving to God, and the blessings. We preach hard on God's blessings to those who give to His church generously. We attack them in every way using the same Bible that we have. If you don't attack their hearts with the right verses, they are not likely to give generously and abundantly. We go straight to the book of Malachi chapter three, from verse eight onwards, and preach about robbing God in tithes and offerings; when they hear such words from God, they give and give till we acknowledge it as actually a harvest time."

"There was another Sunday I told members about aspiring to buy a car because I was commuting from far. They all embraced the idea and organized for a fund-raiser. On the D-Day, they gave all that they had and it was more than three times the money I wanted. I was greatly surprised on how such poor members can give such money. Though at the beginning, I had attacked their hearts and mind with several verses and they feared that God would curse whoever would not give. I used the extra money to take my family out for a tour in London. Leave that aside my friend; there was a day we saw the offering was not enough for all of our needs. Do you know what we did? Waithani prepared a sermon that day, purely on how God has condemned those who visit His place of worship while empty-handed. When they heard the voice of God Himself attacking them from all aspects of life, they gave offerings that compensated what they had failed to offer the previous Sunday and more. The extra contribution could cater for offerings for the following several weeks. We subdivided the extra among the three of us and I used my share to buy my wife a cheap car. So far we have two cars in my family, courtesy of church members."

"So, whenever you see people have slacked their efforts in giving, just use verses and bring them to your feet." "You now remind me of the verses I used the other day to force them to contribute towards my children's school fee." "Hahahaaaa, I remember that my friend. By the way, what made you preach such a gospel?" "Hahahaaaa, that's who I am, I can preach till heaven itself descends to earth. Do you know that it was a gospel of my own? I saw that these people were not willing to help me simply because they too had children who had been chased out of school due to lack of fees. They wanted to equate themselves to me; so they wanted my children to stay at home, just like their children. I saw that as stupidity because my children are more important than theirs. In fact, they were arguing that my children are in private boarding schools and hence more expensive than their children. My children cannot be equated to theirs, never. So, what I did was very simple; I thought for several days and came up with my own gospel. Did you hear me quoting books in the Bible that actually don't exist?" "Yes pastor Mungai, I heard books like Jacob and Joseph." "That's true, I fabricated a sermon and a gospel out of books that don't exist in the Bible because I knew that the congregation could not realize. They don't carry their Bibles along with them and to the few who carry them; they don't open them in church. So, people don't understand what is in the Bible. In case you find few who are trying to search for verses, when you mention them in church, you try to make it quick and read for them from your note book. You must use your wit to win them. You also mix your gospel with the commonly known verses to bring more confusion."

"If a person struggles to find a verse that you have mentioned and you are sure it does not exist, you add another one from another known book; such a person stops from finding what does not exist to what exists. You only make the process as fast as possible. In case you notice that no one is opening their Bibles, then you don't have to hurry in any way; you just preach and read verses at your own pace. That's why you could hear me quoting verses from the book of Jacob and Joseph, sometimes not in a hurry while sometimes in a hurry; just playing around with their psychology. So, in the end, they were 'touched in mind and heart' by 'my gospel'. They contributed more than I wanted. I wanted one-term-fee, but I ended up clearing two-year-fee. That's how we achieve greater things than our expectations. We cannot endure simple problems like anyone else when we can employ our minds and this book called Bible. We have it in our vicinity and must benefit from the same. Or you want to tell me that I should spend nights on empty stomachs with my family when I have the Bible?"

"The Bible is a very powerful tool in acquiring wealth and riches. You live comfortably and happily; in plenty of everything, when you use it wisely. You can buy lands, houses, cars, fly out of country as often as possible, have your children study from abroad, and take your wife for outings every weekend, live in the most prestigious estates in the city and much more. In fact, the benefits thereof are countless. I usually compare them to the countless blessings from God Himself. Sometimes I tend to think that the difference between us, 'wise pastors,' and thugs in the town is that they use guns, knives and other dangerous weapons to rob men when we are only using the Bible and our wit to rob the same men. Again, the difference between us and the government's corrupt men is that we use the Bible and face no risk of going to jail when they use a lot of lies, efforts, collaborators and in the end, they face jail and execution through judiciary. They also live in fear of prosecution while we are always free and safe in 'Jesus' cocoon'. But how did you manage to buy such a huge land in our neighbouring country, yet our income from the church was meagre those days and we had not improved so much in devising our ways of forcing them to offer good offerings?"

Kibe laughed heartily before he could say a word. "My friend, I was very wise those days too. I had a different church back at home that I used to earn a better income. I started the church two weeks before I came to join you in this church. I was given that idea by my friend who had a lot of wealth within one year, all from his church. In fact, a church is better than a job or a business. It has so many advantages, the most important being how fast you get rich without any genuine struggle. Plus, no taxes for Caesar. So, from my church back at home, I accumulated money like never before. Contributions from members were hefty and they used to bring a lot of food stuffs as their gifts to God. That food used to serve all of my family needs and I could sell the excess for more money. In fact, I used to collect all the food they offered, then I could preserve it well and during dry seasons when food was in shortage, I could sell the food to the same people at exorbitant prices. That too accelerated my wealth. Later, I saw it wise to invest in a foreign country by buying a piece of land; I did not want the same people to realize my ways because that would kill their spirit of giving in church. Sometimes I used to misinterpret Bible verses to suit my intentions. Sometimes you preach what they want to hear and you are at peace with them. That way, you ensure they don't hate you. I still use all these ways back in my home church and in this church. I just try to modify here and there to cope with the new generation and become more accommodative. I know you are an expert in that."

"Yes Pastor Kibe, I have experience in some of those vital skills and I used to use them, I also intend to use them later on. I usually tell my friends that if you want to live well with the congregation, ensure you don't preach to them the verses that touch anything to do with their sins, never do that. If you preach against their evil ways, you create enmity between the church and the pastors. People march out of church like soldiers in war. We exercise a lot of wisdom when it comes to selection of verses to be preached each day. And that's why we have a program of pre-selected verses that cover the whole year's sermons to avoid messing up. We have to keep the old members in church and at the same time ensure we are able to increase in number; new members are registered with time. Sometimes we need meetings together as pastors, irrespective of our denominations, to encourage and remind each other of such tactics; otherwise, we might kill 'this lucrative business from heaven' very easily, and that is not the will of Christ."

"You remind me of many things we usually observe in church, but as you said, it's true that we need to be organized to avoid our own unintended ruin. There is something else that you have not mentioned; there was a time members accused the church (the four of us) for misappropriation of funds and lack of accountability. How did you manage to 'cool the congregation's wrath and uproar' down? It's one of the mysteries that I have never understood because we were in danger of losing the job and you saved us so easily." "That was very easy Mr Kibe. I have countless tactics of killing my prey; just as they say that there are many ways of killing a rat. I just took the Bible and searched for some verses that could save us, work that took me days and nights. I found the verse in the Gospel books that talked about muzzling the mouth of an ox; it is a verse that prohibits one from muzzling the mouth of an ox that treads out the corn. Oh, I have remembered it; it is in the book of 1st Corinthians chapter 9 verses 9. I ensured I preached that verse for more than two hours. I really convinced them that as long as we are working with the gospel, then we should also benefit from the same without questions. I also quoted the Law on how the priests were supposed to work in the temple and they were really permitted to eat what they are offering to God. Imagine a priest eating some meat from a lamb of sacrifice which is very holy as it is meant for the Lord? If God permits a priest to do that, then, who are the congregation to question us? I made sure they got ashamed for trying to question our works. We can always employ the Bible to defend our greediness, immorality and devilish acts. I also quoted the same Corinthians and the same chapter but verses 14, "Even so has the Lord ordained that they which preach the gospel should live of the gospel", which made them keep quiet. The verses were so strong that no one spoke anymore."

"Thank you for that advice, I think I only need to practice some of these strategies because sometimes I tend to forget most of them. Before I forget, I wanted to inform you that there was a lady who came here some three days ago. There was another one this morning who came in tears and was carrying a three-month old kid. The first lady was mentally challenged, or insane as you know, but was pregnant. She wanted to talk to you about her expected child so that you could make better plans for the child. She claimed that you impregnated her during those days when you were 'performing miracles' to women and ladies of our church. She wanted to explain everything in details in public but I stopped her and took her to a private place. She briefed me on how you informed her on your ability to restore her mental normalcy but later you spent a night with her in pub's lodging. She is very confused and just wanted to meet you. In fact, she explained all this in tears, bitter tears." Mungai interjected, "Did you tell her any of my whereabouts?" "No, no, no, that is a mistake I cannot afford to make. I lied to her that you were very sick in hospital far from town and that we hadn't received any updates on your progress. I told her that you were run over by a motorcycle and a train concurrently and police took you to hospital in a critical condition. She later left and promised to come back later to me for updates; just in case you are back, she might benefit too."

"The second lady was carrying a child. She was very bitter from the look of the things. Her face showed a picture of someone ready for revenge. She was actually complaining. She told Muturi that you had promised to marry her but you left her immediately she got pregnant. You blocked her calls and messages and she hasn't been able to contact you. You had promised her a good life in church but she has not seen any of those promises being fulfilled. He told her that you left the church long time ago for your village. She was told to come after two years to see if there shall be any news. Pastor Muturi knew that by the time two years are over, she would have recovered from such a disappointment and would not be seeking to revenge anymore; he is very wise too and knows how to handle such delicate cases with care. So far you are safe and secure from any threat. No need for unnecessary stress." "Thank you guys for saving me. Though you kicked me out of the church that we founded together, I know that you still love me and that you are not ready to embarrass me or see me suffer defeat. What about the men and ladies who were seeking for you day and night before I left?"

"Hahahaaaa, you haven't forgotten those things? You know I almost ran away from this town. One lady had recorded a statement with police about what had happened and they were looking for me day and night. You know, the men were seeking to have me prosecuted in court after defiling several girls. But not defiling as such because I always agreed with those girls before they 'offered me the services' and I ensured that I gave them some money as appreciation fee. So, although they were under age of adults, we did it after reaching a consensus. I did not let them down because I also kept my promises, of which I was paying a thousand shillings each. The ladies were not happy because they were complaining that I had 'thrown their marriages into pieces' but I always refute such allegations. You know, if their husbands found out that I had affairs with their wives and kick them out of their marriages, then I should not be blamed. I cannot carry their crosses because the ladies are grown-ups and knew what they were doing when they fell into my traps. So, I have nothing to regret at all. If you are divorced for whatever reason, then, don't lay the blame on me. I have no time or space to accept such non-sense."

"And how did you escape the arm of the police?" "It was really giving me hard time but I finally made it. I met their boss and talked to him in solitude. I fed his pocket beyond what he could expect. He appreciated me so much that he is now one of my greatest friends. He then promised to protect me and asked his juniors to abandon the plans of arresting me." "Where did you get the money from, for feeding his pocket with?" "There was a fund-raiser I organized in the name of contributing towards my child's hospital bill. I borrowed that idea from my friend in another church in our neighbouring town. I told members of my church that my child had been admitted to hospital for some weeks and the bill was beyond what I could afford. When they heard the bad news, they contributed generously and I divided that money into three parts. Two parts of that money went with that police boss. The last part was tangible too; I used it to service my car and renovating my house in this town. So, we can make it in life. I have achieved a lot of my targets so far; courtesy of my church and this Bible you see me holding in hands. My target so far is to become one of the billionaires in this country, and it's possible too. But let me tell you my friend, something you don't know so far; pastor Muturi is already a multi-millionaire and is aiming to be a billionaire in the next one year. The guy is damn rich. I wish I was like him. But he has countless churches all over the country and in all towns. He targets the rich and the poor without discrimination. That's why he has huge incomes per month, ranging from several to hundred millions per month."

After some minutes of silence Mungai's phone rang. It was Wangeci who wanted to talk to him. "Hello pastor Mungai? This is your wife in Christ, Wangeci, calling from home. How have you been?" "Oh, I am doing good, I see you care a lot about my welfare. I am coming and will be there in the next one hour. What are you doing dear?" "I am resting in bed waiting for you. I miss you a lot and just want to see you. Just come without delay, I'm waiting for you dear." "Ok, I am coming." He disconnected the phone call and turned to his friend. "May I go now? We will keep on communicating and I plan to come back soon. Enjoy your time and keep in touch." "Goodbye my friend, see you another day." He went to see him off.

He met Wangeci who welcomed him into her house with a kiss. He felt so warm that he said in his heart, "Why don't I 'devour her'? My wife is not around and I am wasting time like a fool. I need to show some level of maturity!" They went into the table-room where he was served with a piece of coconut, bread and butter, a cup of tea and some fruits. He ate in a hurry and was later served with some rice and a plate of meat stew. He enjoyed till he thanked her unconsciously, calling her 'my wife'. The lady went out of the house to ensure that no one was around and that the children were not anywhere within the vicinity. She pushed the door to its lock and went straight to the bedroom. She called Mungai in a cool and enticing voice. "Pastor Mungai my hubby in Christ, come for a minute." Mungai left the table-room in haste and headed to her bedroom. "Yes my dear, here I am." He was "shocked" to find her naked on the bed, facing the roof. A hot chill went through his veins and he felt paralysed. "Are you sure you can do this to me? I am really weak and you must "help me" because I cannot go back to the sitting-room." "Yes, dear, I cannot endure the 'burning' that I go through each day and you are around. I was not born to endure and persevere in any way. Just come and do not fear anything. I have been waiting for you the whole day. I have confirmed that there is no one around the compound."

He entered the room and after about half an hour of "hard work", he was thirsty. She went to the table room and got a cup of water from the refrigerator. He drank it and felt rejuvenated. He continued with "his mission" till she could "take no more". They bathed together in the in-house-bathroom and got out of the house to bask in the afternoon sun.

They were a "happy couple that Christ had brought together". Each went back to the normal ocean of thoughts. Mungai was delighted for achieving it, "At least I have made it. All I know is that there is nothing that is not possible. We have all it takes to achieve great things. She thought she could escape my long term plans but at least she has shown me that she loves me and means it whenever she calls me husband, dear and so on in Christ. I can take her as my wife for some time before I decide something else." Wangeci was also busy in her thoughts, "He thought he could escape my trap. We must carry this cross together and not as Christ said that each should carry his own cross. I don't have strength to carry crosses alone. We must do it with such idiots. But I have enjoyed the work he has done today; he is like an expert in that field. He seems to have great and precious experience, or it could be because he has defiled many. But I am glad that God heard my cry and gave him into my hands. I have won and I don't care if he leaves me or not. No, but I should enjoy his expertise for some time before I walk to another bastard like him. If he discovers I was sick, I think he might kill me. But that does not worry me as long as I know my days are numbered too. If he dies without achieving his will, let him die. I also got it before I achieved anything substantial, and I started numbering my days on earth from that day."

"How did you see it? Did I do it as you wanted?" He asked her in a whisper. "Yes, of course you did it beyond my expectations. I loved it and that has made me love you even more. I cannot afford to lose you in life. I would encourage you to be doing it daily because I don't see the need to suffer when you are around. We need to be closer to each other each day. I told you that Jesus had good plans on us and cannot fail to assist us whenever we are helpless. I love you dear in Christ." "Thank you, as I told you, as long as we are doing things in Christ, then we are holy and righteous and pure and even peculiar people in His sight. He has even referred to us as "Holy people, peculiar people and precious people, a royal generation of priests"; all in the book of Peter. We are really blessed and if you go to the book of John, He has called us His sons. He even promised Abraham, our father, that He would bless us fully in the latter times, which is today. Therefore, let us enjoy life together in Jesus and we shall remain secure and free from God's wrath." They smiled to each other and kept quiet as they enjoyed the sun's rays that were like medicine to their skins.

Many days passed, with the two "eating the best honey" on earth, and after two months of "good life", Mungai went and constructed a church building in the plot he had preferred from Wangeci's property. He was able to construct a two roomed house on the same plot and he moved there with his entire family. His wife had not spent even a single night with him since the day they were chased out of their former church. The day they occupied the new house on the church-yard, she signalled him that she was very "hungry". They spent the whole day "feeding" as a way of her compensating the lost days. Mungai did not know that he had the worst and most feared disease in the country and beyond. Her wife did not know that her husband had any affair with Wangeci. They went on with their life, knowing everything was a blessing; though he used to visit Wangeci as often as possible.

His church gained popularity within half a year, under the name "The Power and Miracles of Jesus Ministries". They developed faster than many churches did; with countless members. They claimed that Pastor Mungai was blessed and anointed to preach the good news to many. They saw him as god and consequently, their offerings were immeasurable. Many ladies used to visit him on week-days for special prayers and counselling. He was a good counsellor and used to tell them that he received the gift from Jesus Himself through a vision in his room. His family made a big improvement in the first two years; he took his children to the most prestigious schools in that town, his wife purchased several plots and started a factory and car-dealing centres all over the town, several residential homes, established a good number of churches in town under the name "The Power and Miracles of Jesus Ministries" and much more. They became a source of employment and even Wangeci was attending church services there, though for some months before she fell terribly ill. She was baptized in that church as a sign of membership but later on, she could not leave her house. The church used to have some services in her compound to show their togetherness. Before she was unable to move, eat or talk, she met the man of God, Mungai, and gave him a copy of her will. He was given the plot he had built in his church free of charge, of which he appreciated with many thanks. She later asked him to contact her parents and inform them that she was winding up her journey on the earth.

Few weeks later, she was announced dead in the most expensive hospital in town. Mungai's mourned her death for many days as they recalled how her life had been a blessing to them. She was later buried in her compound in a service that was presided by Pastor Mungai and his wife. During the burial ceremony, they praised her until people recognized how dear her life was to them. Her parents were there and could not imagine that they had lost their dear daughter; they loved her so much that they could not help but cry in public. But the main issue among the people who knew her was what had killed her yet she was so young. It was a concern that was never made clear in their minds. Life went on without Wangeci.

One evening, Pastor Muturi paid Mungai a visit. The two were happy to meet each other as they had known each other for quite some time. "I am glad to find you doing great and sorry for coming without a prior notice." "No harm my friend, you are free to visit me any time of the day and night, feel at home and feel most welcome." "Thank you Mungai. I usually hear from my colleagues how you are doing great with a lot of progress since we sent you packing from our church." The two laughed heartily for some time before Mungai could say a word. "Yes, yes, since you threw me out, I have had good times and life has been like adventure. Jesus has been gracious to me and my family as a whole. I have established so many churches under one name in this town and I am planning to expand this "holy business" to other towns." "That's a great idea and please, you make sure you achieve whatever you purpose." "I must do that; I don't settle for anything less than achieving. But I have one request I want from you." "Yes, feel free to air it out. Don't feel shy to share your problem. I am here for you and we can always help each other." "Thank you again my friend. Now, I wanted to know how you get those powers that you use to perform miracles in your churches. It can help me too to keep my herd of sheep growing and not lose any of those that I already have."

"Heheheee, that's the only concern? Let me tell you that that has been very easy for me. As for me, I don't use powers; I use what we call 'the power of deception'. It happens like this; you train some people to pretend to be sick. Then you preach and pray when those trained are seated among the congregation. Later you ask for those who have faith in Jesus Christ of Nazareth and our Saviour to come forward, if any is sick. They appear together with others who don't know what is happening from the side of the normal congregation. Then you offer a strong prayer and announce healing to all. Those trained pretend to have received the Holy Spirit and Power from Christ, they jump with joy; some leave their wheelchairs behind and join you in dancing to praise the name of Christ, some stretch their hands and pretend to recover from paralysis, some pretend to have received forgiveness, some say they have received sight and hearing. Then, you announce the healing of those guys officially in church and insist that they were healed because of their faith in Jesus alone. To those not healed, say it's because their faith was wanting before God. Tell them that Jesus does not condone unbelief in any way. Condemn and reprimand them for testing the Spirit but pray to Christ to forgive them. Then declare forgiveness to them from Christ Himself. Any time you pray, pretend that actually Jesus is communicating with you; use some awkward means to convince them that the Spirit of our Lord is really working in you, like speaking is some language they don't understand (tongues). They actually believe that God has sent you whenever they hear you speak in tongues. You try to make it live and vivid so that the congregation thinks everything is genuine. You stage-manage it until it looks like those described in the miracles of Jesus Christ; in the books of John, Mathew, Luke and Mark. Fake it until you make it, that's what I can say. People don't realize that the whole thing is a total lie. They swarm to your church like flies and even invite more until you are forced to expand your church's room to help accommodate all. Guess what! The returns increase proportionally; the tithes, offerings, gifts and such likes. You can become a trillionaire unknowingly. Yet it's a hoax!"

"It is as simple as that. But make sure you perform 'those miracles' once in like two months so that is does not jeopardize the whole thing. Make sure also that you preach those verses that touch miracles and the power of Jesus. Demonstrate to the congregation fully on how the power of Jesus works to the believers by quoting as many verses and miracles as possible. Sometimes add your own words because they don't even know when you are quoting your verses and when you are quoting Bible verses." "Wow! Ok, thank you. I thought and have believed that you actually use powers." "No, no, no, I have never used powers but when things shall fall apart, I shall move from this town and start life in another town, or I shall start using powers like what my friends do. I have several friends who use those deceiving powers but they pay some fee to get the powers. This is what one of them does; "There is a witch-doctor or more appropriate, they have a doctor who gives them some power that seems to be working miracles but no real miracles."

"Have you ever seen the acrobats who perform some mysterious things like turning papers into handkerchiefs, eating bananas and vomiting them in form of needles, eating fire that does not burn them, walking and riding bicycles on strings and so on? Such powers are not easily understood but they do fake miracles, one thinks they are miracles because they can be seen as so but are not real miracles. So, he buys such power from the doctor and performs miracles in church like once in two months. So, when he uses that power on someone who is lame, people see him walking and completely healed. After leaving the church, the power leaves the healed man and he goes back to his former state. Then the pastor healing them announces at the front of the church and in loud voice that Jesus has healed them because they have faith in Him. Then, he warns them that whoever does not hold on to his faith in Christ, then the "Holy Spirit" would leave him and his final state would be worse than the beginning. He makes sure that he quotes the verses where Jesus said that if an evil spirit is cast out of a man and the house is cleaned, then, that evil spirit goes and calls some other seven evil spirits and they come back, find the house well swept and they occupy in him full, making his final state to be worse than before. I don't remember the verses well but that is the message. So, those healed by these powers get sick again as soon as they leave the church or as soon as the pastor is gone. When they ask him later about falling sick again, of those healed, he quotes those verses I have told you and they keep quiet. That is how he earns and maintains his people in church. Members increase each month until the results are that, he now wants to go and live abroad because of the wealth he has. I therefore advise you to try my ways before you go for those powers. In case you exhaust it then you can try the second one though I doubt the possibility of exhausting it. Or better than that, you can combine both and make the best out of it."

"Oh, I have remembered the exact words and the verses that he quotes. Mathew 12:43-45- "When an unclean spirit goes out of a man, He goes through dry places, seeking rest, and finds none. Then He says, 'I will return to my house from which I came.' And when He comes, He finds it empty, swept, and put in order. Then He goes and takes with him seven other spirits more wicked than himself, and they enter and dwell there; and the last state of that man is worse than the first. So shall it be with this wicked generation." He uses these verses to defend his dark powers."

The discussions went on till it was late in the day. When darkness knocked the doors, Mungai went to see him off. He went back to his home and thought carefully on what Muturi had explained. He decided to continue examining the tactics till he could come to a better conclusion. Few days later, he decided to go for Muturi's tactic; that of 'the Power of Deception'. He also decided to have a special team of both young ladies and men. He could train them in his compound and use them to achieve his agendas in churches. He knew it would work without any challenge.

One evening, he remembered his great friend, Wangeci. He asked his wife to bring him Wangeci's photo that had been lying in the drawers for long. She obeyed her husband's voice without any suspicion. "I have missed this lady and the way she helped us. Imagine giving us a plot in the heart of the town free of charge! She was really a blessing to us. May God rest her soul in eternal peace. Do you still miss her?" His wife replied very fast, "Yes, my dear, I miss her but I have to let it go because no tendency of her mound can lose her spirit from death's gin. Just try and get her memories out of your mind. I know she did great to us but let's move on with life." "Ok, dear, lets sleep then; take the photo back to the drawers." She took the photo back and went straight to bed. He followed her though was not feeling sleepy. In bed, she fell asleep within several minutes while he headed straight to an ocean of thoughts. "She was really beautiful! What could have caused her death? What did the doctor say? I did not ask him though I was in the hospital. Tomorrow, I must visit the hospital and enquire more from the doctor. What shall he say? Shall he not think it weird and insane to ask more about a dead person? But let me just try, if he responds negatively, well and good, if positively, well and even better. I need to understand her death. Such a lady I loved should not die like that. She was supposed to live more years than all of us on earth. I really miss her and need to understand her life better. But I am lucky because there is a lady in church who takes after her; she has a better body shape that is bigger than Wangeci's, she is taller, more light-skinned and sometimes looks like a white lady. I should be consoling my soul with her. I won't stay far from her and I shall never leave her presence. Her husband doesn't have as much money to be compared to mine. I want to "feed her well" till she ignores her husband and that way, I shall achieve my goal. I saw her friend very beautiful too. She even smiled at me when I greeted her. I need to talk to her in private too. What was the name of that lady who likes wearing warm and smart? What was her name, am I forgetting? If I forget her name, it would mean that I am not serious with what I want in life. Oh, her name was Wairimu. Yes, Wairimu was her name. I now remember her, which shows the level of seriousness I have when it comes to ladies. I need to see her for better introduction; I need to know her better. She might make one of my nights "cool", especially when my wife goes for seminars and night-shifts at work."

His mind went over many names and faces of the ladies who were in his church till he fell asleep out of exhaustion. In the morning, he took breakfast that his wife had made at dawn before she left for work. He then prepared to meet the doctor before there was too much work in his office. The doctor was beginning his daily chores when he knocked the door. "Come in please." He entered and closed the door behind him. "Thank you, doctor. My name is Pastor Mungai. I am a man of God and I serve Christ Jesus according to His will. I heard His call long time ago, when I was still young, and obeyed Him. Since then, I have been faithful to Him and have been fighting according to the instructions he has given me. I am His servant and serve Him in my churches, "The Power and Miracles of Jesus Ministries". So far, we have seen His wonder working power and just to mention, the name of my church came down from heaven; Jesus showed me a vision and instructed me on what to call the church. I perform many miracles and many people have benefited from those miracles. Jesus manifests His power in many ways, for example; I have been praying for the sick and they get healed, I preach and multitudes turn from their evil ways to the righteous path. They repent and call upon the name of Christ for help. Those who believe, or have faith in Him, are fully saved and blessed. My prayers touch the heaven and God Himself pours His blessings on His people like rain. Have you ever heard about me?"

"Yes, yes sir, I have heard about you because my wife is one of those who joined your church recently, her name is Wairimu. She has been praising you for preaching the word of God the way it is and nothing else. She even asked me to help her raise some money because she wants to buy you a present. She feels really blessed; the way you preach, the way you expound on complex topic and make it simple, the way you are approachable and much more." "Wow, God is great, my Saviour Jesus Christ is great and marvellous. You mean Wairimu is your wife? She is very humble, Jesus has given her a heart like that of a child and she really loves the word of God. She is always very cooperative and participates actively in all church functions. I like her and most people admire her much. I have even placed her to the position of church lady; to guide and advice all the other ladies, to help me reach all the ladies in church and so on. You are really blessed to have such a wife. And I hope you treat her the way she deserves. Jesus really loves you and I hope you love Him too with an equal measure." "Yes, I am really blessed and I love Jesus as my personal saviour." "Ok, I don't want to take much of your time because I know you have a lot to do. But I really thank you for the warm welcome and the conversation; taking your time to have a discussion with me and letting me know you better"

"Ok, I am also grateful and it's pleasure to meet and know you. Maybe you had an issue you wanted to discuss with me? Or how may I help you, before you leave?" "Yes, yes, doctor, I wanted some clarification from you. There was a time I came to visit a young lady by the name Wangeci. She later died but you were the one who did all the testing and administered medication to her. Do you remember her; her parents came from abroad to meet her?" "Yes, I remember her. You mean that lady who had some wealth like plots in town and was not yet married?" "Exactly doctor, she is the one. Definitely you have remembered her. I just wanted to know what could have caused her death because that time, I was really depressed and could not concentrate on such information. I also had some vision just the day before and Jesus wanted me to go the next day and preach to a certain village whose dwellers were very wicked. He wanted them to hear His voice and turn to Him in repentance. Without explaining a lot, what caused her death?" "Eeeh, ok, I recall her very well and she was really young but finally had to die. Mostly, we don't share such information with anyone unless you are related to a person by blood. Such information is usually very confidential and maybe you tell me how you are related to her and what you intend to do with the information."

"Doctor, I understand all that and I am not related to her by blood but I have been sent with a command to you specifically. Yesterday night, Jesus showed me a vision. In that vision, He sent me to the doctor, you, to gather that information so that He can use it to send me to His servant who is not feeling well in another town. Jesus doesn't want His servant to perish but want me to go and condemn the disease in His name by calling that disease by its name. So, I have instructions from Him, whom I serve faithfully and whole heartedly, to go and chase that infirmity out of His servant. I therefore must know the name of the disease so that I can use it in my holy mission. He also told me that He wants to test your faithfulness in Him. He is to judge you by the kind of information you give me and by your obedience to His word through His servant, I." "Ok, I understand and since it's God Himself who sent you, sorry, Jesus Himself." "The two are one and the same thing. So you haven't made a mistake by calling Him God." He interjected him in a hurry. "Ok, then, what I wanted to say is that, since you have been sent by heaven itself, then I am going to share the confidential information with you. I don't want to attract or invite curses from heaven when I can save myself from the same. I know how Jesus can punish me if I keep the information when He needs it." "Try to be quick because of time, I don't think I have time to waste because His Spirit is pushing me to hurry up before His servant dies, he is in a critical condition. Just mention the disease and that is all that Christ is interested in, not whether you want to avoid curses or not."

The doctor got shocked and shivered a little. He then asked "the Man of God, Servant of Christ and Pastor from Heaven", "Would you please assure me that He won't curse me, because I don't want to die young or suffer in any way? Just ask Him to spare my life and I am ready to honour His voice and command." "Yes, He has assured you, He won't curse you and you shall live till you die, oh I mean, you shall live till you see many generations. God is with you and Jesus has assured you of your security, no need to worry. So, what was that disease?" "Thank you for that assurance, I am willing to obey Him now and forever." "Faster please!" "Ok, let's go to the files and see what I recorded because I cannot recall. I only remember her but not the cause of her death. Come on and help me peruse these countless files. They are so many and one person cannot exhaust them easily." The man of Jesus got angry. He thought the doctor was wasting his time but had to help him see the files. They went to the next room where there were literally countless files. They perused until they found the file. It was the man of God who found it. He opened it before informing the doctor, and guess what! He almost fainted but decided to remain strong. He closed the file in disbelief and handed it over to the doctor. "This has the same names as the one we are looking for. Do people share names, doctor?" "May I have a look at it?" He stretched his hand to take the file from the pastor's hand. "Why is your hand shaking like that? Are you afraid that something is wrong?"

"Hahahaaaa, no doctor, it is the power from the Holy Spirit that guides me that is at work. He is pushing me to hurry up as Jesus' servant is almost losing his life." "Ok, let's hurry up then." He opened the file and confirmed that actually it was the file they were looking for. He then informed him, "Man of God, yes this is the file you want to access. The lady actually died from HIV and AIDS. She could not be treated to recover as you know we don't have its cure yet. I have informed you and you may leave and try to save that servant's life as Jesus has instructed you. Please, do not take much longer in this place as God might punish us with curses. I have done my part, please do yours too. Why are you confused? You don't want to obey God's voice? You want to ignore Jesus' vision?" He came back to his senses, like a person who had just been woken up from deep sleep. He kissed the doctor goodbye and left, almost running like a child. The doctor noticed his eyes were wet with tears and his whole body was shivering and weak. He could not understand "what vision Jesus had given" him while they were looking for the files. He later went back to his office and continued with his work.

Mungai went through stress that he had never gone through since he was born. He was really sure that he had the disease too and had to start numbering his days. "Did the lady know that she was sick and the cause of her death was really that terrible one? If she was sure, why did she want me to fall in love with her? Who passed the disease to her? But I really doubt that she knew it. If she had knowledge on the same, she would have warned me from far not to approach her. Yes, she did not know because she even requested me to be preaching to the whole family when I was in her place. So, she was alright and knew nothing to do with it. What shall I do? I know my days are few and I don't have much to do with the limited time I have. You mean all the wealth I have is going to waste? I remember she also had lot of wealth but she left it having not enjoyed it. You mean I am going to follow the same example? Oh no, my God don't allow it to happen; I still have a lot to achieve and enjoy before I die. What is not happening? I have been fighting so hard in life to pile up all this wealth, and now I am sure of my fate! You mean all these properties and wealth means nothing at last? I don't believe it."

"I am cursed for sure. What shall I do to deliver myself? It is not possible to escape an early death. But I must do something! I don't want my wife to know anything like this, she might swallow me alive. Who shall be left with my children? My very own children shall become orphans? Waaah, I have lost everything in life. Nothing is more important than life yet I am now counting days before I expire. What a curse! And my beautiful wife, shall she die because of what she did not go for? I went for this disease and she has nothing to do with it, is it fair if she is eliminated out of the earth's face by other men's mistakes? There are indeed countless questions without answers. But before I die, I must revenge. Whoever did this to me is cursed, may she die instantly and never come back to the land of the living. I wish I did not pressure the doctor to look for files; it was like a file of curses and demons. But before I leave this world, people must pay for it. They cannot do this to me. They cannot mess up with my precious life and go unpunished. I must punish them for doing such wickedness to me. I am going to start with all the ladies in my church before I reach those in other churches that I have established. I am going to make sure that even that doctor who told me such bad news pays for it. His wife Wairimu will be the first one to face my wrath. I will never tell my wife anything about it; I shall never go to hospital to ensure that my wife does not come to know it. But I feel pity for her; she is really innocent and does not deserve to die. I wish she gets healed through some miracles that I don't know. But it's too late and I cannot save her, she too must die as we don't have an option but to die. My family is going to be wiped out of this earth. But I am lucky too because my children are not infected in any way. That is a blessing and may they live forever to compensate all the years that my wife and I are going to lose. God help them to live longer than any other human being on earth."

Later that week, he called Wairimu for a discussion in his church. Wairimu obeyed the pastor's call and went, ready for whatever the man of God would say. When she arrived, she was welcomed with a deep kiss, something that was not usual as he had never kissed her before. She felt appreciated and great. She could not imagine that she had found favour in the eyes of the servant of Christ Jesus. She was led to a more private room inside the church for some discussions as he put it. "Welcome dear. God has done great things to us and I would like us to start with a word of prayer; to thank Him and ask Him for guidance as we start our discussions. He prayed and she also prayed. "You know, when two guys come together in His name, He is with them and must show His power to them." "I like the way you preach from whatever angel, you are really blessed and I would like to be close to you for the rest of my life. I would like to be blessed the way you are blessed. Help me to be closer to Jesus than before, I know you can and have helped many." "Of course I can, but not by my strength, but through Christ my Lord who strengthens me. I don't want to take much of your time but want to go straight to the vital issues." "Yes please my Lord, tell me what the Lord Jesus has to say today. I am ready to hear His voice and obey it." "Great, great my dear, that is great. He is going to bless you dearly and abundantly. He loves such a heart that is ready to listen and take heed to His commands."

"Now, I know you know me very well because I have been preaching in our church each Sunday, I have prayed for many, I have healed many and counselled many too, and much more. Jesus has been working wonders through me to His children. Of recent, I have been experiencing some challenges as Jesus had explained to me that I would face some hard times for some weeks. My wife has been away for three weeks and I have been suffering as a man. My marriage rights are violated whenever she is not around. I prayed to God to take that pain away by bringing my wife back home but do you know what He answered? He came to me through a vision and explained to me how my wife was busy in another town doing His work. He told me that He had sent her for a mission that would take four more weeks before I could see her. I asked Him what I was supposed to do because I was going through hell and He gave me His reply." He paused to assess her understanding. "Yes my Lord, what did Christ say at last?" "He told me to go to a certain lady called Wairimu and talk to her. I should tell her to help me for several nights before my wife is back and not to fear for He Himself is with us. He told me that she is a wife to a doctor and is very humble and obedient. He told me that He has chosen her among many ladies and shall give her power later in life to help her minister in His vineyard. I could not question Him but to obey. That is why I have called you this evening and that is all that Jesus had given me."

She smiled and answered, "You mean I have found favour in Jesus' sight? You mean I am that great in His presence? I was counting myself worthless and mere human being but I have witnessed that actually, Jesus lifts those who are humble and lowly. May God be praised forever and may His mighty name be blessed among all people on earth." "Ok, that's it my dear. What have you decided?" "Of course I must obey the Lord! I cannot mess up with His word. He is not slack to punish, to punish those who are hard-headed and have stony hearts. I don't want to be one of them. I am willing and ready, do as you wish with me." They spent two hours together that evening, inside the church of God. They "enjoyed" the two hours till they had no strength left. Afterwards, they agreed to be meeting each evening at the same venue and for the same number of hours, till "his wife returns from the Lord's mission". She later drove her to her gate and returned to his wife in their prestigious home, in the church-yard.

After spending several evenings with Wairimu, he was sure that she must have contracted the disease. He then ensured that he was able to trick almost all the ladies in his church. These ladies used to hold him in high esteem and most thought he was really sent from heaven. They were sure that Jesus had anointed him to save His people and had given him all the powers to perform miracles and other great things. They could never challenge him and saw no fault in him; in fact, most thought he was the only infallible man on earth, next to Christ. He used that advantage to lure and trick them to fall victim of his cunning ways. He ensured he spread his disease to all these ladies and consequently, to their families. "They thought they were wise but I have turned their wisdom into folly. They thought I could carry such a cross alone but I feel happy and relieved. I feel the burden gone and I am light as before. At least I have accomplished my missions. If I die now, I have nothing to regret and have nothing to fear. A person who has achieved all his goals is happier than a king and should be ready to die any form of death; be it painful or peaceful one, it doesn't matter. Though I count everything I had gained as loss, I don't regret like a fool. I don't say 'I wish I knew' as that would prove me a fool yet I am not one of the fools."

He lived for some two more years before he fell ill, almost to rest eternally. He kissed goodbye most of his friends. He told his wife to make a will according to her wish. He did not want to write down any will as he counted things after his death as meaningless. One evening, he was rushed to a local medicine-man as he had instructed his family and church members; because he did not want the family or anyone to know what he was suffering from. He was announced a corpse before he even talked to the medicine-man. He was buried in his compound two weeks later. Many church members attended the burial where they mourned greatly and made sure that he was buried with most precious gifts they had brought him in his final journey; suits and caps, a toy-car, a toy-church, necklaces, watches, cakes, money and a huge, well-decorated Bible was buried with him too. They argued that he needed a Bible in his journey to heaven to help defeat the Devil and his followers in case they attacked him to commit sin, and would still require it in heaven. Some even argued that he would be anointed to preach to all angels and were sure that Jesus would be asking him often to conduct sermons in heaven in the evenings before they retired to bed. Some even were heard saying that, he would be one of those in charge of burials whenever angels died in heaven. His wife did not live for more than a year after her husband. She too was buried in their compound, next to her husband's grave. Pastor Kibe came and took the children and lived with them. He also inherited the churches according to the will signed by Mrs Mungai.

JUDAS ISCARIOT
THE SAVIOUR

THE ELECTION DATE WAS FAST APPROACHING AND PREPARATIONS were being made at a tortoise pace. Strategies were being made on how each famous politician would win their seats again. The citizens were also ready to exercise their democratic right in voting in the persons of their choice. It was being preached each day, on radios, televisions and newspapers, how the exercise would be free, fair and transparent. The commission in charge of the elections was also promising everybody of a credible election. Every citizen was complaining how the government in power had failed to deliver its promises and was ready to vote it out. The D-Day was eight months away. People were vowing how they would wake up early that day and send the office-holders packing. They blamed the government for not doing anything to ease the cost of living. The burden was unbearable since it was hard for common citizens to afford basic commodities. Others were squatters in their own nation. There was no justice anywhere for the poor, who were majority. The gap between the poor and the rich was too wide for the poor to cross. This gap came to be known by the poor as 'the valley'. If you were poor, you had to accept that fact because there were no ways you could cross that gap to join the other side. The side of the rich was preserved for the few families, most of whom were politicians and few and mighty businessmen; these were those who worked closely with the politicians, they could fund them during their campaigns in return for tenders and most had been tied to each other through inter-marriages.

They spoke one language; how they were to guard their side to avoid 'unwanted, illegal and unnecessary increase'. In other words, they had only one goal, to ensure that no one could move from the other side to theirs, through maintaining the gap as wide as possible. They owned the country, and the poor people were their 'property and work-tools'. The companies were owned by this 'group of gods'. These cartels owned any fertile piece of land but no one could explain how they got them and most of these lands were only left to forests and bushes. Towns were their properties too. No project could be carried out in the country without their approval, be it of great importance or of no use to citizens. Each had to be examined carefully to see how it would help in furthering their agendas. If a project could not find favour in their eyes, then it was automatically discarded; those that played a big role in lifting these cartels politically and in terms of business were given priority. Those that could widen the gap were discussed day and night and were a 'must be implemented' as fast as possible. It was a routine for such projects to be advertised all over the media, citizens' excitements and reactions being monitored from the dark rooms through judas-holes. Citizens were not discerning the traps behind such projects. They only thought that in such times, the government was very caring. Is it because majority were not thinkers, or were many fools? They used to vote in the same people who were not doing anything to change the citizens' lives. But this time round, there was hope of change as everyone was eager to send these 'cannibals' home.

Those in power had nothing to worry about. It was hard for someone in power to be 'thrown out'. These were cemented ladies and gentlemen who won each time miraculously. One man from the neighbouring countries was heard saying that 'trying to compete with a man seated in power is like trying to cut a fig tree with a razor'. This saying was tested by many 'losers in political power' and found true. They could lose in an unimaginable ways and in broad daylight. There was another saying that in the country, 'it is not the voters who matter but the vote-counters who determine the winner'. These were some of the reasons you could lose in daylight though you be leading in opinion polls. Were things to be different this time round? There were many factors that contributed to winning and losing. For example, you were an automatic loser if you were from the side of the poor because the standards were already set in the valley. You were an express winner if the 'mighty men' were your kin. On the other hand, they were allowing competition to be fair if and only if the competitors were from the side of the rich. That is the only time nature was allowed to take its course. Tactics were countless in these 'kinds of races' to ensure that the results were as planned, as much as possible.

"Now that it is only eight months to election, how are we prepared? Remember that we cannot afford to lose in any way. We must do what it takes to defeat these people. I heard the opinion polls ranked them top and these voters are not happy with our work. Are there new tactics, apart from what I know so far?" The president, Dr Kiongo, asked as he sat down in his office. His assistant, Dr Ngari, sipped tea from his cup and after swallowing, he said, "Dr, we are ready for anything, never worry when I am in charge of anything. Even my name suggests that I am something dangerous, someone terrible, one who can deal with any situation and walk out of it unhurt, I am one of the few who can swallow burning charcoal and never get hurt. We have new strategies and you need not worry." "Could you brief me please? I know you are capable of anything and I do not doubt you in any way. I just want you to sharpen my mind more and more. I need to be updated. Do you remember the tactics we used last time? They were very obvious to all and if we go that way this time, we might fail terribly. Remember that our competitors have never slept since that day. I know they have been mastering our ways, hence the need to come up with something new." Kiongo said as he was served with a cup of tea by his assistant.

"Yes, yes sir. I wanna brief you as you take your tea. Now, since our competitors are from different tribes, we have a plan. We have decided to lure Mr Ngiri with a tangible amount of money. We want him to betray his tribe by dragging it to our side. He has never shown a firm stand when it comes to money. He can abandon any plan or idea and follow you. We need like two million dollars for this plan to be successful. I have been with him and I know him very well. If he says he is supporting us, his tribe would follow him blindly. Maybe the question would be where such an amount of money would come from." "I get you Ngari. That is a wise move. We need not be using one method each day. Now, what about his biggest ally, Dr Ngurwe? He is not easy to be swayed in any way. He is a hard-headed man." Asked Kiongo, as he drunk his tea hurriedly. Ngari laughed sarcastically and said in low voice, "You still doubt me on that? This is something we thought about for some months. We are making calculated moves. He will still be a victim of this trick. Just give me two weeks and you will see." Ngari was really cunning and almost everything was possible to him. In politics, he could perform any miracle including 'raising the dead'. Kiongo was confident with him for a long time. He had demonstrated wit of no comparison to any other person. He had been to many difficult situations before but manoeuvred his ways with ease. He was Kiongo's asset for many years and had never failed him.

Kiongo responded by saying, "I believe everything is possible with you. I want to assure you that money would not be a problem. I will show you where it will come from. I have a funding team composed of my 'other friends'. If you can remember the man I gave the biggest tender last year, then you know where it will come from. He funds our campaigns well but we must give him government tenders as a way of appreciating his efforts. You know it is like a way of saying thank you for the job well done. Tomorrow evening, be sure that the money would be in your account so that you can carry out the plan without delay. You know that we must do what it takes to remain in power. Our nation-founders taught us that leadership is not meant to be handed over haphazardly, one must choose wisely whom to hand over to and why." Ngari nodded his head and relied, "That is it sir, we have to use all means." He then left the office for other businesses. Kiongo walked around the room as he thought over what they were discussing. He walked to the window and stared outside, his eyes fixed on the green, well-levelled grass, flowers and trees. Then he said to himself in a soft voice, as if he was whispering to the window, "I must keep Ngari as close as possible to me. He is a thinking man who can overcome any obstacle. His cunning ways have saved us a lot. If he wins the heart of the two men, then we are assured of victory. We won't need to apply other tactics this time round, as that would be more than enough. This issue of tribalism has helped us so much. If it were not for the well-defined tribal lines, our fate would have been sealed long time ago. But we are very lucky and should not take that for granted."

Before he could continue 'talking to the window and walls', there was a knock on the door. "Come in please", he said as he sat down. It was General Matenjwo who seemed to be sweating. "Yes Matenjwo, how is the going? Any news whatsoever? Relax and have a cup of tea as you explain", Kiongo said as he served him with tea. "Thank you sir, eeeh, so far things are alright and everything went as was planned. The man is down. He thought he would escape but we are capable, yes, we are capable, that is what I can say in your presence", said Matenjwo as he sipped tea from the cup. Kiongo leaped into the air with joy and said to him, "That is a job well done. Truly, it is a mission accomplished. Now that he is gone, let me address the media and send the government's condolences to the family, friends and relatives. Then the ministry should start burial arrangements as soon as today evening. I hope you have already prepared to inform the nation that he was hijacked by thugs and was killed in the process." "Yes, I have sent for the media so that I do it in the next one hour, then we move on with burial arrangements." "That's it. As soon as you send the message, do not talk about it anymore; do not wait for the media to ask you questions. You just pass the message and issue stern warnings to 'thugs' and walk out." "Point taken sir, I understand this as I have experience for a long time." "Good, hurry up!"

Matenjwo walked out of the office and went straight to his office. He wrote the message he was to send to the media and looked himself on the mirror. He adjusted his tie and called his assistant. He ordered him to call his driver and security men. The driver positioned the car next to the office door; the security cars positioned themselves around the boss's car and waited for him. It took him five minutes to get into his car. He was in full uniform but had no cap. The motorcade left and was in the main office in ten minute time. The media was there, waiting for him. He did not waste any time but got out of car and sat on his chair. Then he said, "We regret to announce the death of the minister for 'Tribal Maintenance and Management' to the citizens, which occurred this afternoon along Jihadhari Road. There were thugs who accost his car and shot him. He died on the spot and is in mortuary. We have launched investigations and report will be out soon. As a government, we want to send a word of warning that we are not asleep and won't put up with such kind of malicious acts. These are cowards and must be caught and brought to the court of law for justice to be done. Let everyone remain calm as the investigations are carried out. Let us wait for the report from investigating team without speculations." He then left the media and was driven back to his office. Reporters wanted to ask questions but realized he had no time for such.

Later, the president addressed the media from state-house, sending condolences to the nation. He asked the citizens to be patient with the investigating team and would release their report as soon as it was ready for appropriate action to be taken. The next day, Dr Ngari came at around eight in the morning. They were to discuss the replacement of the minister. Dr Kiongo had hardly settled in his office when he heard a knock on the door. He didn't answer as he knew that whoever knocked would open the door as soon as they knocked. Ngari got in and closed the door behind him. "Good morning Dr Kiongo?" He greeted him as they shook hands. "Good morning Ngari. How are you doing?" "I'm doing good sir. I have remembered that we are to meet this morning and see how we can replace the man. Are you ready for the same or should I go and come later?" He asked as he took out a pen and a note-book from his pocket. "No, no, no, I am ready. This is a too critical issue to be postponed." He then lowered his voice and said, "You see how our plans went smoothly? That is what we want. Now he is gone and we have done the necessary for the sake of formality. We just sent condolences and assured them that the investigations had already started. We know that with such a formality, the citizens would never suspect us. They always think we are holier than Jesus Himself." They both burst into laughter and made a few jokes for some time.

"That is why we have to always show them that we are with them, when actually we are like water and paraffin. For example, if they come to realize the reason as to why we eliminate some of their elites and big-wigs, they would cause chaos that no one would be able to quell. But we are lucky because we always deal with foolish citizens; who cannot think and their minds are always in darkness. All we need to be doing is identifying those who try to enlighten them, whether from our side or theirs, and we do away with such. That way, we are sure of our prosperity and safety. Now, we may tackle our main agenda", said Ngari as he coughed. "Ok, now that we wanted to replace him with someone from the same tribe, who is fit for this? The person we select should not be opposing us as that man was. He should also help in furthering our agenda; which is to create clear divisions among the tribes for the sake of ruling them. You remember how that man wanted to bring togetherness among the big tribes, and enlighten them? He was really a threat to our well-being. We need someone who is a clear opposite of him. We want someone who is there to obey orders and not think on their own. I remember a country where the leader wanted to bring people together but unfortunately, they got enlightenment and a revolution followed. Today, as we speak, the country is a developed one and no one can make fool out of citizens. You make a mistake and you are done. Never go that way my friend. Fight for your side as much as you can and with whatever you have. Do you still remember Dr Nguru? He wanted to bring policies that would have seen a major development in few years. Can you imagine all of us living in such a good country? And that is why Nguru had to pay for his sins."

"Such developments are only meant for us. If you do that to the citizens, you give them a taste of a good life, which is wrong. They might get the courage to demand for good life. They might force us to develop the nation and even replace us with those willing to take them to a better level. Our country must remain in darkness as light is meant for the few and the chosen ones. And of course we are the few and the chosen ones." He concluded as he lean on his chair. Ngari nodded his head and said, "I perfectly remember and understand all this. And that is why I try my best not to make some of those silly mistakes as that would jeopardize all that we have achieved. Now, I think the man with the heart that we want is Dr Ngware. First of all, he has a big influence when it comes to his tribe. Then, he can do anything you order him to, he has never questioned anything; be it right or wrong." "Are you sure, Ngari? And the way Ngware is learned? I cannot imagine such a learned fellow taking instructions just like that. At least a learned person should question some of the things." Ngari laughed and said, "That is the truth of the matter my friend. People are learned but still idiots. If most were not like him, we would have been faced with a revolution because we have so many learned people with us."

"Most are only interested with going to school, studying hard to excel, look for jobs and then earn some good amount of money. Then they make good families and live happily. That is all the learned want. I have never seen any difference between the learned and the unlearned citizens; all are the same in terms of thinking, selfishness, and enjoying the comfort zones. So, Ngware is the same as other idiots. Just as his tribe's people follow him blindly, so does he do to us. They are the same and one thing." Kiongo smiled and said, "You are like gods. You observe a lot and learn a lot from these sheep of ours. So, just call him in the afternoon, inform him our decision, brief him on what to do and what not to do and let him start the job immediately. I will call the media and address them on our appointment of Dr Ngware as the new minister for 'Tribal Maintenance and Management'. I know his tribe would still remain our followers as they would think that we love them and care too much about them. They would never go against us as they always feel involved in government operations. Now, on the other issue, I have worked on the money you requested and the cash is ready in the other office. You remember Mr Ngiri and Ngurwe? Please convince them as early as today and tomorrow. We need to make big moves in the shortest time possible. If he falls into our trap, then we would have nothing to worry about as we are sure of victory. So make haste on that side."

Ngari agreed with him and asked to be given the money. They both walked out of the office and headed to the other office that was a few meters away. There he was given the money in a small briefcase and the secretary was ordered to take it to Ngari's car. They then kissed each other goodbye and he left. In the afternoon, the president briefed the media on the new appointment and replacement of the dead minister by Dr Ngware. His tribe was greatly pleased to hear that and their other leaders vowed to never disappoint the president. They praised him for such a prudent act and assured him of their support come the general election. The president was also glad to hear their promises and knew he had achieved his goal; 'to have them in his pocket all the time'.

Ngari was in his office at around half past three. He asked the secretary to call Mr Ngiri and inform him that it was urgent. She was also instructed to prepare a meal for them before it was late. The secretary did as was asked to. The man took only half an hour to arrive in Ngari's office. He was given a warm welcome. They were happy to meet again as it was long since they sat together in that office. After few words of normal issues, Ngari opened the floor for grave discussions. "I have called you in my office for something we need to reason together. I know you are a man of integrity and can keep secrets. You honour us in every way as you have never let us down. I have never encountered a disappointment from you, and you know when to make a quick decision; which is a very important skill. You are really blessed and we are privileged to have you in our country." He paused to give him time to respond. Ngiri was happy to hear him give him praises which was rare. He appreciated him too and said, "How may

I help you sir? We have been together and you know we 'cook deals till they are cooked'. We must work together for the better of our people. If I do not cooperate, who else would do that? Hahahaaaa, who else? We must be like brothers even when it comes to failing the nation or betraying our people, hahahaaaa. Am I right Ngari?" Ngari was 'dying of laughter' and tears were flowing down the cheeks.

"That's true Ngiri, our agendas and motives are more important than anything else in this country. We can sacrifice anything and anybody for the sake of our advancement. Now, I love the way you reason and the way we are like-minded. There was a deal we wanted to organize and you have to be part of us. You know the elections are very near, less than eight months. We have to win this thing. It is a must because we cannot afford to lose. Losing is too expensive to afford. We have to carry out calculated moves, no mistakes. Our competitors are yearning for the power but have to face the failure of the year." "Yes, I get you and am ready to help as much as possible." "We want you to be part of us in this campaign. You just need to declare that you support our re-election into power and your whole tribe would do exactly what you do, they would be part of us too. Are you getting the trick behind it? You do not even need to campaign for us or be with us everywhere we go, just call the media and brief them on your new move. Tell them that you support us in every way and you are behind us in every move. Your tribe follows you blindly; they do not care if you are taking them to hell or heaven. Or whether you are cursing or blessing them. They will always be with you, in and out of season."

"These are the times you appreciate the beauty of tribalism in our nation. There are plenty of benefits when we allow the people to identify themselves with their tribes. You now understand why we insist that we must have tribal boundaries. They serve us as we wish. You just announce on the media that you are behind our re-election and you will see a miracle. Everyone like a sheep would say they are behind our re-election. They are like warthogs; they forget how we betray them each time with empty promise. But my friend, there is a huge reward in your efforts, and such efforts would not go unpaid. We have raised one million dollars for you! You can take the money with you and just brief the media." Ngiri smiled all over his face. The face brightened like stars. He removed his glasses and said, "Are you sure my honour? You mean one million dollars is mine? You mean I would be one million richer tonight? Ooh my God! How good it is to know how to play politics with your people! But are you serious sir, that by just being a 'helper' to my tribe I would earn me one million dollars?" "Yes Ngiri; that is it. We reward our men and are ready to help them. And any other help you want would be given without delay." "Ooh, I see. My eyes have opened and I see clearly. This is the beauty of working as a team, no division, no objection. I am ready to do it sir." "But not just so, we also want you to convince Mr Ngurwe to be with you so that you make the same move together. We need concerted efforts in achieving all this."

He opened his briefcase and said, "Here is two million dollars. I promised you one million but we are very generous, here are two million dollars, I have decided to boost you further as a friend and for agreeing to work with us. Just take the whole amount and see how much you can share with Ngurwe to bring him to your side." He pushed the briefcase to him. Ngiri responded, "In fact, we are more blessed because Ngurwe does not need any reward for that. He just requires hearing my stand and he would be ready to support me. He does not make decisions on his own, though he is more learned than me. Even I wonder why his sub-tribe follows him. I think the people are either stupid or mad. You cannot follow someone like a fool and tell us you are wise." "Yes, yes, my friend, but the issue of giving them empty promises has helped him a lot. He is very smart is lying to them, and in ensuring that he defines the sub-tribe's boundary by instigating his people against other sub-groups. I think he is 'very wise'." "But I will make sure I give him something to strengthen our bond. Let me go and talk to him next week and then I do the media briefing in the same week. I have so many great men who are my followers and have to talk to them. They cannot fail me but it is good if I fool them by making them see involved in my ideas, plans and moves. I think the deal is clinched." Ngiri concluded. Food was brought and they took it in a hurry. Afterwards, Dr Ngari thanked him a lot and went to see him off.

In his car, he placed the briefcase under his seat and drove off. Ngari remained staring at the direction of the car as he thought hard. Then he talked to himself, "A fool is always a fool. But we are lucky to have them anyway. These are the people who are willing to betray their tribes and closest friends for our sake, and I wish we would have them forever. If we had not had them, things would be different. I hope we remain united, and even as brothers. If he fails to convince them, I think he has to give the money back or lose his life and money all-together. In case of failure, I think he would be forced to see my true colours; that I am actually a chameleon by birth. I cannot afford to disappoint the president." He then went back to the office and arranged some files before leaving for home.

It is in Wanjinga village and the village elders were seated in Wanjinga Wayside Hotel. This was the centre for all the village elders. Elders from the ten villages used to meet here for a cup of tea as they discussed important issues. They were fourteen in number as one of their own was sick in his house. They were served with tea and the first one asked, "Are we really heading in the right direction with this government? I think we should never support it. It has really failed us and betrayed the whole nation. Do you remember all the promises they gave us during the campaigns, yet none has been implemented? We should send them home as early as before we even vote; a government of thugs and cartels, full of evil men and liars, they are beasts. We continue mobilizing our people to vote them out and place in the opposition." "Yes, yes, that is it. We shall never entertain such a government again. See how they loot the country, it's like we do not have laws governing their conduct. Look at the deaths of great men that we have witnessed in the recent months, men of substance just dying on roads in the name of thugs attacking them. These are well planned moves and acts", the second man said in anger. There was some silence before the third one added, "Let us see what they are going to do to convince us to vote for them. Only a fool would go and support them. They are the most corrupt government officials since time immemorial. See what the president does, just say they are working on our problems but does nothing. They offer the best promises but turn them later into excuses; ooh, we don't have enough funds, ooh, the government is working on them, ooh, we are with you and haven't forgotten our promises, ooh …and non-sense. I wish such men were dead so that others would have ruled over us for all those years we have wasted."

The first one interrupted him and said, "We are going to support our man, Mr Ngiri and Ngurwe, at least they saw in advance that this government is taking us to hell, and went to the opposition. They even termed this government as that of 'pigs'. You know how pigs eat anything: that is it with this government; they eat whatever we have as a nation and come later with more empty promises. Ngiri and Ngurwe are visionary, caring and very wise. They promised each other never to be partakers in this government. They have never participated in corruption and I think we can support them till we die and there is need for all of us to pay allegiance to them. They are very generous indeed: do you remember when they gave us two dollars each? They are really with us and part of our lives. I think we cannot live without them. They are able to shed light to the citizens whenever there is darkness." All of these 'wise men' agreed with him and vowed to walk behind their men. The discussion was lengthy but they had other businesses to attend to. They left the hotel after paying for the tea.

After one week, Ngiri was able to convince his men. He had easy time convincing them as they were his friends and not ready to disappoint him. He was really a hero of his own. He went and met the media whereby he gave out his stand to the nation. He explained to the nation how he was behind the re-election of President Kiongo and that his government had done a lot to the citizens. He explained, "I am happy and as a community, we have examined the work of this government and found it excellent. It has done a lot that no any other government has ever done. Look at the education sector, the agricultural sector, the transport sector, just to name a few and be witnesses. Citizens are grateful and are ready to place it again in power. Those opposing the government are selfish and have evil motives. They are jealous that we are making progress in every field as a nation. They have actually been funded by goons and enemies of our nation, to bring down all the efforts that the government has put to ensure we move forward. Let them not lie to you as citizens that they have good plans for us. We are not fools, we know that they do not have any plan for us and are only ready to bring everything to ruins. Let us all be united and move forward as one people under the leadership of Dr Kiongo. Let us support him for the better of our nation."

The news was broadcast on all forms of media. It was actually breaking news all over, with the headlines reading, "Mr Ngiri with president in the race". Many were shocked, especially those who were opposing the president, by the news as he was always known as the opposition figure. This time they were seeing a different Ngiri. It was discussed on media, in towns and in villages too for some days. Political experts were on media for several days trying to elaborate this move to the nation but that was a routine each time an important person made a shocking move. Later, the president and his assistant called Ngiri in their office for further discussions. He availed himself on time. The president shook his hand for several minutes before allowing him to sit on a special chair. Ngari was only smiling for having achieved such a great mission. They all sat down and kept quiet for some minutes. It was so silent that one would have thought that they had nothing to discuss.

Then Kiongo opened his mouth and said, full of joy, "You are a hero, worthy of praises and you shall remain in my heart forever. Today you have done the impossible. You truly deserve glory and honour. Imagine that we are now assured of an easy win during the election! We have no doubt whatsoever. You have helped us greatly; you have saved us from much hardwork and unnecessary toiling and sweating. Let me declare this to you this day, that I shall give you one of these government buildings after I take the office, immediately after the election. I know how I shall organize for a deal of selling it, to fool citizens, and then have the documents transferred to your name. I must reward you better; you are a hero and a patriot of this nation. You will live to be remembered. I say thank you for the mission accomplished." Ngari smiled and said, looking at Ngiri, "Good my friend, you have never let me down. May you live long to serve this country. If everyone understood the beauty of having a person like you, I am sure even our competitors would not compete for power. You have done a great job and we will remain friends forever. Next time we call upon you, just be willing to walk with us. Thank you and be blessed abundantly for saving this country."

Ngiri was greatly pleased to hear the president praising him. He knew that he had earned himself a good part of his heart. He had no much to say but to say thank you to both men. "I want to say thank you to both of you for your offers. I shall always work with you to save the nation. We are one and united forever. I think I have done my part; the rest is just to appear in your campaigns as a way of strengthening our work. Thank you again and be blessed too." They kissed each other goodbye and Ngiri left for other works. When the two mighty men were left behind, they discussed Ngiri in details. They concluded that he was a real friend, as it is always said that a friend in need is a friend in deed. He had proved himself so. Before they dispersed, Kiongo introduced the topic on burial preparations for the late minister. "I hope the burial arrangements are on track because we have only two days to bury him. I want the budget to be tripled and then we see what next." Ngari didn't understand what Kiongo meant but decided to ask before he left. "What do you mean by 'tripling the budget and seeing what next'?" "You have forgotten that we need money for campaigns? We cannot use our salary to campaign! That is very obvious. Though we shall be funded by those we give tenders, we still need our own money as a way of making things secure. We need to feed few men who can campaign for us as we do our part too. Remember we still need something to help pay the goons we hire to cause chaos during the opposition meetings. That is one way of raising such money. So, tell those in charge to make sure that they triple that budget or even make it six times, then we take our share to our bank accounts."

Ngari laughed and answered, "That is why I cannot afford to lose you. You think ahead always. You don't wait till it's too late. I think you have been blessed in many ways. I will inform them as soon as tomorrow morning. Have a great time sir." He left the office smiling and went to his office. Kiongo was left arranging some documents that were not in order on the table. He seemed jovial and energetic. After spending some minutes alone in that office, he left for a meeting with other presidents in state-house.

At Wanjinga Hotel, the fifteen men were gathered to discuss the new move that Ngiri had announced earlier. They were served with tea before they opened the floor for discussions. After drinking half-way, the first one opened the discussion, "We all heard what our men announced last week. They are supporting the president and they gave many reasons as to why they made that decision. We need only give him our support. He knows more than we know, he is our saviour as has been for a long time and we know that he would never betray our tribe. He cannot lead us astray. He knows what he is doing and understands better. I think we are blessed to have Ngiri and Ngurwe, plus other leaders from our tribe." They all agreed with him before another one added, "Remember that if we do not support him, we shall lose as a tribe and the other tribes shall overtake us in everything. Let us guard our independence and freedom. Let us mobilize our community so that we all vote as a block to retain our beloved president. He has really done a lot and we cannot afford to disappoint him nor let our leaders like Ngiri and Ngurwe down." They all gave him a standing ovation as a way of acknowledging that he had great insight.

They continued with discussions for some hours and planning how they would mobilize their tribe for mass voting on that day. Before they left the hotel, one man stood up and said as if he was whispering, "Today morning, I met Honourable Ngiri and Ngurwe. They sent me with your greetings and said that they are with you in this journey. They shall never forsake us and are willing to give us support whenever we need them. They asked us to mobilize our people for our own good. They gave me something which they called sitting allowance. Each one of us is to receive two hundred dollars as the sitting allowance. They said we are doing a good job and should continue in that spirit. These men are very generous and we should really support them in good faith. If anyone would talk evil of these men and our president, may he be cursed with an eternal curse. May he die while walking and still suffer while in the grave. It causes me a lot of pain whenever I hear other tribes condemning our innocent president and leaders. We have to respect them at whatever circumstance." They all stood up and sang a song of joy and celebration. He later gave each their share and they all left praising the president and their tribal leaders.

The day of the burial came and all government officials were ready for the ceremony. All were seated for the service, only waiting for the president and his assistant to arrive. The two were sorting out some few things for the sake of the ceremony. They were also preparing their speeches as they had been busy before. In their office, they called the minister in charge of planning the ceremony to clarify some things to them. The assistant president asked him, "How much was the normal budget?" He answered in low tone, "It was six hundred thousand dollars. We had to spend such because we know the president was attending, which means that his arrangement is more costing." "Ok, no problem with that. Now, did you triple the amount or what happened?" "We actually multiplied by five so that the balance could be a good amount to the president. If we just tripled, it would be very little for campaigns." "Good, that is what we want; the president wants people who are reasoning like you. You just need to wait for your share from that amount later in the week. Did anyone complain about it or was anyone suspicious or curious about it?" "No, no, no, in fact, all were comfortable with it. Some even suggested before that we had to save something for the high office. So, when they heard me mention about it, they suggested we multiply it by five. They know everything because it is not the first time we are doing it." "Thank you and let it not be known beyond the group that was in charge. Nothing should go to the public domain or media."

The president also thanked him and was allowed to leave. The two also followed him and in few minutes time, they were all in the ceremony. It was led by the government spokesman for he had experience in such ceremonies. It was short service because the president had no time for such activities. He only attended for the sake of making it official. Their speeches were poorly organized and they were actually not conveying any idea to the citizens. This was attributed to poor preparation that was done that morning. After the whole thing, the president and his assistant were driven back to the office. In the office, Kiongo seemed to be joyous. He was always smiling and comfortable. Ngari was the first one to speak, "It is done, we have made it and it seems like we have hit many birds with a single stone." "Hahahaaaa, yea, that is true. We have cleared a forest or a flock of birds with a single stone-throw. Heheheee. In fact, when in that ceremony, I was only thinking about the elections and the money we saved from the function itself and nothing else. If it was not for shame, I would have missed the function itself, I don't care if he was a minister or not. After all, many die and we forget them, he was not the first one and won't be the last one." "True, true, Kiongo. You are right. He has no value to us; he does not help us win elections. We are only concerned with victory and nothing less. Let him rest in pieces, peas or beans, whichever he is comfortable with." They both laughed till tears were flowing out of their eyes. They later left for their homes as it was already late in the evening.

In the villages, the fifteen men had divided roles on how they were to mobilize the people to vote for the government when the Election Day was with them. The people seemed comfortable with the instructions they were being given. They had no hard time convincing them to follow Ngiri and Ngurwe, together with other leaders. Things were working out as the president wanted. He had truly won the big tribe.

The Election Day was first approaching and the cabinet was to be dissolved. The two heads thought on how they were to reward their ministers. The cooperation they had shown required to be rewarded. Ngari suggested that they be given a new personal car and five million dollars each. That would be a way of appreciating them and it would also help encourage them to remain loyal to any form of leadership and their nation. Kiongo agreed with him and said, "That is a brilliant idea, so that, for those who won't be ministers in my next government, they would benefit from the work they have done. So, you can order the minister for finance to allocate each such amount of money. Tell the Revenue Collectors to register the most expensive cars in their names. Then we are going to inform the ministers of our decision to reward them." Ngari promised to send the president's orders to the concerned. He added, "I think we should have the meeting next week because you should dissolve the cabinet next week but one. I think we should also have meetings each day for the sake of the sitting allowances. You know the more the meetings, the more the sitting allowances. So we can even double these sitting allowances for the sake of collecting as much as possible." "That's great Ngari. I like the way you think fast and wisely. Tell the cabinet that this is not the time to serve the nation but to see how each can help themselves out of the state resources. Tell them to be ready for daily meetings. You know, we just make the sittings one hour each day just for the sake of recording allowances in our accounts. Those meeting avenues will only serve us as election planning avenues and platforms. We can even use that time to discuss about the next government formation. You go and tell them we start meeting from tomorrow."

Ngari left the president and sent the word to those concerned. He then proceeded to his office for some work. In the next morning, the cabinet met as was planned. They spent that one hour talking about the way their work had been smooth, without pressure, no much to do and the privileges they had enjoyed as ministers. Later, the president informed them that they had earned themselves free supper each day and that would guarantee them a small allowance. They were also to have a party once in two days and that would still earn them allowances. Later, their accounts were credited with allowances, double the usual allowances, and they left in big government cars. The next day, they met in the morning hours for only half an hour because the president wanted to meet a visitor from the neighbouring state. They earned the allowance for the day, reminded of the free supper and the party that was to be held in the afternoon. They were asked to bring their families along too. They were reminded that allowances were always accompanying these parties and supper. They were very pleased with the president and vowed to ensure that he went back in the office even before the elections. They continued with these meetings, parties and suppers until the cabinet was dissolved officially. They 'earned themselves' the cars promised together with the amount of five million dollars. They became extremely rich.

Two months before the Election Day, all the aspirants were allowed to start their campaigns officially. Kiongo and Ngari had very easy time in their campaigns. They had all the necessary support and there was nothing to worry about. Their funding group had given them more than what was required; in form of money, vehicles, airplanes and work-men. Ngiri and Ngurwe organized their tribe well for mass-voting. The campaigns were well conducted without violence. On the D-Day, voting was done and the big tribe under the leadership of Ngiri and Ngurwe backed the president. All these votes together with those from the president's three tribes supporting him gave him a victory even before the counting was hardly three-quarter-way. There was no need to continue with the counting process as all those competing surrendered and coceded early defeat. Those tribes supporting the president went into streets for cerebrations. Later that week, the president was declared winner and sworn in as the president of the nation for the next term.

A big ceremony was held to celebrate the victory officially. It was held in the heart of the city in a five-star hotel which cost the government account almost one thousand million dollars. Many turned up for the party, especially from the supporting tribes. In the party, Kiongo promised to ensure that the nation was stable in terms of security and other issues. He also promised to develop the nation and to help everybody irrespective of their tribe. He promised to fight tribalism and hunger, including poverty. In the process of paying the bill, it was ordered that the amount be tripled and the balance be sent to Ngari's bank account and that of the president.

After all these celebrations, the president and his assistant held a brief meeting with other stakeholders such as the inspector general, permanent secretaries, PCs and DCs among others to discuss on the formation of the national cabinet for the new government. They discussed in length on its composition and other details. Later, it was agreed that the president and his assistant were to nominate the persons they deemed fit to head the ministries; in other words, the formation of the cabinet was left in the hands of the two heads. Ngari praised the decision and termed it as a prudent move and promised the rest that they would make sure it was to be the best ever. Kiongo supported him and added that they were to act for the best interest of the nation. The meeting was concluded with an order to the permanent secretary in the ministry of finance to ensure that the sitting allowance for all those present in that meeting was tripled. They took lunch and left.

Kiongo and Ngari met three weeks later in state house for discussions on cabinet. They invited Ngiri but Ngurwe was left out. Before serious discussions began, they shared jokes and how they had won the election. They praised themselves for being so witty and prudent in dealing with election matters. Later the president began serious discussions, "We have come a long way as winners and not losers. The war was tough but we won easily as if there was no war in the first place. I would like to thank you for the part you played in ensuring that we won in first round and before counting process was over. Now, it is our work to choose the members of the cabinet who are supposed to work hand in hand with us for the next term. It is good we select these men carefully, especially, by considering tribes, age and allegiance to us, tribal betrayal and cunnings. The chosen ones must be from the tribes that supported us during the election period; no one should be from the opposing side. We must punish those tribes by locking them out of 'developing the nation'. Let those lucky to head these ministries be our colleagues; no member from the side of the poor should join our league. Let him or her be rich enough to be counted as those who have tangible money. I hope we are together."

"They must be old enough and if possible, the retired men. We can only have one woman for the sake of making the rest of the women included in leadership, but we shall never let her lead a ministry on her own. She must have a deputy who shall be making all the decisions; in short, a woman is meant to be just a figure. Now, on the issue of paying allegiance to us, it is mandatory that these heads of ministries pay it to us as president and assistant. They shall devote themselves to us fully. Lack of this or trying to violate it shall be like finding a shorter way to grave, that is how serious it is. Tribal betrayal plays a vital role as we saw it when Ngiri betrayed his tribe and guaranteed us early victory. One must find it fun to betray his tribe for the sake of our political game. You betray your tribe as soon as we ask you to do it. Being cunning is going to save us from many unnecessary troubles. For example, you must be able to use lies here and there when defending the government and yourselves. You manoeuvre your ways out of trouble with ease. So, suggest men who have such important traits and we shall move this country forward as a team."

They scratched their heads hard as they thought. Later, several men were suggested and Ngari confirmed that actually, these men were over qualified. They could do anything; they had been prosecuted many times for murder, drug-trafficking, land-grabbing, money laundry, slavery, corruption, raping, practicing tribalism, high-jacking cars, funds embezzling, and other dirty works. No woman was found suitable but they decided to create a new ministry purposely to be headed by a lady. The ministry was named "Ministry of Looting and Purging Looters". A lady was suggested who was actually Ngiri's wife. It was found that she had qualities that were very close to those of Ngiri. Kiongo praised Ngiri for educating his wife to the level of being useful to the society and nation. After the list was confirmed by all, the president gave a vote of thanks for the work completed. He then wrote a text message to the permanent secretary in the ministry of finance. He asked him to credit the bank accounts with one million dollars for each member present in that meeting. They took tea and snacks and then set Ngiri free to go.

Kiongo and his assistant discussed on the date they were to release the list of the appointed cabinet members. They also planned the day they were to brief those chosen before they took their duties officially. They left the state-house for other businesses. That evening, the media reported that the police were boycotting. They were claiming that the salary was meagre and working conditions were poor. The news angered the president and his assistant. They decided to quell it before it took roots. They started by airing threats on the media before they took any other action. Then they investigated and came to know those who were behind the plans. They threatened them of losing their jobs and even possible deaths. They insisted that the government had no money and they were to choose between losing jobs and going back to work. They feared losing jobs and any possible harm that would have occurred. So, they went back to work, having achieved nothing. Many citizens, even those in power, knew the president as a no-non-sense man. No one dared defy his orders.

The day came and the names of the selected members of the cabinet were named on the media from state-house. The news went to all parts of the country but was never received well by those tribes that had no representatives in the cabinet. Their leaders claimed that they were secluded out of leadership for failing to support the government. They were very angry and vowed not to cooperate with it during the whole term. They informed their tribes not to support the government at any point in time. They were also to rely on themselves in solving problems that faced them and ignore the government. There was a big gap and a well-defined boundary between those tribes on the government side and those on the other side. The two heads knew what was happening and decided to take action against those inciting the citizens to be against the government. Ngari informed Kiongo of the four names of those behind all that. The two gave instructions to the Inspector General of Police to see how he could eliminate the four men. The instructions were to be executed as soon as possible. That evening, the Inspector convened a meeting with his men and plotted how the deaths of the four were to occur.

The following morning, the first man was found in his room, having been shot several times on the chest. The news was broadcast on media but the government assured the nation that investigations were to start immediately. Those behind the act would be prosecuted for justice to be done. After three days, before the first man was buried, the second man was found dead in his car along the Jihadhari Road. He had been shot several times in the head and it was hard to recognize him. The government came out and condemned the evil act strongly. It announced that investigations were launched immediately and those behind it were to face the wrath of the law. Later that week, the first man was buried, followed by the second man the following week. In the middle of the service of the burial of the second man, the third man was reported to be found dead in a forest near a garbage pit, at the edge of the town. That news was aired as the service was going on. The government did not comment on that death. Neither was there any assurance of investigations. When the fourth man learned of the deaths and came to know that there were some forces behind their deaths, he fled from the country. That is how he saved himself from the jaws of death.

Two weeks later, the new cabinet was invited to the state house for briefings. No one declined to take the new responsibilities among all those chosen. They all turned up for the meeting with Kiongo and his assistant. Before they were briefed on their duties, Ngari assured them of their security and heavy motorcade wherever they were for the entire time. He assured them of good privileges and hefty salaries and allowances too. Later, they took tea and snacks before the meeting begun officially. After tea, Ngari was asked by the president to take them through the rules guiding the cabinet members. The rules and regulations were clearly stipulated in a special book that was only found in state house. He started briefing them, "I welcome you to these new duties. It is a journey that is adventurous and full of joy, as long as you master the rules. One thing you should know is that; never do anything on your own. For example, never try to solve issues facing the citizens outside what we would advise you. Never betray the government as that shall earn you a quick death. Always be willing to betray the citizens and the opposition; take it as fun and you shall ride smoothly and safely in boisterous waves. In case of executing orders, never question the one who has ordered you. Do as you are ordered and you shall never regret. Know that the government is always right and all the other parties are wrong. Never try to help improve the lives of citizens; always help widen the gap between the rich and the poor through policies and other means. Our goals are given priority; please avoid other priorities to avoid unnecessary conflicts of interests."

"We have the final word; no one else has. Public money and other resources are at your disposal to help yourselves. In case you need anything that belongs to the government, do not ask anyone because the process could be long and time wasting. It is also lack of knowledge and understanding of whom you are and your powers; you are greater than all the others combined. Please, exercise your powers wherever you go. All secrets are meant to be shared in this house and nowhere else; keep secrets as much as even impossible. Letting a secret loose is like telling us that your life is no longer important. Any help you need please call upon us and we shall answer before you call and shall help before you ask. If you have any question or comment, please feel free to ask after the president has finished addressing you. Thank you." Ngari was sweating profusely after addressing the cabinet in loud voice. He ensured that each word and instruction was clearly heard and understood by all. The president was pleased by his assistant especially for tackling on all issues.

He did not have much to say but just added a few things. "I hope you have heard all of the vital instructions. There are other rules but those shall be communicated to you as we move on with this work of serving the nation we love the most. One of those things you need to understand clearly is that you shall strive always to create clear boundaries among different tribes. Let each citizen identify themselves by their tribe and let each tribe know that other tribes are its enemies. That way, we shall succeed in this journey. Our plans shall never fail and you shall leap the benefits of leading a country whose members are divided along tribal lines. If we come to know that your efforts are directed towards unification of these people, I think you shall not believe what shall follow you. Be warned before you get yourselves in a mess. If you shall hear anything that is against the government, you are supposed to inform this office without delay. If we come to know that you have a secret that you have kept to yourself, then I think we shall have a reason to classify you among our enemies. Our enemies vanish like dew in the afternoon. Any question or comment can be aired in this room. Feel free to ask anything." There was some silence which signalled that the message was clearly understood. They took lunch and concluded the meeting. As usual, after the meeting, Ngari informed them that each had one million dollars in their bank accounts already, for attending the king's meeting. They were greatly pleased with the president and his assistant for being so good to them. They later left state house to start their duties officially. It was really a day of blessings.

Later that year, things were not going on well as usual. There was a great famine and drought throughout the country, such as was never encountered before. The rains never fell as per the normal pattern and therefore, no crops grew in the fields. The whole land was bare and dusty. There was no grass for animals, no human food and most rivers were dry. People fed on dying livestock; cows, goats, sheep and chicken, before they turned to donkeys, camels and dogs for food. Everything was starving. Each person was appealing to the government for help. They were asking it to import food to just save lives of its citizens. People began to perish due to lack of food and water. Many succumbed to it while struggling to eat anything. Some were eating tree-leaves in a bid to save themselves. Until this time, the government had not taken any measure to save the situation. The officials were busy with their daily meetings. When more than half a million people were dead, and the media had broadcast the calamity beyond the nation's boundaries, the president convened an emergency meeting. The media had criticised the president and his man for failing to take any measure to help the dying citizens. They had also been reprimanded for setting aside millions of dollars each financial year to go to emergency funds and to help secure food for the nation, but had not combated the situation in advance. The money had not been witnessed helping improve anything like food security. The meeting comprised of the two heads, ministers and every representative from each constituency. These were rich people who did not see any big deal with the famine and drought. Their food was guaranteed in plenty from other countries.

During the meeting, the media was locked out and informed that it was to receive briefings from the minister in charge of agriculture. In the meeting, they had nothing to discuss that was to help the citizens much. After Ngari had opened the meeting with a short prayer, the president began, "This media thing will cause us trouble very soon. It has no respect to the state officials and doesn't know when to criticize us. We need to discuss it first. I do not know why it cannot hide some of these things from the face of the international community. Imagine they reported that we have already lost half a million people since the bad luck began. It cannot try to minimize the figure and talk about like a hundred people so that the other nations can see that we are not yet in trouble as such. Do you know that other countries want to know why I was not acting in advance? They are saying that I am responsible for feeding my people and that I am answerable to them. The media is making them see me like a bad person when I am actually good and doing so much to save my people. I think we should ban it from broadcasting anything like state affairs. This is too much and it is going beyond the set boundaries. What do you suggest my friends?"

Ngiri was the second one to speak as Ngari was quietly thinking hard. "I concur with you. Let the minister for communication revoke the licenses and we do away with media, this way we shall win heavily. This is like a war it has begun with us and we need not relent when we are already in war. Just give the orders and the licenses shall be back to your hands in twelve hour time." At that point, Ngari came back to the meeting, from the world of thoughts. "Actually, they do not know our true colours. If they want to see dust in the sea, let them try my patience. We have been very lenient with them, trying to have pity on those poor bustards of idiots but now they must face the devil himself. We can no longer hold burning charcoal with our tongues. I want us to teach them a lesson that they would never forget. It is high time they start obeying commands like little children do to their parents. I suggest we execute most of them while others go to prisons for the rest of their lives. They think the lives of common people are important to us? They think such lives mean anything to us? Their suffering has nothing to do with us. As long as there is no political importance in saving them from hunger, drought and famine, then I do not think we should even talk about the calamity." He then stood up in anger and sweating as if he wanted to issue commands on the spot. They later agreed unanimously that the licenses were to be revoked with immediate effect. Kiongo told Ngari to ensure he briefed the media about the measures put in place to help the citizens from the disaster. He then added, "You are good in coming up with stories and diverting from the real issues. So, try to make up information and send to the media before we 'do away with it'. Tell it how we have discussed in details how we want to curb more deaths and how we have put measures in place to avoid such a scenario in the near future. You just try to make it as interesting and real as possible." Then, they ordered the finance minister to credit their accounts with the 'right' allowances and called the meeting off. They never discussed anything to do with the national catastrophe, as if citizens actually meant nothing to them.

When the meeting was over, a report was sent to the media by the assistant president. The report read, "We as the government of this republic have had lengthy discussions from yesterday up to this morning. We discussed the calamity that has befallen this nation, as you all know. We have ordered food from the neighbouring countries at no cost as it should be an aid of some kind. No any other citizen should die from hunger, drought and famine. We have also ordered the ministry concerned to build several boreholes in each part of the communities for the sake of plenty of water that is reliable in and out of dry seasons. I ask all of us to help the government in whatever way possible to achieve this. We have also requested the bigger part of international community to assist where possible. We have also decided to declare this bad luck as a national disaster so that we can receive more help from well-wishers and such likes. For those who have lost their loved ones, we say sorry and we are willing to help you and any bill to do with burial and preparations shall be paid by the government. Just be patient with us as we do as we have promised. Therefore, food shall be in plenty from next week."

Few days after the meeting, the media licenses were revoked except for one radio and newspaper. These had close links with the government officials and always 'obeyed commands from above'. Three days after this move by the government, the opposition held their meeting under their leader, Professor Ihuru, in a big hotel in a forest. They met early in the morning as they had many issues, and critical ones to discuss. Ihuru opened the meeting with a word of prayer before he addressed 'his people', "I am glad that all of you have treated this meeting with the importance it deserves. You all know that I hate with passion anyone who does not obey my calls. Today we have to discuss, mostly, on our role in governance. We know how Kiongo terrorized us early in the morning on the Election Day. That is past now; we have to play our part as opposition. It is good to know that the government and opposition is one thing. We are one with Kiongo's government. We are always involved in their meetings, shares, acts, decisions, looting, and any other thing you may name. Our work is to ensure that we get our share as per the agreements. Any time we do not get 'our bread', we have the right to condemn the government in public. In such a case, we get a chance to blind the citizens that we are against the government and that we cannot be united under whatsoever circumstances. We show them that we shall never be united with the government."

"So, my people, let us all cooperate with the government always. Let us monitor them closely for the sake of securing our share. Get me right, that we are not cooperating for the sake of citizens, but for our sake. Citizens are of no use to us, provided that they have no political value to any one of us. Remember also that citizens are on the side of the poor and we are on the side of the rich, with a big gap or gulley, as I may say, between them and us. Let us also strive to widen that gap and this way, our side and league shall be secure. Never try to enlighten them because they shall fight to be like us. This is a game that must have its cards hidden. Let the citizens remain in darkness but try your best to use cunning ways that show them that we are together. You all know how corruption has established roots in the country. It has served us well and all of us are rich because of it. We have looted the nation to a 'point of beyond repair'. All of us have benefited in one way or the other. Therefore, no one should ever try to say that you are fighting it because you shall lose heavily. We shall join forces to ensure that we embarrass you in broad daylight. It is also good to know that we are always paid like any other government official and hence we cannot afford to let anyone mess up with such salaries."

Before he continued, Dr Huhu asked in disbelief, "What do you mean by saying that we are paid? You know I am new in this opposition and would like to understand the rules of the game before I mess up. I would like to play the game like others." Ihuru and his men laughed before he said, "My friend, you need to really learn a lot. As for the opposition officials, we are paid. We receive salaries and allowances, just like the cabinet members. This helps us to be in harmony with the government and ensures equal sharing of the national cake, since all of us are from the side of the rich. But this should never be known by the general public. It might cause chaos. There is a share in the budget that is set aside purposely for us. Note also that, when there is theft in the public funds, we get a share too because we are part of the government. That is why we do not fight with them. We are also allowed to misuse public funds, land, buildings and other resources like vehicles. We only raise our voices against the government whenever they violate the agreements and deny us the right share. Otherwise, welcome to the side of good life and free-style."

"Now, about the state of the nation, we all know how citizens are perishing out there. I do not think we have a role to play there because I know they have no value to any of us. Is there anyone among us who feels like we should intervene and save them? Of course none of us has that mind. Therefore, as long as we are getting our share and are comfortable with the salaries, then we cannot talk ill of the government. Whether they are dying or resurrecting, we have no problem with that. What is important is our welfare and interests. After all, they are too many and when such disasters come, they help reduce their unwanted numbers. I am telling you my friends, these citizens are idiots who only know how to give birth but not how to raise their children; I do not think it is our work to help them bring up these parasites of theirs so called children. Let them die. Sometimes I like the way diseases and other misfortunes come along and sweep these fools out of our land. They can be a big burden to us but thanks be to the nature god for ensuring that they do not come to that point of 'giving us headaches'." He concluded in anger as the members burst out in laughter. They were also very excited to hear all these secrets and vowed to work closely with the government. The discussions of other issues continued until almost afternoon hours.

Before the meeting was called off, Ihuru received a call from the president. It was an invitation to a meeting that was to involve the government and the opposition. Before the telephone call was disconnected, Ihuru was assured of some 'left over'; this was the term used to refer to the funds that had been carried forward from the previous term of the government. He was assured of their share immediately after the meeting. He was also informed of hefty allowances as that was a 'new era'. They were also informed to collect the cheques to help pay the hotel bills after their meeting; this was always agreed that the government was to pay the bills any time the opposition had meetings. This excited everyone in that meeting and they went home praising the president, Kiongo and their leader, Ihuru.

Three weeks after the government promised to import food for the citizens, no sign of help had been witnessed anywhere in the land. Citizens continued to die. The pangs of hunger devoured many while those trying to survive the blows of this monster had to eat soil and leaves. In some families, it was reported that the parents were feeding on their infants' corpses. But this did not shake those in power; they saw it as a good, powerful and most effective iron tool 'provided by God' to help eliminate those 'He was not interested in'. They even declared their social class as the 'Lord's chosen race, breed and precious creatures', whose protector was God Himself. After five months of anguish and pain, the rains descended and watered the land. Later, the whole country became green and citizens had a relief.

The meeting day between the government and opposition came. They all gathered in the most expensive hotel in the city. No one was absent, in fact, all arrived two hours before the scheduled time. Kiongo thanked them for making it to the place. He opened the meeting with a word of prayer to make it official. Then he said, "My friends and colleagues, I am grateful that we have all obeyed the king's voice and kept time. Feel free in this place and more so, feel at home. First of all, before I forget, I want to urge you to use the government resources to construct your own structures such as big hotels with conference halls. We want to be hiring your hotels whenever we have meetings. This would help channel the resources back to your pockets. We do not have to pay these services to 'unknown carnivores' when we can do that to our own friends. It is like a way of boosting each other to grow financially. That's what I thought when I realized that most of us do not have these ideas as most are new to the cabinet. It is good to think outside the box."

"The other thing is, whenever you have meetings, let them be conducted in luxurious places because the better the place, the higher the bills. Imagine if you construct a very luxurious hotel and we hire rooms for two to three weeks! How much do you think you are going to earn from that? I tell you it is in plenty. So, Dr Ihuru, try to have your meetings in these nice places and as often as possible because the more the meetings, the more the allowances. You do not need to worry about the bills as that is our burden as the government. Your work is to attend the meetings and earn allowances. This term, we have decided to increase the allowances so that for a two hour sitting, the allowance is four times of what we used to earn before. So you see how we are trying our best to make your life enjoyable and better!"

"Another thing that I wanted to share with you is about the government tenders and contracts, including employment. In the previous government, we used to give these tenders to your own companies and those who usually fund our campaigns during the election periods, including our allies who are not part of this government. This time we want to continue with the same trend but more shares of these tenders should go to your companies. In fact, as long as you have your company, you qualify direct for any tender. If you do not have a substantial number of companies, you can suggest your friends' companies so that you later share the 'blessings' with them. The other option is to just register a number of them, even if they do not exist physically, and we shall be giving tenders to them as they come. We only need to be discussing how we shall be sharing them as time goes by. Then, on the payment of these tenders, you remember we were paying you the entire amount as long as you did the work half-way. This time we want to be paying tenders before any work is done. From there, whether the work is done or not, we do not want to follow that. If you receive the payment and fail to do the work, you only make sure that ten per cent of the payment comes back to the government. Those were the most important issues I saw I could easily forget."

"Let me tell you as my friends, we have a lot to share today. Do not be tired as this is the day of the 'Good News' that we have been waiting for in this life. Before we continue, let us be served with snacks to rejuvenate our minds." Tea, coffee, bread, eggs, all types of fruits, sausages, and pan-cakes were served on the tables. They ate until they could hardly breathe. They took a short break that lasted for half an hour before they resumed in the meeting room. Afterwards, Kiongo continued, "As the opposition in this country, you have a big role to play. Play your role wisely, that's what I can say. You need to show the general public that you are really against us and our deeds, but we all understand that is not the case. Remember that we are one and we must rule this nation as a team. Know that you are only against the citizens and not the government, just as we are. So, I would urge you to cooperate. You need to use propaganda when necessary for the sake of our side. Once in a while you are allowed to complain in public that we have failed as a government in fulfilling our promises but do not take any action like going to court to prosecute those involved in gross misconduct in the government. Do not even try to demonstrate and mobilizing the citizens to be against the government. Never try to enlighten any person on the side of the poor, or attempt to inform and educate them of their rights. You know they are there to serve our interests when necessary."

"I am planning to have a meeting with the judiciary next week to give them advice on how they should discharge their duties, not as judges but as our servants. You know what we want is a stage-managed drama involving the opposition, government, judiciary, Anti-corruption commission, the police, and other commissions that we have in this country. We want you people once in a while to be raising your voices against the government. You complain that there is corruption in the government or some funds have been misused. You pin-point a specific scandal and we as the government, should come out boldly, condemning the act and issue threats to those involved. Then, the Anti-Corruption Commission should be ordered to investigate the matter and prosecute those culprits. The police should come in to help this commission with the investigations. These police departments should take their time pretending to be investigating, this way they should take time that is enough to earn them enough allowances. Finally, they should give their report to the Anti-corruption commission for prosecution. In the court of law, the judges should request the president to form a commission of enquiry to investigate, those prosecuted, further. Such a commission of enquiry should take their time too for the sake of allowances."

"This commission should request the president to ask those mentioned in the report to step aside for fruitful investigations. I shall grant their request and the culprits shall step aside, waiting to be cleared. When that commission has finally submitted their report, the judges take their time pretending to be going through the report. Then they shall ask the chief justice to form a commission of judges to hear and determine the case. It shall be done so and such judges shall determine the reasons to give when acquitting the prosecuted men. Later, they shall call the media in court and declare those involved innocent. They shall order the government to pay them some good amount of money for tainting their reputation. Then I shall reshuffle them back to the cabinet and their salaries shall be paid with interests. Then we as the government shall make sure they are paid as the court shall order but shall make it ten times. The extra amount shall be sent to our bank accounts equally. This way, we shall have benefited, and at the same time, fooled the citizens that our opposition is never part of us and are playing their roles appropriately. We shall have killed countless birds with a single stone."

"This way, we are sure that the citizens shall have faith in our opposition so that when they do not elect us back to the offices, then they elect those from opposition and we become the new opposition. You see the cycle? It is like an endless loop because finally it is our own that shall be in the government and we are in opposition and vice versa. You see all these plans? They are meant for our togetherness. And note that, the process I have just described was in summary. We shall make sure that is as long as possible and shall involve many people, commissions and resources. Each one of us must benefit from such a process. These commissions shall sometimes acquit the guilty through funny, funny ways and reasons. For example; a commission from the police department can say that they have lacked access to important information and that has hindered their investigations. At that point, the guilty is set free! You see my friends? That is what we are saying in details. Another case could be that the court sits to hear the evidence provided and declares it as unsubstantial; hence the case is dismissed on the grounds of lack of evidence. In another way, the accused could claim to the judge that the allegations have no grounds and are only meant to bring him down politically. This way, the judge dismisses the case. In another way again, the accused can rush to court and ask for the court orders to stop those investigating them from doing so as his or her rights would be violated. In that situation, the judge orders the investigations to stop with immediate effect. This way, the accused win without trail. And so on, and so on; there are many fake ways of making it to that point of confusing these idiots. In other situations, we can have the cases going on for like ten years while many are 'receiving their share from sittings, investigations etc."

"So, my people open your eyes wide and stop dozing during daytime. We are the heads and shall remain so forever. Let me not continue without you people saying something." When he paused to welcome remarks from the members, Ihuru was the first one to speak his heart out, "Yes, yes, your excellency. You are very right and I believe that had it not been for your able leadership and wit, we would be in a different country. These citizens would have over-turned us and mostly, we would be on the other side while they would be on our side. You have brought us a long way and I would encourage you to continue with that spirit. You must be God's chosen leader to deliver this country out of calamities and sufferings. I pray that He may bless you to live forever to serve Him and His people. On the other hand, I would assure all of you in this meeting that if we win during the next election that is only around the corner, we are going to work together and as a team for all the days. I shall ensure that tough measures are in place to maintain the standards you have set so far. I can say that these citizens are ignorant, forget faster than warthogs, they are not enlightened and do not learn from past mistakes. In fact, most have never known their rights and I would like to say that we should always strive to maximize our benefits on their weaknesses. God has given us these men and women of little minds so that we can live happily and without stress. Sometimes when I see them suffer great losses and repeat the same mistakes, I tend to think that even God Himself is not interested in such stupidity. He no longer needs or values them and they are curses themselves. Let me not talk much about them because even in talking about them I suffer a loss." The silence in the room was turned into laughter and they all praised Ihuru for such 'words of wisdom.

"The other thing I would like to stress on is that of maintaining the tribal lines", Ihuru went on talking in high tone for everyone to hear him clearly. "We need to dominate these people and one way to do it is to have them divided along their tribes and other means possible. Remember that you cannot rule without first dividing those to be ruled. So, help us in defining these citizens with their ethnic groups as we have been doing since independence. Let each one of us rule over their groups and whoever tries to unite one tribe with another for no reason except election purposes should 'shake the ancestors' hands before dawn. I hope we are together that the only time we should have them together is only when we want them to vote as a block." Kiongo was very excited and started praising Ihuru for his wisdom. He added with finality, "I think we shall never fight among ourselves to be in office. All of us are like-minded and have one common goal. We should always campaign peacefully and whoever is elected as the president shall be supported by all. I want to declare this to all of you today, that if Ihuru defeats me in the forth-coming elections, I shall hand-over to him peacefully and work with him like my brother. Live long Dr Ihuru. Is there anyone with something else to add before I continue with other plans?"

No one had anything to say. Kiongo smiled at his men and added, "We have helped this country greatly and would want to continue with that spirit. So, whenever you see us working together is because we need concerted efforts in taking this nation to a better level. Other things shall be discussed privately as we go on with our daily chores." They dispersed for other duties with Kiongo and Ngari being assured of great victory.

At Wanjinga Village, we find the Wayside Hotel open although it is still at dawn. The village Representatives are gathered for serious discussions.

They had spent the whole night discussing the move they were to make during the forthcoming election that was only two weeks away. They were not happy with the way the government had failed to deliver its promises and the hard life the citizens had been forced to live. They were having extremely difficult lives and the government seemed not to care. These men vowed to send the government home and elect Dr Ihuru as their president. They decided to mobilize their tribes to support Ihuru. The first elder was first to say in low tone, "What do we do? This is a government of animals and not human beings. They are extremely insensitive and inhumane. We have to deliver ourselves out of these pigs' hands. We are in slavery and have been in bondage since independence. So many years after independence and life is worse than it was before independence. I wish we could go back to colonial era. It's only Ihuru and his men who can be our saviour once and for all. Do you remember how he tries to disclose all the filth in this government? He has been trying to get impunity uncovered since time immemorial. Although there were times we had him as our president and his government was also accused day and night for corruption issues, I think he is better than Kiongo. Let us have him as our saviour and we shall never regret. I also think that when his government was constantly being accused of gross misconduct, it was not true but his enemies were trying to bring his efforts down. It was his enemies who were trying to sabotage his plans, promises and projects so that the citizens don't benefit from the same. Furthermore, he is one of our own. Remember that he is from our tribe and has been fighting for us when others try to fight us. I like him and love him. He always had great dreams for our country. Let us support him and we shall live happily. What do you say my friends?" All the other members agreed with him and promised to do so. The sixth elder spoke too, "Let us not be swayed from what we have purposed to do. We bring our people together for mass voting on that morning. We should send these government officials home and forget about them. With Ihuru, everything shall be new and we shall forget the past. We are not fools anymore." There was a long silence in the hotel before the fourth elder called the attendants to serve them with tea as it was already seven in the morning.

After tea and a short break, the elders resumed with the meeting. This time, they were not even smiling. Their faces were gloomy and dull. They seemed like people who were ready for war and revenge. Their faces spoke a lot about the pain that was in their hearts. The tenth elder spoke softly, "What the hell does this government think is doing? Kiongo thinks we don't have the power to send him packing? He will go home before dawn of that morning. We should teach him a lesson he would never forget. It's high time he learns from his mistakes. It's high time he joins his wife for the sake of concentrating on his children. He is very insensitive and ought not to be in any public office. Let's do our best to throw them out of office for the rest of their lives." All the elders agreed with him and their faces brightened. The sun was already high in the sky and they decided to call off the meeting till another day. They left with only one aim, to bring the government down and have Ihuru in power.

The Election Day was only one week away. Kiongo met with Ngari in his office for someone discussions. The two met before six in the morning and were ready for a heavy task ahead. Ngari began the conversation, "Should we not strive for this seat? Sometimes I am stranded whether to fight hard for another term or let it go to Ihuru. After all, we are one and it doesn't matter who takes the wheel. We shall still be receiving salaries and allowances even when in opposition. Or what do you say sir?" Kiongo shook his head and laughed sacarstically. "We cannot afford to let it go. You only know the importance of something you have when you lose it. Please come back to your senses. Don't dream at daytime, Ngari. Just think about all the privileges you have had and the authority you have been exercising for all those thirty-five years. If you lose, you shall regret for the rest of your life. Let us 'sit on these people' for only one more term. Then we can let it go. So, what do we do because we have only one week to go. Please use your wit to solve this riddle." Ngari laughed and replied, "If that's the case, let me suggest some possible means of winning. We need drastic measures because time is not on our side anymore. You know that Ihuru is not our friend though we eat and drink together. If given the chance to be above us, he can roast us alive. Do you recall what we did to him during our first term when he tried to compete with us as if he was the press? He still has that bitterness in his heart. In fact, reliable sources revealed to me that he has vowed to revenge. But after the next term, I am sure he would be interested no more in revenge as we shall have aged beyond his expectations. We can therefore find a way of winning this time round." Before he could continue, Kiongo interjected, "We do not make assumptions or work with guess works my friend. We cannot say we shall be old enough for him not to revenge. Let us think like sober men and not like young girls. Can you suggest better ways of surviving till we die? Power is meant to be guarded like life, it's so precious and prestigious that it's not meant to be handed over or lost like a piece of wood. I told Ihuru that I would hand-over power to him peacefully in case he wins but it was only a white lie. Let him continue believing so but we know that that shall never happen." He kept quiet and stared on the table.

Ngari lowered his voice and whispered, "If that's the case and we have tight moment, why don't we do away with him this night? Remember that there are only three men in this competition and Ihuru is your greatest threat. If you don't win, he wins with his running-mate, Matenjwo, and vice versa. The third man is Ngiri with his running-mate as Ngurwe. These can be defeated with ease and hence are not a threat to you at all. So, let us eliminate this man and you shall be assured of the victory early in the morning. I have many ways of achieving that plan. What do you say before I go on speaking?" "I don't oppose anything, in fact, that has been my idea since long time ago. We can do away with him this night. Just tell me how we should achieve it and I would assist you where and when necessary." "Ok, thank you. Now, you know very well how we usually do it but I would suggest a new way of doing it this time round. Our Jihadhari Road should still serve us in our mission. I would suggest that we use a truck this time. We should park a long vehicle at Jihadhari Road's sharpest corner. Then, since his vehicle is always driven at a neck breaking speed, it should knock the truck out of its way and that would give him a direct ticket to hell or heaven, whichever is appropriate. I think no one would blame us because it shall be seen as a normal accident and we would not be required to clarify anything to the public. That's very easy and achievable." "Good, let us do it tonight but for the sake of ensuring that the mighty man becomes past tense, we should have some men lurking in the scene so that if he survives, bullets should be rained on him like sand. He must perish if that is the way we have decided to go. We should be achievers in whatever we do. With those remarks, just go and organize everything, I am only waiting for final report. You know where all the resources are for the work." Ngari kissed him goodbye and left in a hurry as if he was taking a patient to hospital. Even the guard at the door was shocked to see him half-walking and half-running, something he had never seen him do before. He wondered as to why such a high profile person could be almost running. He even thought that maybe it could be that he was suffering from diarrhoea and wanted to be in loo before things fell apart. But he could not ask the president the reason for his assistant to run.

Ngari went straight to Matenjwo's office. Matenjwo was known for his prowess in setting traps that never missed the prey. His expertise had served the government for a long time and had even received many 'awards and prizes' for jobs well done. Ngari didn't knock the office door but went straight inside. He greeted him and sat down on the office table. Then he said in a whisper, "We have to make a quick move. This is a critical time and no second should go to waste and unutilized. Ihuru should not see the sunrise on the morrow. You are his running-mate but should help us. Organize your men to park a truck at our corner on Jihadhari Road. You know it because it's not your first time to do it. You know people like Iguru and Iguna among others and how they succumbed to accidents in that corner. Place also some men, heavily armed with sophisticated guns, in the nearby bush to finish the mission in case of any attempt to survive the tragedy. With those few words, do as I have ordered you and your reward shall be immeasurable. Thank you and all the best, I have other businesses to attend to." "Ok, but Ihuru being my friend and I being his running-mate doesn't mean much; I can do away with him any time, after all, I am not much interested in overthrowing your leadership." He laughed loudly and left the office at a tortoise pace. Matenjwo thought for a while before he called his men to implement the plan. He briefed them on what they were supposed to do and sent them to the job. He then called Ngari and talked with him for some minutes. "Hallo Dr Ngari? Now, I have a concern about our plan. You know, we do not know if the man would pass the place this evening. We do not have any information about his itinerary this evening. If he doesn't fall victim of our trap, what shall we do? Is there any need for going to his house and shoot him on the spot?" Ngari was responding like someone who was really thinking hard, "Ok, thank you for the concern, but if he doesn't appear tonight, then our mission would be counted as mission failed. I shall give more instructions and guidelines from tonight's outcome. Let's hope for the best. You just do your part." After the talk, Matenjwo disconnected the telephone and relaxed in the office.

The men supposed to do the work did as they were instructed but they were not lucky at all. They lay in watch till dawn without Ihuru passing by. In the morning, report was sent to Matenjwo who informed Ngari in advance. Ngari was not much shocked by the news although it was not good news at all. He called Matenjwo, "Hello Matenjwo? I have heard the news but it's not encouraging at all. It seems like gods have been merciful to this man; they haven't yet finished with him on earth. Let me talk to Kiongo and signal you once we have better plans. You just wait till I talk to you later." Ngari left his office that early morning and met Kiongo. The two, in a hurry, discussed on how they could 'help themselves' before things could turn pepper on the D-Day. Kiongo was depressed but had plans too, "My friend, we are blessed with brains and money. Do you know that money can clear any obstacle like a bush is cleared with a panga? Let's think about it in terms money and obstacle. Now, clear the bush." Ngari smiled and shouted, "We are lucky, thank you for the great insight. If gods had mercy on him, then we can also show some kind of mercy and generosity to him. Let's call him to this office and talk to him together. I want us to convince him to give up the race. We should suggest to him how he should step down and let you compete with Ngiri. This way, you shall win very easily and we shall only be required to reward him positively and abundantly. He should betray his followers and convince them as to why they should vote you in. If that fails, though I doubt, we should kill him in broad daylight or rig the elections to your favour. We cannot exhaust our wit, it's only that time is swiftly passing by, leaving us with only six days."

"Yes, yes, call him very fast. This time you are very right, Dr Ngari. Just have him to this office in the next half an hour." Ngari rushed out of office and sent a word to Ihuru. Ihuru was already at Wanjinga Wayside Hotel, campaigning for presidential seat. He had gathered a crowd so large that no one could count them. They were eager to listen to him and vote him in too. As he was half way with his presentations to the multitude, he received a call. It was Ngari's secretary. He informed him that he was urgently needed at State House. His face turned pale. His mind started working tirelessly and nonstop, wondering what the president could have to share with him so urgently. Could he be sick and wanted him to be the acting president? Could he be in danger and wanted to share a secret with him? He wondered. So many questions were running in his mind but had no answers. He made up his mind and decided to excuse himself from the meeting. He left his running-mate in charge of the campaign and left to meet the president. His supporters were left doubting his unplanned exit out of the meeting. They could not understand why he had to leave the meeting halfway.

He was in State House after twenty minutes. He was warmly welcomed by the two heads who were already taking tea. Kiongo was very excited to see him and started by thanking him for making it to the place within the shortest time possible. "I am glad that you have treated my call with agency. You must be a wise person who can be relied on by the mighty and the weak. The country needs men like you. May God bless you sir, may your days be full of joy and may you see many of your generations. Ngari, serve our visitor with a cup of tea. Let him have an easy time in this office." Ngari did as was instructed before Kiongo went on, "I have something to share with you because you are a man of integrity. You can keep secrets and you cooperate when necessary. Now, you know that something must be sacrificed for one to be successful. I hope you have great insight and we are together, and that you understand what I mean. Are we sailing on the same boat, or we are traveling on parallel paths?" Ihuru nodded his head as a sign of being in accord with Kiongo. "Definitely sir, we are really sailing on the same boat. I get what you are saying. It's true that success requires sacrifice. How may I help you?" "Ok, thank you Ihuru for your understanding. What I want to say can be expressed in very few words because you have all the insight that is required in this conversation. I would like to win this election and I need your help. How do you intend to help me? I have thought for many months about it and I can only find you as the right man to offer assistance. I shall surely reward you handsomely. Any idea on how you are planning to assist me?" Ihuru thought for some seconds before he answered, "Ok Dr Kiongo. But the problem is that I am also in the race. Unless I quit, I don't see how I can assist you. And if I quit, then it would mean I betray my followers and supporters. Unless you assist me in suggesting some other means that I can use to help you, I can only quit."

Kiongo laughed and looked at Ngari who was smiling like a small child. After some silence, Kiongo lowered his voice as he explained, "You are right Dr Ihuru. You are ultimately right. In fact, it's like you have hit the nail by the head. That's why I love you more than my brothers and my wife. You remind me of another day I was telling my mother how I have a person and a friend called Ihuru who means more to me than my family. So, that's exactly what we want you to do. You can quit and support me for only this round, and then we stand with you in the next election as my brother. You are really a friend and I have no doubt about it. Just help me and five million dollars shall be in your bank account immediately after the D-Day. You shall also receive government tenders and contracts in plenty. I shall also make sure that you shall never be prosecuted for the grave crimes you committed. My government shall provide your security and you shall be immune to any state forces and institutions, including commissions. Other privileges shall follow you for the rest of your life; till you become the next president after I leave the office. Just think about it and make quick decision before you finish your tea. They always say that knowing when to make quick decisions is an important skill, and I know you have the skill itself and much more." Ihuru smiled before he said what was to change the fate of the nation for the rest of time. It was also to mark his destiny.

"You know who I am because you have already said it all. I know that without concerted efforts, we cannot achieve anything as a country. I have heard the good deals and goodies you have in store for me and all of us as a nation and I see you as a leader sent from heaven by God Himself. You are really a blessing to us and I wish you could live forever for the sake of this nation. Your able leadership is crucial for this nation's development. We have gone through precious moments as a nation under your great leadership and wisdom. We want to keep the country on the same track and this way can only be achieved through your experience and expertise, wisdom, patriotism and so on. No one can doubt your ability. We shall be together as brothers and more than a family. Today, I can boldly confirm that I shall be on your side because no one is better than your Excellency. I shall stand with you once and for all. I have assured you of victory and my people are yours."

He then lowered his voice and whispered to his ears, "We are experts in betraying these imbeciles called citizens. They are never wise and shall remain in our cocoons until they learn from their own mistakes. Let me betray them once again for your advantage. Just send the money to my account and everything is going to work in your favour. As long as the citizens have no brains to help discern what game of politics and selfishness we are playing, they shall remain losers forever. They think we are losers when we are on the opposition side when indeed they are the losers. I have never witnessed such kind of persons who never learn from past mistakes. They suffer each day and live a life full of hardship but they still follow what we say like cursed idiots. I wish they die each day and live miserably like animals. Let me betray them once again for their folly. I have done it many times before and I am ready to do it again. So, your Excellency let me declare tomorrow morning that I have quitted the competition and I am supporting your re-election. Then shall I ask my people to show love to you as they do to me by voting you in. I hope everything is as you wanted."

Kiongo and Ngari were so excited that Ihuru thought that he was a hero who had found favour in the presence of the king. He had saved Kiongo and his team from early morning defeat. He had assured them what no one else could have assured them. They rejoiced together as a family and took lunch together. When they finished taking lunch, Ngari gave thanks to Ihuru and Kiongo for the work just completed. "I'm the happiest man in this country. I love it, I love it. Job well done by smart people and great results obtained within half an hour. God bless both of you. Kiongo is a great man and leader and we ought to praise him. Ihuru is a legend of his own; he is a rare hero from heaven itself, sent by God to show his wisdom in times of need. Be blessed. I want to request the president to offer you transport and security as you invite the media to declare your new move to the public." "Yes, yes, just let him use some of the government's vehicles and security personnel. He is a great man who deserves honour and other goodies. Just make sure that he takes supper with us after his life changing announcement. We are one people and shall remain united forever, whether or not, or not or whether the devil and gods like it. I wish we could live forever; this life is so good that no one would want to part with it. Thank you once again Dr Ihuru. You have proved to all that your wisdom is from heaven and you are learned for the benefit of your country. Just go and make the announcement, then come and dine with me."

Ngari led Ihuru out of office after kissing Kiongo goodbye. The government vehicles were already arrayed outside. Ihuru boarded and was under heavy security. The security was beafed up to almost that of the president and his assistant. Ihuru felt like he was the president. He was driven to his office at the heart of the city where he was expected to make his final declaration to the nation. At State House, Ngari laughed like a hyena before they went on with private discussions with the president. "Finally we have made it. It was a wise move. Well calculated move has changed our fate. This is the beauty of great insight and quick thinking. But, above all, the sweet taste of having 'good money' in your pocket. Thanks to colossal amounts of money that we have. If we have changed the game within such a short time, in a blink of an eye, then we are God's chosen and shall never lose in any way." Kiongo smiled before he made his comments. "Life is all about decisions and achievements. He has really saved us. Now, about the money we have promised and other goodies, I think it's wise if we don't waste our time trying to think about them. Once he has made the famous declaration, make sure that his name is removed from the voting register with immediate effect. Then have all the government vehicles and security personnel revoked. Then the electoral commission should declare that once out of register, no more bringing of your name back to register, no reinstatement. That it is an irreversible move. This way, we shall guard our expected victory just in case he changes his mind - you know these people are like chameleons, changing their colours every day. We cannot trust them in any way. After elections and our victory, we can start harassing him through commissions and judiciary, including police. This shall help us avoid paying anything that we have promised him. He thinks we can give him five million dollars, what for? Never! That's like a waste and I don't think we can afford it."

"I believe in thinking twice before you make such a move. They think the white man was a fool when he said you should think twice whenever a deal is too good? He also advised us that we should never think that whatever glitters is gold. An idiot, just like these citizens and he calls himself wise. Let him perish in his folly and let him fall a victim of his own trap. We don't care!" Ngari laughed until his ribs were aching. He could laugh no more and was already kneeling on the floor for lack of energy to sit upright. Then in tears of laughter he said, "I wish you were my brother forever I also wish we could purchase our freedom from death so that we could live in this country until Jesus comes back to have us rule with Him in heaven." They left the office after taking some tea.

Ihuru gathered the media to make his declaration. He gave a long speech that meant to pave way for his final words. Then the unexpected came out of his mouth. "I have taken several months, mulling day and night, just trying to make the right decision. And today I am pleased to announce to you that I have quit the presidential race and ready to offer my support to the current president, His Excellency Dr Kiongo and his assistant, Dr Ngari. These are men of integrity whose leadership is direct from heaven to us. We cannot afford to have them out of office. Let us all support them and I humbly request all of my supporters to support Kiongo as you would have done to me. Let us not be greedy of leadership, let's not be selfish and blind, because that can make us not see the great works these two men are doing to all of us. They have made the cost of living as affordable as possible. Please help them achieve and fulfil their goals for our benefit. Thank you." He got into the motorcade to be driven back to the office and later to the state house for dinner. The news spread like cancer over the whole land. People were confused and didn't understand why Ihuru made such a move. But they all decided to support Kiongo as was the wish of Ihuru. They decided to die and resurrect with him.

They took the evening meal as was promised by Kiongo. They were all happy and kept praising each other throughout the entire period of taking meals. Later that night, Ihuru visited Ngiri and had a discussion with him. "My friend, I have withdrawn from the race and now you are competing with Kiongo. I have seen he is a great man who deserves to be given a new term. Don't you think so too? Why don't you take the same course, yet I have set a good example to you?" Ngiri was not surprised but thought for some minutes before he responded to Ihuru. "I think I can quit too but I don't know how. People might see me a coward and I don't want them to see me so. Let me fight to the last minute although I know I can't win in any way; whether heaven wants it or not. I already know I shall lose but let me just remain in the ballot papers for the sake of it. You know you are the only one who was sure of winning this election but you have shifted the victory to Kiongo and not to me. But he is also a good man and we shall work with his government hand-in-hand as usual; our main concern is the salaries, allowances and other privileges that we receive always."

Ihuru laughed heartily and said, "That's true Ngiri. Your insight is great. But you can 'struggle to remain in the race' as you have said. As for me, I thought Kiongo deserves to be given another chance and that is why I have decided to step aside for him." The discussions went on till almost dawn when they dispersed to face the new day that was fast approaching.

The next day, all the government vehicles and the security personnel that were guarding Ihuru were revoked. That afternoon, the Electoral Commission's chairman addressed the media. "As all of us are aware, Dr Ihuru withdrew himself from the presidential competition and hence his name has been removed from the register. He is no longer part of the competitors and hence his name shall not be in the ballot papers. Bearing in mind the short time that is remaining before we conduct the elections, in case of anything, we cannot bring his name back to the register. Once out of the register, always out of register. Therefore, you can make your decision based on Kiongo and Ngiri, who are the only competitors in this race. I want to assure you that the election shall be fair and transparent, and that we are committed to deliver a credible election. Thank you and I wish you a peaceful election." Ihuru did not understand what was happening but his friends informed him that it was normal and that his security would be beefed up once a new government was formed. He believed this advice and hence continued supporting the government.

On the D-Day, the citizens woke up early that morning and cast their votes. Kiongo won very easily and there was a cerebration as was never before. All the towns and villages were full of citizens, carrying Kiongo's bill-boards and singing praises to him. Kiongo, Ngari, Ngiri, Ihuru and others were in the most expensive hotel in the city, celebrating the victory. It was later reported that more that eighty million dollars was spent that day, in the hotel alone. Few weeks after a new government was formed under Kiongo, Ihuru visited the state house. He was welcomed warmly and the discussions started after some tea. "I saw it wise to come and have a discussion with you. First, I would like to congratulate you for making a history in winning with a landslide. It was great. The other issue was to remind you of our shares in the government. Remember to ensure that we get tenders as usual, our salaries should never be reduced but if you wish, you can increase the allowances. We rely on these allowances greatly. There was also the issue of hiring our hotels and conference rooms whenever you have meetings. On our side as opposition, we will cooperate and help you as much as you need us. Ngiri is my friend and I shall ensure that we shall never let you down." Kiongo smiled and later called Ngiri in his office. Ngari was present too.

Kiongo addressed them with joy. "As I had promised earlier, we shall work as a team. Let no one be against us as a government because that shall not be taken lightly. Now, there was something you didn't know. In the years past, we used to reward our allies with vast pieces of land and government properties. But of recent, we have been rewarding them with money. This is because we no longer have land to share. Therefore, let us be sharing money and anything else available like tenders and privileges. Land is very rare nowadays as you all know. I also reward my cabinet members with the same; hence you should also accept that way. In fact, there was a time we were forced to reward our great friend with the cemetery's land when he insisted that he wanted a piece of land and not money. It was a great embarrassment to us when the media broadcast the information to the nation. There was another friend who insisted the same but we were again forced to do the unexpected. We gave him the land and offices in our neighbouring country, meant for our ambassador's offices. Guess what! We were out for another disappointment when the information leaked. So far, we do not want to taint our name over such issues. Just take money as we offer and our life shall be simple and enjoyable." Kiongo's men were grateful to hear their president being so clear to them. They continued with the discussions and finally, Kiongo promised them hefty allowances for the day. It was really a great experience and they promised to work with him once more.

One year later, heavy rains were predicted by the meteorological department. The report was handed over to the State House and the Ministry of Agriculture. The president called his men for a meeting to discuss the report. The media was informed to announce to the public on how the government was preparing to curb the impact of the heavy rains. The report sent to the media was prepared by the assistant president, Ihuru and Ngiri and read, "As the government, we want to assure all of our citizens that no one shall perish in the floods. We are prepared and have set measures in place to ensure that all of our people are secure. We have plenty of food in store and things such as medical equipment, clothing, houses and anything else possible is in place to help the same. We have set aside enough money out of the budget to help in fighting any calamity. We have learnt from past mistakes and have enough experience. Rest assured that we are ready for anything." The news spread all over the land and the citizens were happy to hear the plans the government had.

Few days after the report was read, the president called his men for a meeting before the rains fell. They discussed the issue in depth. "We sent our report to the nation and it's good to plan ahead. What do you suggest?" Ihuru was the first one to contribute his thoughts. "I think we should wait to see what shall happen. I remember there was a time the meteorology gave their report but things turned opposite. Although they are using advanced technology and have improved their predictions and forecasting, we cannot rely on that. Of recent they have not made a mistake but that is not to be used in making our decision. We have our own way. I heard you say that we have set aside more than eight hundred million dollars for the sake of this calamity. That amount is tangible and we cannot afford to waste it on people who have no political importance to us. We have other needs that have not been met. In fact, I have a piece of land I wanted to purchase in town and have not been able to do so. It was very expensive but I think my share from the eight hundred million dollars can be of great help to me." Ngiri laughed and added his voice. "I also have a friend who wanted me to help him in marriage. His son wants to have a wedding next month but the dowry was out of proportion. He is asking me to assist him and he shall help me later. Once the dowry is cleared, he shall have the wedding day as soon as possible. I cannot afford to let him down or disappoint him simply because the citizens are in trouble when the rains descend. Citizens' interests cannot be considered when we have important issues at hand. My share will assist a lot. Remember that I have to scratch his back so that he too shall scratch mine later."

Kiongo nodded his head and a big smile covered his whole face. "I see, I see. We have the same challenges and I was wondering how such money could go to such a waste. Citizens mean nothing to us but our needs are much more important, in fact, cannot be compared with the life of citizens." There was a loud laughter in the office before he continued. "Before I forget, it is good that you take heed to my advice. I have heard my brother Ihuru say that he wanted to purchase a land in town. Let me tell you this, whenever you want to invest, please ensure that you make your investments but in foreign countries. You shall never carry all of your eggs in one basket. Things change and the only way to be secure from such un-expectations is to have your wealth distributed in different countries so that if things shall go against any one of us and investigations be done, then it shall be difficult to trace your wealth. Ensure that you buy lands, houses, businesses and companies in many countries and in different continents. Register your properties in different names in your family and friends. Have many bank accounts in different banks in diverse nations. Spread your wealth as much as possible. It is only a fool who puts all his money in one bank. Remember that you have a lot of money that we give you in different ways such as allowances, salaries, tenders and properties. All these we receive illegally and things can change and be against us one day. Therefore, try your best to bury all these in as far as possible." There was silence as everyone was trying to cogitate on the wise message from the wise man.

The discussions continued till it was agreed on how the money was to be shared among the mighty. Two weeks after the meeting, the rains descended. They were so heavy that their impact was felt heavily after the first three days. Everywhere, especially in the villages were floods. Cholera broke out and many perished. The floods swept more than seven hundred thousand of the poor citizens within the first one month. No voice was heard from the government or from the opposition. Many villages and villagers were swept, leaving behind only rocks and well-rooted trees. Livestock was swept too. Many perished while crying to the government for help. Some ran for their lives to the neighbouring countries. After three months of anguish and sufferings, the rains stopped and those still alive got a relief. It was nature's mercy that they survived. Finally, after the floods, the government and opposition's voices were heard for the first time.

The president was the first one to address the issue. "As a government we send our heart-felt condolences to the families affected. We are very sorry to those who lost their loved ones and we promise to be with them during this time of great sorrow. We assure them our support and we shall be responsible for every hospital bill and burial expenses. We ask the Red-Cross Organization to do as much as they can to help our citizens. Let us stand with those affected." Later that evening, the opposition gave their message to the citizens through the media. It was Ihuru who read the message. "As opposition, we are very concerned with those affected and want to offer our condolences to families, friends and others who have lost their people. Receive our condolences and be sure that we are trying our best to see how to work with government in helping our people. We would appeal to all citizens to contribute whatever each can afford so that we can use the same to help those greatly affected. We have an active bank account to which you can send your contributions and shall be received with many thanks. Be generous as the Holy Books teach us that God loves a cheerful giver. Save our citizens and you shall be blessed."

Many citizens contributed towards the saving of their fellow citizens as they were asked by Ihuru. Money, clothing, food, and prayers were offered in plenty. Later on, it was reported on media that the money they contributed was missing; had been 'sucked out of accounts' by the 'big men'. There was nothing to offer to those affected by the floods. Food and clothing had been sold to the neighbouring country. That is when the citizens realized that no one was there for them in times of need, except nature. After the calamity and corresponding scams, Kiongo gathered his men for a brief meeting. It was on Sunday morning when the meeting took place in State House. Kiongo informed his men that there were several issues that needed attention.

"You all know the floods are gone and we need to share the eight hundred million dollars we had set aside. Those citizens who were meant to die are already in graves and those alive are recovering well. They no longer need our attention and I see it an appropriate time to share our blessings. You know that God has been gracious to us and His generosity and mercies are following us wherever we are going and in whatever we are doing. We need to be happy over the same. Now, I want you to suggest how we can share that money as we wait for more blessings." Ngari was smiling as he was making his suggestions. "Ok, as for me, I see we should share it among the six men; Kiongo, Ihuru, Ngiri and their respective running-mates. That way we can each get one hundred million dollars and the remaining amount can go to Kiongo's account." Ihuru interjected him, "Yes, yes, but later we can discuss the remaining amount rather than have it in one person's account. We need to meet our needs as early as possible." Kiongo smiled and added his voice, "Yes, we need first get the one hundred million dollars each and later we can see where to take the remaining two hundred million dollars." As was agreed by all, each received his share and Kiongo added, "But remember we are to get allowances for this sitting. I have ordered the minister concerned to ensure we all get allowances that are eight times of what we usually get. We need to enjoy these things before we leave this world."

"There was a time I remember how citizens used to reject those people who used to do great things for the sake of this nation. Do you remember Dr Mwega? He was a visionary man who could do anything for the sake of his country. He was the most patriotic guy I have ever seen. We voted him in and within the first two years, he had introduced free education from primary to secondary school. He then ensured that the economy of our country was stable, people could afford the cost of living and there was great peace throughout the nation. He built roads to open up the rural areas for development, he revived industries, he collaborated with countless foreign countries, opened up markets, and agriculture was boosted to unbelievable level among other things. He was determined to move the country to the greatest heights ever. But guess what happened! He was rejected after his first term. No one wanted to vote him in for another term. The same citizens decided to vote in unpopular thugs, cartels, dogs, hyenas and vultures. These cannibals devoured the nation in their presence, day and night. That is what taught me a lesson; that these idiots are never interested in good people. They don't care about you whenever you sacrifice yourself for their sake. So, why should I waste my time and efforts trying to save them? Why should I think about improving their lives or even treating them like human beings? Never! Even the Holy Books tell us never to give our pearls to pigs because they will only trample the pearls under their feet, or never even throw what is holy to dogs because they would only turn back and rend us. We should never adopt their folly because theirs is like a curse from both heaven and hell." All of the men laughed loudly and heartily till tears flowed down their cheeks.

"These imbeciles don't learn from the past mistakes. We do not improve their lives yet when it comes to voting, they only consider us, only the three of us, and follow what we say and do like parrots. I don't like them; I hate them with passion! Let us direct all of our efforts towards their suffering and destruction. We shall never show mercy to them, come rain come sunshine. We cannot struggle to improve the lives of the cursed, even God and His Son have rejected them. Therefore, what God and His Son have rejected, let no man accept!" Kiongo concluded with finality. The loudest laughter ensured from that room till the men were helpless. They could not believe Kiongo was that funny since they had never experienced him cracking dirty jokes. The discussions went on with Ngari's contribution. "We have good plans for all of us present and for anyone who is on our side, the rich. One thing we have in mind is subjecting our country to debts. We have to borrow as much as possible to ensure that we are constantly paying the loans. The money we borrow from international communities shall be divided among us equally. Then we have to force the citizens to pay it through their loans. We have to make them borrow money from us through cooperatives and banks. This shall ensure that all the citizens have debts that they pay continuously. Then we shall be taking that money (I mean interests) they pay to us and we repay the international loans with it. The interest charged on their loans should be exorbitant to make it impossible for them to live without paying something. Therefore, in general, I mean that they are the ones to pay the international loans through the interests we charge their loans."

"When it comes to general elections, the funds needed shall be raised from these idiots. We shall increase the prices of basic commodities towards the time of the elections. The extra taxes we get from these basic goods like water, flour, cooking oil, petroleum products and services shall be divided among us for campaign costs. We do not have to get back into our pockets to have the work done. This has an advantage in that, we do not have to rely on well-wishers and friends to fund our campaigns because most of them are becoming unpredictable and cannot be trusted. So, whenever you see the prices of the very basic goods and services sky-rocketing, do not complain, just know that we are doing it for your own good. Another plan is to ensure that the embarrassments we got ourselves into shall never be witnessed again. If you find yourself in trouble for misappropriation of funds, let me advise you as my friends whom I love dearly. Sometimes information leak and get to the media. At such a time, never admit the fault. Try to defend yourselves as much as possible but if things turn pepper and pressure to resign increases to unbearable levels, just keep calm. We shall reshuffle the cabinet and commissions where necessary, just to silence the public and media. Reshuffling these commissions and cabinet shall help hide you, and you shall look innocent in their eyes when we place you in a new ministry or commission, and we shall be seen like people who are really working hard towards improving the nation. We have done it and it has worked before, countless times."

"In fact, commissions are political parties in disguise. They are all headed and managed by our friends and relatives. The cabinet is one big and powerful political party that we use to save ourselves from the evil forces and powers. The judiciary is another tool we use to cleanse ourselves. It plays a very vital role in acquitting the defeated person in allegations. In short, you face the judiciary when you are evil, wicked, tainted and filth, then you come out of it righteous, glorious, stronger, untainted, and holy. You see how important the tool is? In general, they all serve our interests; hence no need to worry at all. We are in control, we hold the helm and there is nothing that can go wrong." He explained a lot to the men. The discussions took the rest of the day. They dispersed in the evening for other activities. They continued with these kinds of meetings, receiving heavy allowances and their salaries were being increased each day. Ihuru was always reminding the president to honour his words and give him the money he had promised together with the tight security and motorcades. But Kiongo never kept his word; he was always telling him to wait till some things were set in order. The citizens were always suffering and whenever there was a calamity, they perished in large numbers. Life was hard always; they continued making the same mistakes whenever there was a general or a by-election.

At the end of Kiongo's term, there was to be an election. Few months before the elections, campaigns began. This time round, a meeting was held in State House to discuss on how Kiongo would support Ihuru as he had promised. Ihuru was determined to be the succeeding president as he had many followers who were willing to support him. At State House, it was only Kiongo, Ngari and Ihuru who were present. It was supposed to be a private discussion. In the meeting, Ihuru was the first one to speak, "I have been patient with you for all those years. You never fulfilled any promise as we had agreed. This time round, you are the one to scratch my back; I scratched yours and you don't have an option but to stand with me." He said in anger. Kiongo and Ngari kept quiet for some seconds before Ngari said few words. "I think you are mad, you don't just come to our presence and demand things. We are also patient with you but we shall support you by ensuring that we don't campaign that hard to come back to State House. Therefore, campaign as hard as you can and let us just campaign lazily and you win, knowing that all of us shall be in the ballot. When you win we shall hand over the power to you peacefully and in broad daytime." "Yes, as long as you shall hand over to me peacefully, then I don't have a problem. I just need to campaign; after all, I am capable of making it to State House easily and without anyone's support." Ihuru said in joy. Kiongo just nodded his head smiling. Ihuru left in a hurry to meet his running-mate, Matenjwo, and the campaign team.

Kiongo talked to Ngari in a very low voice that forced him to lean his head towards Kiongo's mouth for the sake of not missing a single word. "I think Ihuru is an animal. Don't you think he shall not revenge when he gets to power? I think he shall be on our necks if we let him be above us. I always see revenge in his heart and mind whenever I see his face." Ngari thought for some minutes before he said his thoughts. "Let us not risk anything my friend. We cannot make mistakes that are likely to put our lives in jeopardy. Let us rig these elections in your favour. Then, we start looking for a man who can take over after you." Kiongo's face brightened after the words. He ordered him to ensure that the plans were well-made to ensure a victory. They later dispersed when Ngari had assured him of his efforts towards what they had discussed.

In Ihuru's office, Matenjwo was present with Hiti. Ihuru wanted to have a meeting with the two to discuss a few things that were considered as burning issues. The three were served with tea before they started their discussions. After the tea, Ihuru addressed his men. "I want to thank you as my friends for answering my call this morning. The Election Day is just around the corner and that means we do not have time to waste. We are determined to win this election and losing it is like losing our lives. That is how important it is to us. We should not entertain any form of mistakes. I appeal to all of you to support our work and rewards shall be great. Let me tell you my friends, Kiongo has been sitting in office for the last many years, we cannot continue to be under him anymore. And I want you to treat this meeting's discussions as confidential. Keep the secrets tight within your minds. I want to assure you that I shall reward you with many pieces of land that we shall revoke from these men in office. They own vast lands and that should not be the case. Look at the privileges they enjoy! Look at the money they have in foreign lands, the structures like hotels, companies and industries, all in foreign countries. If we get to power, we shall have these properties as ours. I want to inform you that they shall become as poor as church mice. Wait and see!"

"As Kiongo was, so I shall be; no common citizen shall benefit from my leadership. I am not aiming at enlightening any citizen, or helping them to have easy life, but I want to have our tribe and my friends in power and owning everything important in this country. I shall use the judiciary, police and other powerful commissions to harass these Kiongo's men till some flee out of this nation. Others shall land in prison for the rest of their lives while most shall succumb to bullets. I shall show no mercy to most of these people. They think they can own this country but wait and see what shall happen when I get to power. You just support me and your rewards are great. I remember how Kiongo's tribe has been ruling this nation without mercy and compassion to my tribe. How many of my tribe are in high offices? None, except ten of us. This shall be reversed. I shall make sure that my tribe dominates this country; in all offices and as ambassadors. I shall make sure that none from the opposition gets allowances except from my side. I think it's my 'time to eat'. It's my tribe's time to 'feed on the country'. It's our time my friends."

There was a long silence in the room as the other men thought deeply on what their leader was saying. Ihuru continued expressing himself to his men till lunch-time. They took lunch before they dispersed out of the office. Matenjwo went to his room with a heavy head. All of Ihuru's words were ringing and resonating in his head like a bell. He could not believe what Ihuru had explained to them that morning. He made up his mind but did not inform anyone of what he came up with. That night, he went to Kiongo and met him together with Ngari. They sat in a private room where even cooks could not access. Kiongo trusted Matenjwo so much that he never ignored him whenever he wanted to meet him in private. He had served him with loyalty and determination more than any other high-ranking person in his government. "Yes, Matenjwo, you must be having good news because you have never called me in vain", Kiongo whispered. Matenjwo smiled and replied, "I have some shocking news today, the good news I no longer good. Ihuru called us this morning for a meeting and his thoughts were astonishing. If he gets to the power, he is determined to destroy and revenge. He has no any other mission but to leave everything up-side-down. Your life is in danger if you are not careful. He has vowed to kill both of you, kill your families and wipe all of your generations and friends out of the face of this country. He wants to replace your tribe with his tribe in all offices; in fact, he has said that your tribe shall serve his tribe as slaves forever. He has also vowed to have you in prison suffering for some ten years. You shall be tortured slowly till you give up your spirit due to too much agony, pain and lack of strength. He wants you to go without food for many days and you shall faint due to lack of water. He says you have treated him and his tribe like animals and that you have never helped him. Your property shall be divided among all of his allies. Your men shall never have allowances, or take part in his government; in fact, they shall be running for their dear lives, just to save themselves from his wrath. If you have ears, hear what I am saying, if you have eyes, see what I am saying and if you have brains, discern what is in his mind."

Ngari fainted in the room. His ears could not accept what was being said and explained. His mind failed to comprehend the reality. After some first aid to him, he recovered but looked drunk. He seemed confused and lost. Kiongo made him sit on a sofa set for some minutes, without a shirt or vest. He turned lights off to reduce the amount of light in the room. Kiongo had been strong for his entire life but this time round, he was already sweating profusely. Blood vessels were all over his body and eyes were red. Ngari was a very brave man but the words made him like a child. He used to think that there was no news, situation, calamity or sight that could make him a child, but things were different this day. The two men had no words, their strength was gone and they looked helpless. Matenjwo was feeding the two with lukewarm water to help them recover faster. After half an hour, the two were strong and could speak but still trembling and feeble. They vowed never to hand-over power to Ihuru, come rain come sunshine, come God come Devil and come death come resurrection. They thanked Matenjwo and promised to work with him for the rest of his life.

During the elections, there was a massive rigging such as was never seen before. Ihuru complained bitterly but things were done. He later went to court for justice but the judge dismissed the case on lack of substantial evidence. This way, Kiongo got another chance to lead the nation. When his term was almost over, they decided to get a man who could be trusted with the nation's secrets. The man was Matenjwo. Matenjwo was helped in his campaigns and in rigging. He got into power to help guard the interests of 'the mighty men'. This way, Kiongo and Ngari together with their filthy men were safe and secure from all alarms. They rested in their precious homes peacefully, receiving salaries and many other benefits from the government. Matenjwo was a man of their choice. He followed their footsteps and never brought a change in favour of the poor, poor helpless citizens. Their lives remained unchanged until they could not see any difference in leadership. They gave up participating actively in state affairs like elections. They were only concerned with their daily bread.

THE WICKED GOD

———◆•◆•◆———

SHE WAS VERY YOUNG WHEN MANY REALIZED HOW FAR SHE COULD go in this life. Many people saw her as a shining light that would illuminate the whole village, nation and world at large. Her parents had also seen a family's and generation's saviour in her. They had great hopes in her since the early stages of her development. They had been waiting for someone who would come and deliver them out of the curses of poverty. Her mother was once heard 'praising time' for paying her dearly with the gift of this amazing girl. Time had really gone and the mother was really aging, but still believed that a day would come when time would step in as a cure for this malady called poverty. Most of her friends who were 'pure in heart' knew she would be an asset to many. They respected her a lot and didn't want to be far from her in any day. Everyone longed to be associated with her to the fullest.

Muthoni was brought up in a very hard life. Her parents were examples of what it means to be poor. Her father died when she was only 4 years old. He was suffering from unknown disease that had been a big challenge to him and the whole family since he was still a youth. Her mother had nothing left to make the child's life bright or admirable. The small piece of land they had was only for inadequate subsistence farming. But this peasant-farming life-style did not discourage her mother from struggling to make her child's life better. The unwavering hope in her made her stronger every day, and knew that one day she would be one of the most valuable persons in Kenya. At the normal age of five years, Muthoni was taken to nursery school to join her age-mates, though the mother didn't know how she would support her up to the last step in the academic-ladder.

The mother used to wake up at dawn. She would make her a cup of porridge without sugar; which was just some water and small amount of maize flour. Sometimes; when situation was challenging and life difficult to unbearable conditions, she would grind some dry leaves and use it as tea-leaves to prepare a cup of sugarless and milk-less tea, for her. They spent at least three days in a week without food, but the mother used to give the whole family some hope to help them carry out the daily chores strong. She used to say, "The mouth that doesn't feed well today is the same mouth that shall eat like a king on the morrow". There was no hope of heavy meals or balanced diet; the main diet was porridge, day in day out. She believed that porridge could help them survive longer because it didn't consume a lot of flour. The inadequate produce from the small piece of land; like cabbages and onions, arrow-roots, bananas, potatoes and maize, was like a celebration to the family.

At primary school, she became the brightest pupil in every class and the teachers also joined others in praising her. She was very disciplined and respectful, very industrious and obedient, which made the whole school set her as a beacon of an ideal pupil. She astonished her teachers in the manner she used to ask questions and the great insight she had shown them in academic field. She was very retentive and curious in all fields of subjects. Though her mother could not pay her fees to the fullest, the school decided to pay her fees out of harambees and school development funds. Even if she could miss classes due to other activities, such as games and other official duties, this did not bring her performance down. She ever remained top of her class. She rarely failed to get a question right, whether asked out of class or in class, whether asked out of surprise or not, whether asked in examinations or out of them, she was aware and rarely failed to answer correctly. Many prizes were brought to her mother, which inspired her more and more. She collected all of the awards offered in their school both in form of money and materials.

After securing good marks in her final examination, she secured a scholarship to secondary school. At that level, she used to help her teachers in many ways such as setting experiments for other students. She participated in games, which made her an all-rounded-person. She excelled in all these which added her favour in the eyes of many. She got to the leadership as early as she got to form one. In the final two years in that school, she became the school's head-girl. At science and mathematics congresses, she emerged as the most creative and innovative student in her province. She could come up with models in science that were really applicable in solving daily problems facing the society. The formulae she invented in mathematics were always making work in calculations as simple as possible and were always efficient. One of the adjudicators in a congress described her as 'a genius of the time'. Many admired her ways, leadership, performance, achievements and even her beauty.

In the last days in school, the school hosted a big party in honour of her contribution to the school. Many parents attended the party just to see this great girl that students used to narrate at their homes. At the party, she was seated at the high-table and laureled. Her face attracted many parents and visitors for her uniqueness. The principal and chair of the board of governors led the group in this great occasion. Her life story was read to the people followed by praises from the other teachers and parents who knew her well. Photos were taken together with her mother who declared that it was a great honour to be recognized through her child. She saw it as her greatest day since she was born.

She was able to get the best grade in her final examination. This set a new record that school had in performance. She got a scholarship to join university and many villagers really contributed to her finances. They wanted her to study until she would be recognized in the whole world. No one wanted her to lack anything in her life's journey, till she had fulfilled her dreams. Many were aware of her dreams especially the biggest of all; she wanted to liberate her country out of many challenges that seemed to cloud and block its path to development. Her mother's wish was also in her mind and had plans to bring more honour to her with time. She could not forget the many people who supported her along the way in life such as teachers and villagers. She wanted to turn their dishonour, poverty, hopelessness and dismay into glory and honour. Their under-development and backwardness would turn into development and enlightenment. Their challenges would be changed into success. Truly, she was what everyone in the family, village, nation and international levels needed.

The D-Day came when she was to join campus. All the preparations had been made and many people congregated in their compound to see her off. Many gave her their last advice and reminded her that she carried every hope of the village in herself, that she had the nation's burden on her shoulders. After all this, she left and was accompanied by her brothers and sisters. They registered at the university and kissed her good-bye. She was now in a new environment. But she really knew why she was in the new environment. Life was not that challenging to her as she had a stock left from the contributions made by well-wishers and villagers. She could manage herself without difficulties because the help from the sponsors was also boosting her in meeting the daily needs. Many students admired her life-style which was simple though she had everything. She didn't allow the environment to change her but took advantage and redefined her ways for the better.

She used to see many gentlemen and ladies trying funny life-styles that were really affecting their general life. Some used to bleach their bodies, as soon as they joined the campus, using different chemicals and perfumes. Most smelled like decaying carcasses due to unknown perfumes of all types. You could not tell the true skin of a student because most of them had become Caucasians in campus though they were typical Africans. The funny thing with them was how they had white skins but the body-joints betrayed them because they were as black as coal. The mode of dressing was wanting. Skirts that hardly covered private parts and most found it a challenge to sit in public. The ladies' bosoms were never covered and Muthoni was always astonished with this kind of life. She had not seen it before but it was a norm in campus.

Different hair styles made her wonder if these people really knew what they were doing. Many people had wigs on their heads that made their heads go unwashed for even three months. This was not only unethical, but also made congested areas, such as classes, unconducive for learning. It was very difficult to sit next to a person with a wig because of the choking smell that streamed out of their heads. She had noticed that actually it is true that, 'a lady's head is the most expensive part of her body, but the dirtiest'. Many spent thousands of shillings on heads per month only to create unfavourable environment in school. Unnecessary decorations were also part of their lives. Heavy chains on necks, earrings and pins on noses made her to realize that truly the young generation was lost. The shoes they wore were out of order. Extremely high-heeled shoes were the most noise-makers as one made their way along aisles and in any room.

To many ladies, tight trousers, called pencils in campus and streets, were more important than skirts. You could not use the idea of trousers to differentiate between a lady and a man.

She also noticed that men were also drawn into this quagmire of lifestyle. Most had their trousers slit at knees and full of patches which they used to say was a new fashion. Bangles, necklaces, earrings and chemical-haired designs were order of the day. Different hair-cuts were seen all over and lip-sticks were used by majority. They could colour eyelids, trim eyebrows, and most were always in sleepers even when on official duties. Some were always drunk, used other drugs such as cigarettes, and most were seen idling all the time. Most men were in shackles of doom; wasted most precious time in games that were of no value to their lives. She could see them packed to the maximum in pool-games, in video halls, in bars, play-stations and dancing halls. In cyber-cafes, the trend was the same. You could think that students were busy downloading course-work and doing research on the internet, only to realize that they were busy betting online. Betting was another game that had swept most students' mind and spent a lot of money in the game. They thought they were making money but most lost dearly and messed up with their lives. Some used school-fees to bet while others borrowed money from their friends for the same work. This is the only game that made many become thieves and pick-pockets-men for the sake of getting something for betting.

She used to see the nearby town-centres always flooded with students walking up and down without a definite direction. You could be tempted to think they were part of intelligence unit charged with the duty of monitoring the towns. In the school pavements, classes, hostels, streets and everywhere, students were giving the picture we hear from holy books on how it was in entering the Noah's ark. Many were 'married for seasons' and could not help but accompany their companions everywhere. Things were in deed terrible in night-hours because it was hard to find them in rooms. Most were 'resting in long grasses and 'supporting each other' in dark corners. There was no need for clothing to ladies at night because that would 'spoil the broth'. Weekend was another mystery to Muthoni, who didn't understand where her friends and most ladies disappeared to. It was like they were swallowed by unknown monster just after the Friday-lessons.

The hostels became as silent as a grave. No noise, no movements, no usual long phone calls, only darkness covered most of the rooms.

One of her friends, during a discussion said to her, "Don't you think students should have easy moments to release stress? We are living in school like a prison; a lot of work like waking up early for lessons, 'sponsors' are far from us in week-days, we are in a clouded environment and the bitter truth is, books are not interesting. We need some time away from them. Furthermore, we are in school because it is a requirement you be in school until you get to the age of marriage. Don't you know this? I thought you knew because you seem to be sharp." She did not respond to her in an angry manner but said to her, "Yea, books are not that friendly but we do our part so that we don't end up regretting for the lost opportunities." What her friend was saying is that, ladies were not available during weekend because they were busy elsewhere. In short, life at campus was a total mess but she did not allow any influence from anybody; neither did she adopt any life-style that had no meaning.

She studied hard with a clear goal in life, to change the life of many for the better. After the first year, results were out and she had an outstanding performance. She celebrated her achievement with her room-mates who really praised her for the hard work. She reminded them the saying that 'hard work pays or shall never go unrewarded'. Many admired her and wished they were like her. By the time she was starting her second year of study, she was really used to campus life and had defined her way of life. She had many friends and had a good working network with her lecturers. Most lecturers had noticed her talent in academics and offered her advice frequently. They wanted her to go far in life and no one wanted her entangled in 'campus briers and thorns'. The general trend to many students was the way to destruction and many lecturers knew this very well. That's the reason they could not let her go without their advice. She used to ask many meaningful questions and lecturers had hard time with her in terms of the way they were required to prepare for any subject before they went to class. She had great insight into what was taught and lecturers were well pleased with her.

After second year's results were out, she got the highest average in school with most of the subjects scoring grade A. The school came to know her better and started monitoring her closely. Life continued and many students started to realize they were lost during their 3rd year of study, but life was 'too sweet' to change their ways at that time. Though many were members of religious groups established in campus, they were the kind of people who preached salt while taking honey. It was difficult for one to differentiate between a student in those groups and any other 'lost sheep'. There was a lot of hypocrisy among them, immorality, envy, hatred, back-biting, leadership-wrangles and such likes. They only dressed well during services like on Sunday when they were to 'meet their Master'. Muthoni was also part of these groups but was never influenced by their ways. She remained a good example to all. Though the class work was becoming difficult to many, she was able to maintain her performance as was evidenced in continuous assessment tests and assignments. Things became so hard and complex that most students turned to 'Mwakenya' as was known in campus. Mwakenya was in different forms including phones, pieces of papers, full hand-outs, exercise books, inner clothing, body parts, walls, desks, group formations and zooming. Cheating in examinations and CATs became order of the day simply because students had no time for books. They were too busy with other activities to have contact with the real issues that brought them to campus. Other new students (Freshers) were being admitted each year but were easily and quickly introduced to the new destructive life. It was hard to find a good student like Muthoni in campus. Almost everyone was rotten, corrupted and incorrigibly damaged.

Finally, the third year was over and results were out. Many students had to take supplementary examinations and their performance was really poor. Quite a number of them could not continue to fourth year but were to retake a whole year of study in third year. This scenario forced many to realize that things were not right. As a fluke, Muthoni emerged with the best grade than all the other years she had been in school. As usual, many came to congratulate her for the outstanding performance. She was shocked to hear many 'naughty crooks' asking for her advice on how to get a good performance. But it was too late to correct them-selves in just a year because they had a poor foundation in course work. They had realized how time was far much spent and it was almost near to go out and present the fruits of their labour to parents and other interested groups in their villages. They also knew that they had missed the necessary skills to help serve the community after graduation. But Muthoni was really proud of her work during the past three years.

She joined the fourth year with a lot of vigour. She had the right spirit in academics and knew she would make it too in that year. Her dream this time round was to pass the examinations with flying colours and wanted to set a new record in that campus. She longed to surprise many with her excellence that would out-shine the previous students' records. She would have her name recorded in history books as one of the academic giants of the times. She was determined not to put her hardworking lecturers, parent and family at large, friends and all those who wanted to see her excel in her endeavours, to shame. She longed to open new doors that would take her to greater heights in life. She had the desire to put all of her enemies to an open shame. If she had managed to manoeuvre her path in campus for three years without tainting her image and ways, she could manage herself in this final year with a lot of ease. Bearing in mind that most of the crooked students were changing for the better after realizing how limited time was to improve in academics, then there was no way she could go astray. She just wanted to prove herself that what most people thought of herself, she was actually so; a great person and a legend. In short, she just wanted to kill many birds with a single stone-throw, even better, kill countless birds without even throwing the stone itself.

The final journey began well and after few CATs, she had excellent results. This encouraged her a lot and was a proof that she was really in the right track and would make it according to her plans. One day, early in the evening, a group of students knocked her room's door and she gave them a warm welcome. They were not familiar to her but she understood how the campus had a large number of students, making it hard for anyone to have met all of them. Her two friends and room-mates were also not in a position to recognize the visitors but didn't mind since they had received many visitors before, having not met them previously. The five visitors were glad for being welcomed because it was rare to be welcomed in many rooms since students were ever busy if not out. They were well dressed but the two ladies in the group were in tight trousers, braided hair, high-heeled shoes, earrings and the scent of their perfumes filed the room. Men were in ties, suits and black-shining shoes; really presentable. Each of the five had a huge smart-phone, a notebook, a pen and a Bible. The presence of a

Bible eased the tension in Muthoni because she had no reason to fear or be suspicious of anything. Before they said anything, one of her room-mates said, "Today we are lucky. We usually hear from our neighbours how you come to this place often but have never found us in. We are blessed to have you people spreading the good news. I know today is the day that our Lord has made. We are lucky because you have found us and we can hear the good news before we leave for a meeting. You are highly welcome and feel at home. Some of us usually don't have time to worship or study bible, though we have them in our lockers, but this is a sign that God has not given up on us. Please, be free and feel at home."

The visitors felt comfortable and introduced themselves as men and ladies of God sent to proclaim the gospel. Their leader began, "We would like to share the word of God with you this evening because God has given us this opportunity to spread His word to all mankind. We are the chosen generation and we have an obligation as people of God. According to the book of Mathew, we are to spread God's word and as many as would believe and get baptised shall be saved. We should not only preach to people, but also baptise them in the name of the Father, the Son and the Holy Ghost. In this way, people are saved. If you visit the book of Romans, you will find God telling us how men got lost and became so filthy that He also ignored them. But in Hebrews, He is asking us not to harden our hearts today if we get to hear his voice." At that point, he started to raise his voice to the point of shouting like they do in churches. Sweat was now flowing down his face and his voice was 'shaking' the room and all that were inside.

"Many times do we hear his voice but we never soften our hearts for his word to have a room", he continued. "We value other voices and take heed to them rather than to that of God. Oh man, how deceiving is your heart. Who can understand the heart of man? Let us open our bibles to the book of John, just at the beginning of that book. What do we find? That Jesus is the word of God and was with God since the beginning. Everything was created by him and without Him, nothing was created that we see. But He came to this world and we never recognized Him. We ended up crucifying Him in broad day-light. Oooooii, just imagine!" At that point tears started flowing down his cheeks and everybody in that room became weak and emotions drove them to sobbing. The man was really preaching the love of God and the wickedness of man that could not allow him to recognize his creator. He continued after some seconds of tears, "We need to love our creator back and not be so blind that we end up fooling ourselves while in this world. How often do we see a man really toiling throughout his life just to die and leave everything with us, but without peace with his Maker? The bible clearly asks us in the book of Mathew, "What shall a man gain if he gains the whole world and loses his own life?" Because there's nothing you can give in return, my friend."

"Open your eyes and let not the devil deceive you. You cannot be working like you want to own the whole world and really forget your Creator. Your own Creator who gives you the breath of life you are enjoying every day, the peace you have in whatever you do, the healthy body you have, parents and friends who care, the many blessings since you were born. Imagine the many people who are perishing each day in grisly road accidents and others are in hospitals, yet He has kept you safe. Not that you have pleased Him more than others, no, but simply because He is giving you a chance each day to recognize His mercies and greatness. Please, today, harden not your heart. Accept Him and serve Him with all of your might, strength, breath, body and everything that you have, because all of these are His. You own nothing and you are not even creating time with Him! You don't even want to participate in His work of preaching to others to be saved. Let not the devil lie to you, you shall give account to God at the end of everything; in His judgement day, that is coming soon. We need to equip ourselves with every good work for the sake of God's work. We don't have time to waste because our salvation is nearer than when we believed."

"We do not have to work for earthly things that shall be destroyed at Jesus' coming. We need to work for God's kingdom and as he said in the book of Mathew, we should seek the kingdom of God first and everything shall be added to us. Think about it my dear brothers and sisters. Imagine, whatever you are working hard to get, in terms of earthly things, the same is being given to a man of God freely as an addition to his work in seeking the kingdom. How ironical is that! That you spend sleepless nights to acquire things that others are getting freely! Ooh, my God, how great thou art! That you have hidden these things to the wise and mighty, just to reveal them to the simple and humble! Thank you Lord Jesus, thank you and I adore you, I praise you and magnify your name!" At that time, he paused for some time and Muthoni seemed to have been touched to the inner most nerves. She seemed motionless and lost in thoughts. The man went on, "Our God is able to save. Jesus is calling us to open our hearts to Him and He would heal us to return to Him. He knows our hearts, thoughts and intents as is written in His word in Hebrews that "His word is sharper than any double edged sword, He is able to discern our inner being, dividing asunder the marrow and bones, exposing the very inner things of man". We cannot hide anything out of His presence but need to fear Him for His greatness. He is saying in the book of Isaiah, "Come let us reason together and though your sins be as red as scarlet, I shall make them whiter than snow." We only need to abandon our usual ways and return to Him. We have sinned and we are full of sins but we only need to repent. The bible puts it very clearly that "All have sinned and fallen short of the glory of God", in the book of Romans. Please my friends, let us not be so selfish that we waste our precious times in toils and pains for earthly things and goodies, yet we forget the owner of those things and goodies. He shall not hesitate to throw us into the Hell fire if we do not recognise His voice as early as this, before the grace period is over."

"Today, God has brought us together to share His word and rectify the path of each other so that all of us may be saved. The blood of Jesus is still flowing down the cross at Calvary for your sake. Just imagine, an innocent man being killed because of your filthy and crooked ways. Uuuuuuuii! God Help, please help! We don't want to leave this room tonight unchanged! We want you to destroy our hearts and create new ones in us, today and not tomorrow!" He let out a cry that sent all of the people in that room filled with sorrow. They were wailing and Muthoni went on her knees. She pleaded with the rest to pray for her because she had ignored God and the blood of Jesus for so long. She said in bitter tears, "I have wandered far from God, I have counted the blood of Jesus worthless and need forgiveness. I have really sinned and God has had mercy on me tonight. I promise never to go back to the wrong path any other time in my life. I thought I was working so hard to save my family, community and nation. I thought that the world needed me but I was fooling to myself. I was listening to the devil's voice and ignoring that of God. Please God, forgive me, I leave everything in your hands, guide me, tame me, I am yours and I must serve you from this moment. My brothers and sisters, pray for me, lay your hands on me and place me in God's hands. I have heard Jesus calling me and I must obey His voice. I must love Jesus back. I must be with God."

All of the visitors and her room-mates praised God in a song for helping Muthoni realize her ways. They conducted a long prayer and sang several songs as a way of appreciating what God had done to them that day. After that, Muthoni stood up but still full of tears in her eyes. She seemed lost in thoughts and full of bitterness. She then said to them, "I feel pity to myself and have a lot of bitterness inside. I hate myself for being such a fool. How can I be so blind and deaf? I wish I had known these things earlier for I would have made my ways right before God. But I once more thank Him for not judging my stupidity. Today I have received the necessary light in this life. I have felt the presence of God, I feel filled with the Holy-Ghost, and my heart and conscience are clear that Jesus saves and he has done so to me today. I shall never enter into the wrong path, I just want to serve God my saviour for His mercies and grace to me. How I wish that every one of us would realize the free gift of God, His grace and long-suffering, His ways of doing things and the great wisdom He has! I am glad that He didn't destroy me in my foolishness and stupidity. May He be praised forever, may His name be glorified and magnified by all. Praise God you people, praise Him once more you living and non-living things!"

They later took a cup of tea and the visitors left. The room-mates also left for a meeting and Muthoni was all alone in the room. There was a lot of silence in the room and hostel as she pondered on the events of that evening. It was really the greatest day in her life; marking the beginning of a new dawn. She really felt empty and started cursing herself bitterly in the room. Tears were flowing down the cheeks and she knelt down to ask for forgiveness in prayers. She did not prepare anything for supper that day but got into bed and slept immediately. In the morning, she did not wake up as usual; she was awake by four in the morning but not for the usual study. She took her bible and studied till sunrise. Her friends were astonished by her move and declared that she had really been 'touched by the gospel'. One said to the other, "God works wonders and in different ways. He can change anything and we really need to fear Him. Did you see how Muthoni didn't bother with her books? It's like books are her greatest enemies from yesterday evening! This is what we refer to as true conversion, and God wants such converts to worship Him."

The other lady answered and said, "Yes, yes my dear, you are right. But this is something of great concern. Remember how she has been in the past years; her hard-work, her performance, her great name, she is a role-model to many- the mentors like lecturers and many more. Such a U-turn in life can cause shock to many. I feel like it is not an appropriate move in her final year. Is there a way we can help her so that she may first finish her great work?"

The other answered, "My dear, remember this is God's work. God is greater than anything and all of us. Let her keep the books aside and serve God. Maybe this is the Lord's final call on her to serve Him before God's anger is kindled against her. We need to help her serve God. Furthermore, if she doesn't work hard, or if she ignores her books completely, or even if she doesn't graduate, who cares? Don't you remember how she works so hard until we are seen as jokers when compared to her? I am glad that she won't work hard anymore except in God's work. This is God who is slowing her down so that we, as jokers or joy-riders, may at least have peace of mind. I hate such kind of her hard-work and performance. She is so smart until we are equated to dull students. May God never allow her to go back to books any other time, may He keep her busy with His work once and for all. Let us not conspire against God's mighty hand. Are you not happy Mary my dear?" She concluded smiling and springing into the air with joy.

Mary was saddened by her friend's words and she responded to her saying, "Jane, there is no good news in Muthoni's new move. Remember how many people rely on her as their role-model. I thought you are a good friend but it seems you were only a hypocrite. Do you know that a hypocrite is worse than a murderer? If you are her friend and my friend too, please, let's approach and advise her. Remember she shall have enough time with God; to serve Him without books waiting for her, after she is through with her final year. It is not wise to bring down the house she has built for three years, just in one day. Which God would allow someone He loves to demolish such great works in one minute? Such God would even taint His reputation. Her performance is a show of someone to be relied on by many in the future. Though we don't have a lot of information about her background, we can be sure that many students who work hard and are talented come from needy families and they are there to uplift their families. I know her family, friends and relatives are waiting for her to deliver them out of some kind of poverty or such a misery. There is nothing to celebrate about her drastic change in direction."

Jane laughed like an idiot and said with a loud voice and full of anger, "What are you saying? Are you greater than God? Do you have more wisdom than Him? If so, go and advise God Himself. I don't care if there are people relying on her or not. It is not my business to give unnecessary advice to anyone. Are we together my friend? I hate her, to hell with her. She thinks she is the brightest girl in this world? I heard her say she wanted to set a new record in academics, may she fail to achieve it terribly. If she was like us, I would not hate her; but she is never with us in clubs for some beers, she has not bleached her skin, she is ever against our ways and more so, she is admired by many and most of us are never approached by any boy. Don't you recall how she turned many boys down when they wanted to 'push with her' in this campus? Many boys praise her so much until they wear my ears out. All the lecturers tell us to emulate her ways as if we are kids. I hate all this non-sense from the bottom of my heart. Don't you remember that she is also on scholarship? And I know she got it from her hard-work. This is a proof that she has been doing great since she was a child. May that God take away the scholarship too! Have you understood now? Have I opened your eyes like Jesus did when His disciples ate bread on the way to Emmaus? Hahahaaaa, uuuuuuiiii!"

Mary wept bitterly and vowed to talk to Muthoni privately. After this conversation, Muthoni came back from washroom. The two friends left the room for classes and Muthoni was alone. She put on her gorgeous clothes and took her bible instead of class-work books. She headed to church to pray and worship because of 'the new revelation from the Holy One'. She read several verses in the book of Romans, and again she started sobbing when she saw how man was far from God's glory. She also read the book of revelation and saw how Jesus would return and reward His servants. There she vowed to serve Jesus and remain faithful to Him rather than serving the worldly glory. After some rest from the 'new kind of study', she opened the book of Isaiah. There she found a verse that talked about obedience to God and how He would let His people eat the best fruits out of the land.

She later turned to the book of Mathew and found some encouraging message. It was about seeking and finding, knocking and getting the door opened, asking and receiving. Then another verse in the bible that talked about those who leave everything for Jesus' sake and getting rewarded one hundred fold times. All this sounded new and promising. She started building hope and faith in God, knowing well that she would receive whatever she asked for as was stated in Mathew.

She later offered a long prayer to God; asking for forgiveness, thanking Him and asking for a good life that many would admire. She asked Him not to put her to any kind of shame and that He should manifest Himself in her so that His glory may be shining among all around her. She committed everything to God. She was determined to serve and live for Him. She asked for blessings so that her enemies may glorify God and praise Jesus - the Crucified Saviour. She concluded her service with a song of praise and left for lunch. In the room, she found Mary back and greeted her in Jesus name as other Christians used to do. Mary got a shock when she realized that Muthoni was not from class but somewhere else. They sat on the same bed and Mary started crying. "What is the matter my friend? Are you sick? Has anyone hurt you? Tell me dear, don't hide anything from me." Mary replied in tears, "You are the one who has hurt me. My heart is heavy. Please Muthoni, do not let the water get poured when already at the door-step. Do not destroy all the work you have done like this. I feel that you have left the right track and you are now in a thicket inside a dense forest. I love you and I must help you to my level best. Please, I plead with you, serve God after fourth year. He won't condemn you for delaying to serve Him. It is only this final year, and then you shall have all the time with Jesus. There are many ways of serving God. Your ways are enough to glorify God. You do not have crooked ways and that is what God is pleased with. Please, please Muthoni, go back to books and finish the race. I look up to you as my role model, though I fail to live up to your standards."

"Do not let things fall apart at this time. This is a critical point in your life. We need you as a friend, your family, community and nation need you as a saviour, while outsiders need you as their role-model. God will still bless you even if you don't serve Him by ignoring the books. Have you forgotten that many are helping you and sponsors do so to you because of your hard-work, talent in academics and good behaviour? I do not see

Jesus standing with you if you neglect your talent, which is academics." Muthoni kept quiet for some minutes and later said, "My dear, God has called me and I feel that I must tool-down everything in hands, then follow my Jesus. I have heard His voice and can no longer harden my heart. God can make me greater than before even if I neglect everything. He has power for miracles and can give me anything I ask in Jesus name." Mary said in a very low voice as if she was whispering, "You are lost my dear friend. Please, tell God to be patient with you until you finish this year. Then He can make you, not just a servant to Him, but a slave as He wishes. If He wishes to curse you by not leaving your books aside, then, let that curse come to me. I am ready to bear your punishment. You should continue shining to many like before. This calling is not promising anything. I know how God is merciful, long-suffering and caring. He hears and would want us to explore our talents for the betterment of all. Please hear my voice and harken to it. Let us ask God to curse me on your behalf so that you may continue like before. If He does not listen to this prayer from the bottom of my heart, I better not be one of His children. I love you and want the best out of you. Prepare lunch and go for classes, I will plead with God on your behalf."

Muthoni kept silent for the next five minutes. Then she stood up to prepare lunch. They later ate together and continued with their previous discussion. She tried to defend her enlightenment from God and how she wanted to serve Jesus as a way of saying 'thank you' for saving her on the cross. She started, "Let me carry my own cross and follow Jesus. I feel that I love the Holy Trinity more than before." Mary was not happy at all and she took the bible from Muthoni's hands. She said in a low voice, "If this is the word of God, Jesus and Holy Spirit; that has changed your life like this, that will cause great sorrow to many, that will ruin your life, that will cause your down-fall, that will tremble my heart day and night, that will put out the light that many have been waiting for, that will destroy our saviour, that has made my room-mate utter words that no one would want to wish even their enemies, then, today have I lost faith in God unless He changes His mind and restores your former state. I don't want to be associated with Him. May He curse me and let me die at this moment as I speak these words to you. I will tear this bible into pieces, burn it in fire and would never worship Him. I will do all this for your sake. I cannot afford to see the light we have been waiting for so long, burn dim." Muthoni said quickly, "No, no, no my dear, do not bother with my life. Just relax. God is great and wise but I would rather serve Him because I feel His presence so strong."

There was a long silence and Mary rose up holding the bible in hands. She tore it into pieces and threw the pieces in dirty water in a nearby bucket. Muthoni could not believe what she was seeing. She thought she was dreaming but it was a real drama. She exclaimed, "Are you doing this because of me, dear? Please relax and take time to think deeply about it. You do not have to fight for me, God is there for me. But is it possible to destroy a bible and go unpunished? He is going to curse you my friend." Mary interjected and shouted, "Let Him curse me. I no longer need Him if this is what He is going to do His work. He cannot destroy the light meant for many. Your family has been waiting for you to deliver them, the world needs you to light it up and here He is trying to extinguish the brightest candle in our times, no sane person can allow that. If He is bitter with me, let Him kill me now and not tomorrow. We cannot continue like this and it is most likely that we cannot be friends if you do not turn back to your books."

The two did not talk to each other for many days though they were in the same room. Mary was one of those who were trying to struggle with books to at least better her grades. But though she had lost her way like any other student, she had great wishes towards Muthoni. She wanted her to continue with her good ways and hard-work. She wanted Muthoni to be a beacon of a good student until the end. But unfortunately, Muthoni didn't go back to books. She spent each day with her bible, attending church services, missions, meetings and visitations. At the end of the semester, just before the final examinations, they had to do the CATs on all subjects. She spent a night in church; reminding God how she had served Him since the revelation and that it was God's turn to reward her. She asked Him to put her enemies into shame by giving her an exemplary performance. After the night in church, she went back to room at dawn. She slept for some hours before she went to do the CATs that afternoon. All the students were preparing thoroughly, some through the normal study others through 'group formations' and the rest were busy writing 'Mwakenya'. Muthoni took out a hand-out and started to peruse through in a hurry before the lecturer came in with the question papers.

When he came in, he distributed the papers and students started to write the CATs' answers on special papers meant for CATs. What surprised everyone was the fact that Muthoni had not carried those papers. She asked for permission to go and get some but the lecturer was shocked to hear that from Muthoni. He responded, "Are you sure Muthoni? What happened? I have never heard nor seen that from you. You are always ready and you have been a good example to many. I don't believe what you are saying. Or maybe you are sick but do not want to disclose it?" Muthoni kept quiet for some seconds like someone who did not understand English language. The lecturer, Mr Mwema, spoke to her in Kikuyu in a bid to make her understand what he was asking and that is when she responded saying, "Sir, I am not sick. I just forgot them on my table where I was studying from." The lecturer said, "Have you forgotten that once I have distributed the papers you are not supposed to walk out anymore, till the CAT answers are collected? We do not allow that because once a student has seen the questions, they can walk out with different fake excuses with an aim of consulting books in rooms, toilets or in other class-rooms. Please, take only two minutes to get the papers but see me after the CAT."

She ran out of class and headed to the nearest canteen. She asked the shop-keeper for five papers and the shop-keeper wrapped them in a nylon-paper. She then realized that she had no money in her pockets as was usual. She started to sweat because the two minutes were far much spent. She asked the shop-keeper to help her and she would come to pay later but he strongly refused saying, "Young lady, are you new in this campus? Which year are you in? We do not trust students because of their cunning ways. But if you are a student, you must be knowing all this." She told him she was a fourth year student and she had a CAT waiting for her and that time was running out. When he heard her say she was a fourth year student, she said in a loud voice, "What the hell are you talking about? I do not understand you. Are you trying to trick me because you are a fourth year? Who can trust a fourth year student? This is how you fourth years hoax us and force us to pay for your debts. Do you want me to call the security personnel so that you can be forced to explain whatever you are up to?"

Many people hard the shop-keeper shouting at her and a large crowd gathered around the shop. By that time, almost ten minutes had been spent. She was sure she could not be allowed into that examination room. The crowd demanded to know her better and threatened to take an action against her for trying to con the shop-keeper in broad daylight. University students had no good reputation anywhere in the campus and neighbouring towns. Muthoni prayed to God to help her. She said in her heart, "God, please do not let me be embarrassed anymore. I trust in you, show thyself. Deliver me out of this mess. I know it is the devil trying to fight me but he won't win this war. Every power belongs to you, save me." After the short prayer, she felt relieved and wanted to see her Jesus perform a miracle. But the crowd was becoming impatient with her silence. Those who had not seen her before started collecting stones ready to rain them on her for such a brave immoral move. When she realized things were turning pepper, she said in tears, "I was not trying to lie to him; I just found myself in a hurry to class and thought I could ask him in a polite way to help me. I promise you before God that I wasn't hoaxing him. Please forgive me."

The mob could not believe her and one of them said in an angry voice, "What are you telling us, you think you can use the name of God to scare us or convince us? We know students very well. They are only thugs in the name of students." At that moment, she wet herself out of fear. In her mind, she was very sure that she could no longer be allowed into the examination room. Her body started to shake like a feeble twig on a windy day. The crowd was so rowdy that more and more people flooded into the place. The security personnel heard the noise and sent some men to help calm the crowd. They found the lady at the centre of the mob, she was sobbing, sweating and wet. They calmed the people down, explained to them how they should follow the lawful procedure in seeking justice and took the lady to their office for interrogations. The crowd dropped the stones and left for other activities. By this time, the students had finished their CAT and the lecturer asked the students why Muthoni behaved in such an unusual way. No one seemed to understand her but some said that the lecturer should ask her room-mates, Mary and Jane. He called the two ladies and went to the office together.

At the office, Jane said she should never be asked anything about Muthoni because they are not friends at all. She then left the office, leaving Mary and the lecturer alone. The lecturer seemed to be lost in thoughts but later said, "Mary, do you really know anything about Muthoni? Could she be suffering in any way? Please, share with me so that we can see how we can help her. Remember she is one of the best students in this campus and we have great hope in her." Mary kept quiet for some seconds before she replied, "Yes my teacher. There is something I know about her and I also do not have peace. I tried to advise her but in vain. I even tore her bible and threw it in dirty water after realizing that I was going to lose the most shining star in this life. But sir, all was fruitless." The lecturer opened his eyes wide as if he wanted to overcome some mist that was blocking his sight. He whispered to her, "What is it Mary? Has she lost anyone in her family?" "No sir", she said in low tone, "She was 'saved' and that changed everything for the worse. She has found God and Saviour. She does not value books anymore." They continued with the discussion privately. She explained everything to him and he really pitied Muthoni for the unwise decision. He promised to advise Muthoni later after the second CAT. Mary left the office for other activities.

At the security office, one of them said, "We should take her to the police station as this involves criminal charges, we need not meddle with the case. Let the police be notified of what happened so that they can start investigations with immediate effect. I know that if we leave her in the hands of law enforcing body, she would not hesitate to explain why she was a con-woman at day-time. They would also teach her a lesson she would never forget. Is there any objection to my suggestion?" Most of his colleagues agreed with him but few were against it. Another one said in a low tone, "I think we need to deal with her case because she is still our student and 'acted unwisely' within the school. The management would not be pleased with the case taking roots outside the school's domain. Let us have our intelligence unit interrogate her." Later, all agreed to have her write a report and take the case before the school's disciplinary committee for appropriate measures to be taken against her. She was interrogated thoroughly and after she had prepared a report, she was released for classes. She was informed that she would receive a letter from them later in the semester.

Muthoni no longer had peace of mind in whatever she was doing from that moment onwards. She did not know what direction the case would take but decided to commit it into the hands of the Lord. She continued with her prayers and bible study without bothering with her books. Mary did not advise her anymore. Jane was only making mockery of her previous efforts to advise her. During the next CAT, Muthoni was called by Mr Mwema before she could sit for the CAT. She was informed that she could not sit for the CAT without writing a comprehensive report with valid reasons concerning her previous CAT's disappearance. She tried to plead with him in tears and her cry was heard. She was allowed to sit for the CAT but was to immediately follow the lecturer to the office after the CAT. She felt relieved but was always thinking on what she would tell the lecturer in the office. During the CAT, she seemed confused. She had no ideas on what to write on the answer sheets simply because she hadn't done any preparation. She had spent the most precious time on bible study and prayers. But 'lucky' to her, she remembered what God had promised in the bible; that He would answer if she called upon Him, He would make His child a head and not a tail, He would open the door if she knocked and other good promises. With that thought, she gained some strength and decided to pray for God to open her mind. After a short prayer, she was able to smile knowing that God had really heard her prayer and would answer immediately.

After a short while, 'her Saviour gave her insight'. She remembered one of the calculations she had done in third year of study and how she could do it with ease. By this time, Mr Mwema was out to collect attendance sheet from the office. She decided to borrow a calculator from her neighbour to compute the idea that came on her mind. She asked the nearest person in whispers but he responded angrily. He was so stubborn to her that he even shouted at her, creating some noise in class. It happened that, as soon as the noise began, Mr Hasira was passing by the class-room trying to ensure that the environment was conducive for students to do CATs. He heard the noise and stood by the window to witness whatever was happening. Muthoni did not answer the student back but stretched her neck to call upon another student at the front. The student seemed to be in deep concentration on his work and could not hear her calling. She decided to stretch her neck further to him and raised her voice to be heard. All the students turned to her direction wondering what she was doing. They thought she was either copying from him or she wanted him to assist her with his answers. They wondered why she was talking in class when it was against the rules to talk to anybody during CATs. There was some murmuring among students and this forced Mr Hasira to shout at the class. He instructed her angrily to walk out and head straight to the office for causing commotion during CAT. He then issued stern warning to them and proceeded to the office after her.

At the office, Hasira could not listen to Muthoni's explanations. She gave her the hand-book on examination and CATs' rules and regulations. She agreed she was familiar with them and tried to offer some reasons as to why she was talking during CAT. He could not entertain her excuses but instructed her to sit down in the office and write a report on the incidence. No sooner had she started writing the report than when Mr Mwema came in. He was shocked to find her writing a report under the heading, 'CAUSING COMMOTION DURING CAT'. He could not believe what he was seeing. He said in shock but in a whisper, "My child, what is happening and what is not happening? Is there a demon haunting you? Last time you lied to me and never came back for the CAT, today you are writing a report on another incidence. What is it Muthoni? May I know something so that I can see how I can help?" Muthoni kept silent for some seconds and then said, "Sir, I wanted to ask for calculator but Mr Hasira doesn't want to listen. There was some noise at that time and he said I was causing commotion during CAT. During your CAT last time, I went for answer sheets but something else happened. Please understand sir." He replied, "I do not understand you Muthoni. Does it mean that you forgot calculator and last time you forgot answer sheets? What are you doing if you can forget such vital tools? Which farmer heads to field without a panga and a jembe? How can you be a secretary without a pen and a book? How can it be that all this is happening in your final year and all of a sudden? Things are out of control on your side. Has a witch done their works on you? I need to understand you more than before. After this, please, write a report on last CAT's incidence, submit to me and be ready to explain more. See how you are going to miss two consecutive CATs!"

He then left Muthoni there and went to invigilate the CAT. She was already in tears and sobbing loudly in the office. She was weak and seemed like someone tormented. Her body was slightly slim from great sorrow. She could not write the report that was legible due to too much shivering. Later, she was able to compose a report of few sentences but hand-writing was not clear. She took another paper and wrote the one for Mwema. This one was to be long enough as she had a lot to explain. In both reports, she concluded with a sentence that read, "May God have mercy on me, may He help me out of troubles and may he touch the reader of this report to have a forgiving heart." Later, Mr Mwema came in and took his report from her. He instructed her to see the school counsellor and bring him a report on the same, not later than the following morning. Mr Hasira came in before she left the room. He also took his report from her and went through it. His anger was kindled when he saw the very last sentence in the report. He tore it in pieces out of anger and shouted, "What the hell is this you have written? Is this a report? Who taught you to write such a non-sense in reports? Write another one in the next few minutes and attach a copy of your national and school IDs. Very fast and never include your feelings and religion in it. Your opinion has no place in such a report." He then threw the pieces of the report in the dustbin and left.

Mr Mwema watched her face keenly and said, "Please, avoid more trouble. Life creates enough troubles for all of us, but if you add more troubles, you suffer. Let your life take the former course. It was well defined and predictable. Today, we cannot tell or understand where you are heading to. It takes many years to build but can take seconds to destroy one's life. When you become a candle to many, you do not try to extinguish it because many would be left in utter darkness. Never try to turn people's hope into hopelessness. They say that, as water finds its own level, so have you your own level. Why do you want to occupy another level that is not yours? We need to be careful so that we don't bring our mansions down like fools. God has given us brains to use them in reasoning and doing things. We have to maximize on that, knowing that He also expects a lot from us when He has given us a lot. So, Muthoni, be careful that you do not let the water gourd break at door step. Write the report he has instructed you and do not include your opinions. I do not want you to re-write mine. But remember to see a counsellor and submit a report on the progress. Have a great day." He left for other businesses, leaving Muthoni alone in the office. Later, Mr Hasira came and collected the report, left for other works without saying a single word to her and she felt relieved. She dismissed herself for other activities but seemed like someone living in misery. She seemed utterly lost.

She did not go to room for anything but straight to church for some quiet time with Jesus. There, she knelt down and said a short prayer in bitterness. Tears hardly came out because she was hungry and exhausted. She had cried enough in the office and eyes were already red and dry. After the prayer, she sat down for some minutes just staring at the church-roof. She then fell down on her belly and cried to God saying, "God, you talked to me that night and I softened my heart for you to come in and dine with me. I made you my hope and defender, shield and provider, and most of all, everything to me. I made a decision to walk with you and here I am in trouble. Please, let your power be manifested in me. I really need you at this time to intervene in my life. It has taken a new direction and would like you to take control over it. Let me not be disappointed. Christ the great Saviour, you saved me on the cross when you suffered on my behalf, please, save me from these troubles that the devil has cast on me. I now commit these things into your hands."

With those words, she sat on the floor waiting for the voice of God to assure her victory over her calamities. After a long silence, she went to her room and found the friends making supper. She only said hi to them and got into bed without supper. Mary was surprised and said to Jane, "What is not happening? Her eyes are red as canker, she has not asked for supper, she did not do today's CAT and last time she ran out of class having not done the CAT. What God is this that convinced her to serve Him in such a way? Things are falling apart faster than expected and at the wrong time. I better serve the devil than such a God who does not feel what people are going through." Jane smiled and said in sarcastic manner, "Heheheee that is the way to go my dear. Let her serve God at this time. This will slow her progress down and even kill her mentally. I used to fear she would become one of the greatest persons and many would use her as reference to success. I'm glad that Jesus has come at the right time to destroy such works and has relieved me. If she does not take supper, we can as well understand that it is Christ who is instructing her to do so. Remember she got saved and is now under the Holy Spirit, so He might tell her to avoid supper for the sake of the Spirit to give her good dreams. The Spirit might also tell her to fast for some days to cleanse her-self from the filth that comes from food. Remember Jesus is holy and would be defiled by earthly food. I know that soon she will be taking heavenly food to be closer to God, hahahaaaa!"

Mary did not like what her friend was saying but didn't comment on her words. They took supper and retired to bed.

That weekend, the students left hostels as usual for raving in the nearest clubs in town. Muthoni was left alone but decided it was the best time to be closer to her Saviour. She had quiet time studying the word of God and praying indoor. But she never touched any class work. On Sunday, she went to church and the pastor encouraged people to have enough time with their Creator saying, "My brothers and sisters in Christ, spare your time and understand our Saviour. He has done marvellous to us and we need to remember Him in every day. We do not have to be mean but should always remember that time spent at the feet of Jesus is not time wasted, He rewards His people dearly." She felt greatly encouraged by that day's sermon and vowed to herself that she would really serve God and live for her Christ. After two days of the new week, another CAT was to be done in the morning hours. In the previous night, she had spent sleeping hours in church praying to and praising God. She was encouraged by the pastor's words of spending time with Jesus who would later reward dearly and in diverse ways. At dawn, she went to bed to at least have a nap before CAT time as she was extremely exhausted with the night's service.

At seven in the morning, her friends woke up and prepared breakfast. They left at eight for the CAT that was to start in half an hour time. Muthoni was left sleeping because she had just fallen asleep when the others were waking up. At 8.30 am, the alarm she had set in her phone rang and she got out of bed confused due to heavy sleep. She prepared in a hurry, said a prayer and left the room. No sooner had she stepped out of the room than when she realized she had not picked her answer sheets from the bag. She went back to the room in a hurry, checked her sheets but was not there. She panicked. She started overturning her bags and books and the noise from the hurry made one of her neighbours thought she was in trouble. She came and asked her in surprise, "I thought you had a CAT from 8.30 am and it is already quarter past nine. Or are you not part of the students doing your course? You seem to be looking for something, share the problem please. You are getting late." Muthoni replied in a melancholic voice, "I had some papers for my CAT but cannot find them. Could you please help me with some?" She answered, "Yes I can, please come and have mine. You are really late for this CAT. Most students who get late do

158

so due to lack of proper preparation. Don't let yourself be counted among such students yet you know how the whole school has faith in you. Always prepare such 'academic tools' in advance because last minutes' rush can mess you up. Once you get them, do not waste time anymore."

She gave her few sheets and sent her to class saying, "Success dear, God be with you". She left the hostel at a neck-breaking speed. She looked confused and was not careful with the path that was full of stones and potholes. As she approached the class, she stepped in a pothole and went flying to the ground. She fell with thud! She broke her leg and let everything she was carrying out of her hands. The sheets flew in the wind and Muthoni laid there like a log, screaming in anguish. Many students rushed there to help her. By this time, she was late for the CAT by three-quarters of an hour. According to the rules and regulations, she could not be allowed in, bearing in mind that she had some other issues before. The crowd took her to the school's dispensary where she received some treatment. The nurse referred her to the nearest hospital for closer examination by a doctor though she didn't inform her anything substantial. After the ambulance had taken her to the hospital, she was admitted immediately. The doctor was able to examine her carefully and she was really shocked to hear him inform her that she had to undergo some kind of special surgery because it seemed like the fracture was almost incorrigible. He further said that they had to try to mend the situation by placing thin pieces of metal within and without the leg-bones and monitor the progress for some months. If no improvement was to be recorded, then the leg was to be dismembered after six months.

She broke into tears and exclaimed, "Didn't I find God and Christ Jesus the Saviour? God, please show thy-self. Jesus Christ, your healing power is no less today. You healed many and today I call upon you to have mercy on me. Please, save me Christ. Restore my leg and I shall live the rest of my life for you, serving you as you wish. I heard your voice when you whispered to me not to harden my heart. Hear me today as you are capable of doing great things." This prayer was followed by a moment of great silence in the presence of the doctor. Then the doctor said in low tone, "My dear child, weep not, I am going to do my best to help you regain your former state. Worry less. And it is good to have faith in God because He can help even when things turn impossible. He can bring light out of nowhere to chase darkness out of its place. He is able to lift anything fallen not to rise again. Trust in Him and Christ as your Saviour and things shall go well. Let me inform your parent and school about what you should undergo in the next five hours." He left to meet the parent and the school representative. Muthoni was left on the bed, depressed like never before.

Her parent agreed with the doctor and the school representative saw it reasonable too. Her mother enquired about the total cost of the operation and she almost fainted when the doctor quoted the figure. Thirty thousand Kenyan Shillings was an amount she had never touched since she was born. She wailed as if she was bereaved for the second time. The school representative, Mr Mwema, tried to console her and tried to convince her that all would be alright. With those words from Mr Mwema, she found solace and asked him to try his best to help the family. Mwema agreed and the deal was clinched between the two. The two informed the doctor to do his part as they went to raise the said amount. They conducted a short prayer session in the hospital and left her in the hands of God. They left the room and headed straight to school. The management was informed the whole thing and decided to conduct a fundraiser on the day before the doctor asked for the money. The lecturers availed themselves and raised forty-five thousands towards her surgery. The next day, Mr Mwema and her mother went to hospital and paid the bill as were instructed by the doctor. They found the surgery was successful but she had to remain with the doctor for one month for close-monitoring of the recovery.

Her mother was later called in school for some discussions with the management and lecturers about the situation and the number of incidences Muthoni was off-side in the past few weeks. There she was informed how Muthoni had changed for the worse and was shown the letters she had written addressing Mr Mwema and Mr Hasira. It was also discussed how the accident happened that day and the student who was a witness of how Muthoni was late that morning for the CAT, narrated her part of the story to them. The room-mates were also called and briefed them on how Muthoni changed after "meeting God and shaking Jesus' right hand". Her mother listened carefully and most of the time she seemed lost in a tide of thoughts. Her eyes turned pale and the face became cold. She later said, "I thought she was doing alright but now I see that Muthoni is no longer the little girl I knew and have been waiting for to deliver us out of poverty.

Which God did she find? Which Jesus is this? What are they up to? If she found them, then let us see where they want to take her to." With those words, she was allowed to go home and was promised to be kept abreast on any progress in hospital and in school. She was assured that Muthoni would still be answerable when back to school because management could not condone any act that breaks rules and regulations set. She assured the management that she was not against any decision made by the school and no objection whatsoever on any action taken against Muthoni. She then left for home before three in the afternoon.

In the hospital, some students, who called themselves 'Evangelists of the Most High and Soldiers of Christ Jesus', from her university, visited her. It was on a cool afternoon and there were rainy clouds all over the sky. She was glad to see her school-mates and welcomed them warmly. After some brief introduction, they comforted her with many stories on how God had seen many people through difficult situations. Finally, their leader stood amongst them to crown the whole thing with the word of God. To her joy, it was the man who preached to her that night when she met God. He talked for some minutes trying to praise her for accepting Jesus into her life and remaining steadfast in Him. Then he gave a brief sermon, "My dear friends, let's go into our bibles and see what God has for us this afternoon. Before we read any verse, see how great He is, see how gracious He has been to us, that today we are expecting rains though we don't deserve any blessing from Him. He lets His sunshine and rains fall on both the wicked and the righteous. Is that not His mercy at work? Open your eyes wide and see, He has made Himself manifest to all of us so that no one would be tempted to say, 'there is no God', as it is written in at the beginning of the book of Romans. And that we cannot pretend not to see His power at work every day. Let me ask you my dear sister in Christ Muthoni, is Jesus not working on you when you are in this hospital, and you see some being taken out of their beds in this room to morgue, and yet you haven't been taken there too? Or is it because you are more righteous than them? Have you bribed Him so that He has spared your life too? When you fell to the ground in school, who held you not to break your skull or backbone? Is it not the Lord Himself? Remember my friends how Job was questioned by God about His power, greatness, mercy and grace, wisdom and such things. Was Job able to answer God back? In fact, he humbled himself and declared His greatness and His infallibility. Who are we then before Jesus?"

After a pause that lasted for few seconds, he continued, "Answer me if you can. Who will cause the rain to fall on us and later stop it and bring sunshine on all? Jesus is the same every other day. As he allowed Job to be tested, so is He allowing Muthoni to be strengthened because of the love He has for her. He would let her faith get strong and stronger each day so that in the end, He would shower His blessings on her like He did on Job. Muthoni, you shall recover soon as Jesus willeth and thou shallt come out of hospitals, stronger, wiser, richer, healthier and fully blessed; only singing praises to Christ the risen King. You shall be a blessing to all and a head, not a tail, in whatever you do. With those remarks, let's all stand up, join hands, believe and call upon the Lord to descend and heal the little child, Muthoni." They all did as were instructed and he began, "Jesus the Son of God, we have sinned and left the paths of righteousness and are far from thy will. Forgive us. Let your mercy cover us and thy wisdom be shining in us. God, guide us, fill us with thy Holy Spirit and always show us the way. Touch your child Muthoni to see your power tonight. Let the leg recover because you are able, your greatness will last forever. Heal her and let her live to praise you forever. Be with us all and help us to keep your word in our mind always. Thank you and we glorify your name, in Jesus' name we do pray and believe, Amen, amen, amen."

Muthoni was very delighted and tears of joy flowed down her cheeks and wet her blouse. She praised the preacher of the day and asked him to consider paying her another visit. They later kissed each other good-bye and left the hospital. She sat there the whole night pondering on what was preached that day. It was really good news and she considered herself most blessed since she accepted Christ into her life. She later fell asleep although it was almost morning hours.

After several months in hospital, the doctor informed the school and her mother that she could be discharged out of hospital but had to remain with the metallic pieces in her leg for the rest of her life. She was also to walk on wheel-chair for one year to let the leg recover and strengthen bones. The news was not good news at all. No one could imagine her on wheel-chair for a whole year and metals in leg for life-time. But it was said and had to be done. She left the hospital and went home. Her mother was growing weaker each day and sorrow was like a veil on her face. She could not believe what her daughter was going through. Stress clouded her mind and after a few weeks, she was rushed to hospital due to what was reported by her neighbour as 'fainting'. At the hospital, nurses did first aid on her and the doctor examined her. After some blood test, it was declared that she had high blood pressure and attributed it to stress. She had to be under medication at the hospital for some weeks before she could be allowed to continue with the same at home. The relatives could not believe that the devil was actually out to ruin the family. Meanwhile, Muthoni's brother, Maina, was taking care of her. The sisters were schooling in primary and secondary schools and were not available to take care of her at day time; hence Maina was the only option. He was through with form four and was waiting for examination results to know his fate.

With the mother in the hospital, no one could provide for the family. Food became the biggest issue and that forced Maina to ask the neighbours for help every now and then, almost every day. After some weeks, their mother was brought home by a hospital van. Maina and Muthoni were glad to see their mother back. It renewed some hope in Maina's heart. A note indicating the hospital bill was left behind together with some medicines to be used for five months. They took with them her ID card and said the money was supposed to be paid not later than one month from that day. The bill was huge and required a harambee to raise the amount. Their mother seemed extremely weak and unhealthy, as if she had not taken any food for a week.

Maina ran to their closest neighbour, Mr Waithaka. He handed him the note indicating the bill and asked him for some food to help feed his mother for the day. Mr Waithaka put the note in his pocket and gave him some maize flour and a cabbage to help prepare a meal for his family. Maina prepared a meal for the family and fed his mother and sister. Later in the evening, Waithaka visited them with a can of milk he bought at the market centre. Maina prepared some tea for all of them. After some discussions with all of them, Waithaka left and decided to mobilize the villagers for a harambee. After some days, a harambee was done and the required amount was raised. Mr Waithaka and Maina went to the hospital and cleared the bill. They were given the ID card and left the hospital. Maina was grateful and sent a note to Waithaka expressing gratitude to the whole village on behalf of the family. With the bill sorted out, Maina knew that the biggest challenge that remained with the family was daily food.

He continued begging many villagers for food though most of the days they went without any. Life became difficult and fully unmanageable. His siblings dropped out of school and joined him at home. Now the whole family was locked in another form of poverty, hunger and poor health. When their mother saw the situation was out of control, her health deteriorated faster than before. She was unable to eat anything and hardly did she take water too. They all became confused. One day, Muthoni remembered the preaching on Job's trial and she gained some strength. She encouraged the family members based on those words and told them that God was really in control. She said one evening, "My mother, brothers and sisters, God has a plan, to build us and not to ruin us. Our family shall grow strong and stronger at God's appointed time. We are God's chosen people and He cannot disappoint us. It's only today that we do not have food and anything like basic needs, but tomorrow shall be brighter than today. Just remember God's servant Job. God let him be tested to prove his faith in Him and He blessed him in one day. He did not require many days or years to change his situation, but just a single day. I want to assure you that Jesus is watching, our situation is not yet to that of Job and we are serving a great Saviour. He can provide us with daily bread at all times. We need not fear because God is always by our side. Just pray always in your hearts, just keep on thanking Him and rejoicing even in calamities, for we know that He is a wonderful Saviour." She then offered a short prayer and they went to bed on empty stomachs.

Maina was really busy moving from house to house asking for food. He had no time for any other activity save keeping each family's soul alive. He used to say in his heart, 'After all, life is more important than clothing and shelter, education is a luxury when it comes to our situation'. His concern was only food. After four days had passed without food, he realized his mother's life was at a critical point. She was sick and had gone without food for so many days. She had also stopped taking medicines because it was clear that she was to take them after each meal. Bitter tears oozed out of eyes and he left the room hurriedly. He could not believe that his mother could die in his sight. He ran out of the compound and went along the path that headed to the river. As he was going down, he saw banana trees that were not yet matured in the neighbour's field. He rushed there and plucked few bananas. He ran back home and prepared some banana stew for the family. They ate and his mother was able to take the medicine as was instructed by the doctor.

One evening, as Muthoni was heading to sleep, she erred out of the wheel-chair in a bid to get into her bed. She went flying to the floor but was not lucky. Her mending leg struck the bed-bar and the whole body fell on it; breaking it till the pieces of metal that were placed in it made their way out through the skin. The bones were now in pieces. She let out a loud cry that left the whole house shaking. The pain was really unbearable. The siblings came and found her helpless on the floor. The mother was too weak to get there fast enough. When she later managed to get to the room, the sight of her leg left her breathless. She fainted and fell on the wheel-chair. Maina took her very fast and placed her on the bed. He also took Muthoni to the table room and placed her on a sack on the floor. He left his siblings in charge of them and went straight to Waithaka's. He called Waithaka who responded urgently to the call. They ran to the house and found everything was really in a mess. Waithaka called few other men and they called an ambulance. The ambulance took long to appear though the hospital was not far from the village. Finally, it came and the nurses took Muthoni into the van. They were shown the room where the mother was lying and when they took her by the hand, she was too cold. She was no longer breathing, the heart was no longer beating and every part was very stiff. She was gone and the spirit had departed long time ago; as soon as she fainted.

They called few men and informed them in secret that she was long gone but had to take her with them. There was no objection but to help them carry the body wrapped on a blanket to the van. Maina was not informed immediately but left in charge of his siblings. Mr Waithaka was left with them too, trying to give them the company they needed. Maina narrated to him how difficult it was to survive and how things happened that evening. The other members fell asleep. He stayed with them until morning. The morning came and many villagers arrived. They were carrying food stuffs and this made Maina stronger as he was assured that 'his people' would suffer no more. At around ten in the morning, Mr Waithaka took Maina for a short walk in the garden. He tried to inform him a lot and that is when he realized that his mother was dead. He shed tears but he remained strong. After some time, they went back home and burial preparation started. It was a big loss to Maina but he said to himself, "But I tried my best, at least my mother didn't die due to hunger. It seems the 'Gods of luck have departed' and left us alone. They have left us in utter darkness. Each day is more cursed than the previous. But we have to keep on moving till there is no more strength in us."

The burial was scheduled to take place after four days because the bill at the mortuary would be high if more days were spent there. Furthermore, the family had no members who needed to be waited for so long. When the day came, a simple ceremony was conducted which was officiated by the village elder who had some bible knowledge. The body was brought by the hospital van because no one could hire a vehicle. It took two hours and she was laid to rest. There were only a few villagers who attended and Muthoni could not see her mother being buried eternally; she was still in hospital in a critical condition and great pain. In the evening, Maina was left with the siblings as the others left but Waithaka stayed with them for one more night. He left the next day in the morning after they had taken breakfast together. He decided to mobilize the villagers once more for a harambee to raise money to clear the mortuary bill. They contributed but they were unable to raise twelve thousand. The seven thousand they raised was taken to the concerned and they assured them that they were determined to raise the remaining before one year was gone. After two weeks, the food that had been brought during the tragedy ran out. Maina had to go back to his struggles trying feed the family. By this time, he received a letter of admission to university. He had passed his KCSE well and secured himself a place in institutions of higher learning, just like Muthoni had done.

He went through the letter and saw that he was supposed to report in the next three months and the fee that was required. This letter didn't make any sense to him. He knew he could not make it and could not leave the family dying of hunger. He kept the letter in a safe place in the room, inside his secondary school's books. He made up his mind to inform few villagers about the letter but also ask them to employ him for the sake of feeding the family. He did so and most did not comment on that in any way. Mr Waithaka informed him to keep the letter safe with hopes that things would change one day and he would be able to report to school.

On employment, no one suggested anything because they were very poor villagers. He went slightly far from their village. He found a man who seemed to be wealthy from the look of the appearance. Maina discussed with him about his life briefly but could not offer a solution. He told him to pray to God harder for assistance and left in his car in a hurry. Maina felt like giving up but decided to approach other people. But it is true that bad luck was lurking behind him. He was unsuccessful in every way. He was asking for something to eat for he had spent the last five days without food, save water. He also remembered that his siblings were still at home waiting for him to bring something and his sister Muthoni was in hospital and he could not tell himself how she was recovering. All this news broke his heart.

As he was leaving that village for home, he came across the village garbage pit. He stood there for some minutes thinking whether to take something with him from the garbage or not. He made up his mind to take whatever was there as long as it could help his family live for another day. He chased the dogs and vultures that were feeding themselves from the waste, jumped into the pit and crouched there, perusing through the wastes. He took one paper-bag from there, searched for pieces of ugali, bread and anything else that is edible. He got half of the paper he had, wrapped it neatly and put it in another paper and left for home. Along the way, he was greedily eating a piece of rotten ugali which revived his spirit and body. After three hours of walk, he arrived at home. The children were happy to see him back and their hope was renewed. He found the youngest child asleep. The rest could hardly speak. He sat down and opened his 'living luggage'. He distributed pieces of decaying food to them which they attacked like hyenas. After they were all full, he wrapped the remains for the next few days. Their lives and spirits were rejuvenated and could speak. They informed him that their youngest sister slept the previous day in the morning and has not woken up. He was shocked to hear what they were saying but did not show them. He sat there still shocked in his mind, his heart throbbing with unbelief.

After gaining some courage, he prayed to God and said, "Our Father in heaven, keep her alive until she has slept enough. I have brought her food and she needs it too. I struggle hard for their sake and it is good if they enjoy the labour of my hands. Thank you in Jesus name". After the prayer, he went to wake her up. He called her a few times, "Wanjiru, Wanjiru, Wanjiru, wake up, I am back with a lot of food for you and us all. Wanjiru, Wanjiru, wake up!" When he realized that she was not responding, he went closer but a foul smell sent him few steps back. He did not understand where it was coming from. He gained a new strength and went closer but the smell was choking. He decided to put up with it and wake her up. When he touched her, the body was like a stick and cold as snow. When he shook the body to lift her up, so many worms dispersed from underneath and he realized that she wasn't with them anymore. He almost fainted. He dropped the body and rushed to Waithaka's.

He found him taking a cup of tea and was welcomed into the room. He took the first few minutes explaining to him how he went to search for a greener pasture for the sake of the children. Then he invited him to their house for closer examination of his sister. When he arrived there, the smell and worms from the room kept him at a distance. He enquired more from the rest and later called several villagers. He briefed them and they called for an ambulance. The body was wrapped on a blanket and taken to the mortuary, for she was dead. Mr Waithaka shed some tears that evening and expressed his great concern to Maina. This time round, Maina was weak and could not stand on his own. His eyes were red and blood-vessels were all over his body. He was wondering what was happening and thousands of questions were running on his mind without answers. The villagers organized for the burial bearing in mind that the previous bill had not been cleared and Muthoni was still in hospital. The villagers could not believe that the family was feeding on garbage due to such a poverty-level. But they had nothing to offer to save the situation. The child was buried after three days. Muthoni was not informed about it as she was still in a bad condition. Only few people appeared for the burial that was led by Mr Waithaka himself, though he had no much to preach.

After few days, Maina felt deserted and utterly lost. He realized he was fighting a losing battle and was all alone. But he gave himself some sort of strength and decided to gather all the effort he had and fight for the remaining members of the family. He went to Mr Waithaka and asked him to take him to hospital when he had time the following week. He then went on with his daily chores in searching for the family. He went to the garbage pit he had visited before in the neighbouring village. When he was heading there, he said a short prayer in his native language, saying, "God of our ancestors, help me. I just need food, anything else at this time is not necessary, only survival is important. My family members are very important to me, I need them. Help us, not forgetting Muthoni in hospital. She too is part of us. Remember all of us once and for all." He then continued with his journey to the place. This time round, he was not lucky. Misfortune was with him. He found the garbage pit emptied and there was nothing he could take. He felt discouraged and out of place. He thought of where he could head to at the moment but no idea came on his mind. He did not want any other child to perish due to lack of food.

After one hour of hard thinking, he thought of going back home to see the rest. He went in haste though hunger was slowing him down every now and then. After a four-hour journey, he arrived empty handed. The rest were asleep and he decided not to wake anyone up as he had nothing to offer. He took some minutes in the room, and then went out though it was night time. The moon was high in the sky but fully covered in black clouds making the whole land dark. He thought for some minutes of how he could get food for the family, seeing that if they woke up and found nothing, they would get discouraged. Tears flowed down his cheeks when he realized how hopeless and helpless he was. At that time, strong wind blew over the land and swept the black clouds far away from the moon. Now, the land was clearly visible. He could see far and the three graves in the compound were visible too. The crosses on the graves were shining brighter than before, not because they had been re-painted, but because he had taken no time before to look at any grave since he was ever busy in search for food.

He went closer to the graves and read the inscription on each cross. Then he said a prayer, softly, "I have lost so many of my people, who were precious to me and here I am without any hope. My father is not known to me, my mother left me without goodbye and my sister left me without tasting the food I brought home. Where do I belong? Is there anyone who is seeing what I am going through? If so, what are they waiting for, that I die or suffer more? My sister is in hospital and I do not know her welfare. I am supposed to be in school yet I am here in dark, struggling to live, my only concern being food."

Cold wind was now stronger than before but he seemed not to feel it. He continued with his prayer, "Where is God at this time of need? I think I need His comfort or His final word before I rest with my mother and sister. I do not need to see any other day. I won't wait to see my family die simply because of food. God, keep the family and take care of it, I am long gone too. Why should I be born just to live in inadequacy of food?" With those words, Maina left the graves and went straight to the kitchen. He untied the firewood and went with the rope. There was a tree near the graves whose branches hung over the graves. He climbed and tied one end to the branches. He made a loop on the other end and put it on his neck. Then he said his last words, "May our children live. May they not follow me", and jumped out of the branches. The knot tightened the loop on his neck before he almost landed on the mother's grave and he gave up his ghost in great pain. The life was lost, another one in that family. It was really terrible. The next day, people gathered around the graves. The administration was informed and permit was issued to bury the body. The villagers dug a shallow grave near the mother's on that day and buried Maina without a coffin; having not seen Muthoni anymore.

Mr Waithaka saw that things were really hard and asked the chief to take the children to the nearest orphanage. The chief agreed after lengthy discussion with the villagers. The three children were taken to orphanage but Muthoni remained in hospital. Later that year, the chief conducted a harambee to help clear the bills in mortuary. Many people showed up from several villages, not like that conducted by Mr Waithaka who was not known beyond the village. Enough money was raised but could not pay Muthoni's bill at the hospital. The homestead was left deserted. After two years, Muthoni's leg was recovering but the pieces of metal could only be reinforced with more if she was to walk out of hospital. Mr Waithaka decided to approach the chief and inform him about Muthoni's bill. It was so big that villagers could not even think of a harambee. The chief informed the PC and DC who decided to contact the minister in charge of health. The minister promised to clear the bill with the government funds as soon as she left the hospital.

Later on, after spending two and a half years in hospital, she was discharged in the presence of Mr Waithaka. He informed the doctor that Muthoni had no place to call home and that she needed assistance. They discussed the calamities that befell the family in details and the doctor finally decided to help her. Mr Waithaka thanked him and left. He took her to his sister's home far from the village. There she had a normal life but the lady, Mercy, informed her later that she needed to decide if she could go back to school or not. Muthoni asked for some time to think about the matter and promised to give her feedback after one month. Mercy did not argue but agreed and told her that she had all the time with her to decide, and that there was no hurry. Muthoni decided to consult God as her guide. She asked Mercy to buy her a bible to help her in understanding Him more. A bible was bought for her and she was very grateful. She could wake up at two in the morning to pray and praise God. She made sure that she gave her supplications to God each day. She asked Him to show her how she would serve Him for the rest of her life. She prayed harder and more earnestly each day for God to speak to her. She eagerly waited for His voice each day and night but in vain.

She decided to be reading God's promises each night before she prayed so that she could be heard and answered. The end month was fast approaching but she had not yet gotten Jesus' reply. She became confused and decided to keep praying. The last day of the month came and she had nothing to tell her mistress, Mercy. That night, she did not eat anything and never slept. She locked herself in the bed-room and decided to call upon Christ. She started with the verse in Jeremiah 33:3 and found hope to drive her through the night. She clung on that promise of God as she prayed. She prayed until she could kneel down no more, hot sweat flowing down from the eyes. The night was far much spent and morning was fast approaching. She hoped that God would answer her that night as she trusted in Him and relied on His promises and word. The morning came and she knew Mercy would want to know something that day. The day came and she had not heard anything from God whom she was serving. At seven that morning, Mercy left for work but reminded Muthoni not to forget to give her decision as she had promised. She left and Muthoni went to bed as she was extremely exhausted. Her eyes were red and face was full of wrinkles. She slept like dead person till four in the evening.

Mercy came back at six and as they were taking a cup of tea together, she asked her to inform her about her decision. Muthoni had nothing to offer. The Lord she had waited for so long did not respond to her in any way. She thought for some seconds and said, "My aunt Mercy, I have a story to share with you. There was a time God called me to be part of His flock. Since then, I have been longing to serve Him just as I vowed to Him. I decided to be a follower of Christ Jesus forever. I have been praying each day and night for their guidance but haven't heard anything yet. Maybe you help me see any way I can serve the Lord through." Mercy was somehow confused but didn't express it openly. She asked her, "How did this God reveal Himself to you? Was it through a dream or a vision?" She laughed and said, "Not that way aunt, not in any way as you have suggested. I just heard a preaching from the book of Hebrew one evening and I decided to soften my heart for His sake. I saw I had been selfish and had not served Him since I was born. I saw I had been fighting for earthly things instead of His kingdom and I decided not to harden my heart anymore. That is how I found the Lord and made Jesus my Saviour, Holy Spirit my guide. But I…" She paused for a while and looked down as if she wanted to cry. Her 'aunt' said in a low voice, "But what my child? Don't fear anything, say it. Some things we keep to ourselves 'eat us up'. They don't give us peace in the mind and heart plus the spirit. The spirit becomes troubled until we share them with others, that's when we are relieved. Tell me please."

She shed tears and said, sobbing, "Since that time, life has not been good. Since then, I have had some bad times, lived through some sad times and I live a dark life. It's like I found Demon rather than God. The way my life has been worsening is at an alarming rate. Troubles all over and not a day have I found joy. I pray heard but I am never answered. Tell me if there is something I still lack to help me converse with Him as I would." She sobbed louder and louder but her aunt gave her comfort saying, "Don't worry, God is great. He has many ways of doing His work and no one can fully understand Him. Just be patient and He would never forsake thee. But I would prefer that you keep on thinking and see what you feel like doing at best. Do not wait that at a specific time He would answer you, no, just see what you can do and that is it. Take supper and go have rest, then you can think carefully and inform us. We are ready to pay any course for you and in whatever university or college you wish. If you feel like you want to start a business, well and good, tell us to provide capital for you." She then went to bedroom and came back with a wallet. She showed her a photo of herself in school uniform and said to her, "That's me, I liked schooling too much. If you feel you like schooling, tell me and we would support you. You are talented in academics and I would prefer you major there. Education is the best provision for old age, as they put it. If I was not fully educated, my life would be very difficult and unmanageable. So, my dear, think about it and let me know."

They took supper and went to sleep. Muthoni thought about the aunt's words for a while but fell asleep later. In the morning, an idea came to her mind, she decided to take a walk to a pastor who used to neighbour them and share with him a few things to help see the way forward. She took breakfast and after her aunt was gone, she also left to meet the pastor. She was lucky to find him indoor and was given a warm welcome. The pastor was shocked to see her beauty in the first sight. Muthoni's face was like that of an angle. His wife was not around for she had left for work in the field. He made her a heavy breakfast, composed of two eggs, two slices of bread, blue-band, a cup of milk, a mango, a banana, a passion-fruit, a chapatti and a sausage. Muthoni was glad and thanked the pastor, Mr Okoth, for such a meal. She celebrated it and afterwards, she opened her heart for discussions. She briefly gave her life story and current situation. To her surprise, Okoth had no hard time in getting what to say in line with what she had explained. He said in soft and sweet tone, "My dear, there's nothing hard with the Lord we serve. Jesus is mighty to save, very powerful. He has done great things and is still doing them in our lives. He has been speaking to me so many times and I always deliver the message to the concerned. In offering a single prayer, an answer is provided."

Her face brightened and a big smile was on her face. It was like she had found a man of God who was also His representative on earth. He took some minutes preaching to her and quoting so many verses that Muthoni had not heard before. Later, he said he wanted to offer a prayer to Jesus to open her ways and turn her into a blessing. They knelt down and prayed for three minutes. Then he told her not to worry anymore for an answer had been provided. He informed her that there was a choir in his church and she could visit the church and see if there is any role she could play to help her serve God. This multiplied her joy and really admitted to him that she had found God for the second time. She declared to him that she would be glad to serve Christ forever in church and other ways possible. They parted ways later in the day and Muthoni promised to visit them in church the following Sunday. It was really a blessing to Muthoni meeting a pastor like Okoth.

On Sunday morning, she woke up early and prepared for church. She informed Mercy where she was going and was allowed. At church, she found multitude of congregation under Mr Okoth. She fellowshipped with them and was later introduced to the members by Okoth himself. The church was delighted to welcome her and promised to help in orientation process. She was happy and learnt few things that day about the church. The pastor later introduced his wife and son, Wanjala, to Muthoni; Wanjala was the choir leader. They went for lunch together in pastor's house. In the evening she went back home. It was really a great experience to her as she felt relieved in her mind and heart. She had found a family and a great company in life.

After many days in church and as an assistant-choir leader, Wanjala found himself attracted to her and proposed for future consideration in terms of marriage. Muthoni had also examined him and had not identified any flaw in him. She accepted him into her life and since they were of age, the church could not oppose it on any ground. After two years of engagement, a wedding was arranged but since she had no parents, the doctor and Mercy, were in charge of everything. The wedding was done and a family was found. It was joyful to be in a marriage at the beginning since both were church members and dedicated their life to God. They used to pray each day and night; after every meal, before getting out of bed, before sleeping and before undertaking any activity, be it at night or day-time. Truly, it was God-found family. Everything was being provided by the pastor and his wife. They lacked nothing at all.

Later on, before a year was gone, the pastor fell ill and could not attend any service. This meant that, the offerings he used to collect were collected by others. Division arose in church and the leaders who were in charge could no more speak or act in accord. It turned into chaos, each saying their own things and acting differently. There was a great rift in church. Majority of the members marched out of the well-founded church and joined other denominations. The church was left 'empty'. Poverty struck the pastor's family beyond what he could imagine. The illness was like a curse; it never recognized any kind of treatment and finally the man of God surrendered his life to it. Sorrow covered the family members like garments, not really understanding what was happening. Muthoni and Wanjala had no source of livelihood any more. They mourned the death of the man of God for two weeks and finally laid him to rest.

The two decided to ask God for guidance as they sought for menial jobs in the village. They ensured that they started each day by calling upon Jesus to show them the way. They were not lucky at all. It was extremely hard to get jobs even those that were poorly paid. Poverty struck them in all directions, leaving them without food, clothing or anything else useful in life. It so happened that all these problems struck when Muthoni was already expectant. Wanjala didn't know what to do with such a life. They dedicated themselves more and more to prayers for God's intervention. His mother was also suffering from hunger only living on the little she got from the small piece of garden. She could hardly help them. She could rarely give offering in church and she decided to remain at home rather than go and get embarrassment when time for offering and tithing 'passed her seated'. Life turned out to be very difficult for all of them.

Wanjala decided to go to town for any kind of job for the sake of feeding the family. He left Muthoni in the village pregnant. She suffered beyond measure. Food was a problem. Malnutrition changed her body to that of a child, yet, she was pregnant. She prayed to her Saviour more earnestly for just food. She remembered her brother Maina who struggled for food for quit a long time, when she was on a wheel-chair. She thought of asking the doctor to take her to their home to just see her brother. And she did as she thought. The next day, she asked Mrs Okoth to take her to the doctor's house for a word with any of their family members. Unfortunately, she was informed that the doctor's moved to town long time ago, and that they had sold their piece of land too. Darkness! This time round, her life was in a snare. She asked her if there was no way she could get to see her brothers and sisters. Mrs Okoth felt sorry for her but decided to tell her the truth and what happened when she was in hospital. It was at that time she heard that her brother, Maina, was long gone to the land of no return. She cried bitterly when she knew that he committed suicide after food became a real challenge, just as was to her now. Her mother perished after seeing her leg in pieces, her youngest sister succumbed to hunger and the rest were in an orphanage that was not known to Mrs Okoth.

After getting the whole story, she returned home feeling like she was a curse in this world. Dark clouds covered her mind and she felt completely lost. Life ceased to have meaning to her and she felt abandoned. After several days without food, she decided to beg from neighbouring homes. Sometimes she was lucky and could get something, while in other days, she went home empty handed. Things got tuff but she never gave up. One day, she sat down and thought her life back. She remembered how she was bright in school, how she won prizes in school, how people had hope in her, how she was hard-working, how her mother struggled to raise her up and all her room-mates in campus together with their advice. She wept. She fell down on her belly and called on God to see her through the challenges. She said in a short prayer, "Lord God almighty, remember me. Just help me; I do not want to die of hunger. Provide me with food, please Lord, my life changed so drastically and I no longer value myself. I do not understand myself anymore, please have mercy on me. I have gone through so many changes and challenges in my life till I have no strength anymore. Save me good Lord, in Jesus's name." She finished her prayer and cried for some minutes, her heart being extremely heavy. Her heart and mind were burdened beyond measure. That evening, there was a knock on the door. She thought it was God who had heard her cry and was answering her as He did to His servants, prophets and kings and priests narrated in the Bible.

When she opened the door, it was Mrs Okoth, though she was empty-handed. It was not her norm to visit her as she had never done that before. She gave her a welcome and said, "What is it my lord? Has God answered your prayers and you felt like sharing the blessings with me? Mrs Okoth broke into tears and said, "My child, the tide is against us, blessings left us long time ago. We are fighting without weapons and strength, in a losing battle. I feel better if I were dead!" She got shocked at her words and asked, "What is it mum? Why should you say so? Please share the problem." "My dear", she continued, sobbing, "We have lost him." "Who?" She asked, astonished. Mrs Okoth kept silent for one minute before she said, "My son Wanjala has left us. He was run over by a bus in town as he was crossing the road." She got a shock that forced her to miscarry. She became breathless and remained like a statue. Mrs Okoth got a double shock when she saw the miscarriage. She fainted. Muthoni let out a loud scream that helped gather villagers to her room. The villagers rushed the two to hospital where

Mrs Okoth was declared dead on arrival. Muthoni did not speak for a whole week. Doctors did a lot of testing and treatments until she gained her normality. Burial was done in her absence as she was still in hospital.

Two months later, she was discharged from the hospital but the bill was to be left unpaid. Her leg was still giving her hard time as it was still painful from within. She went home and found the place deserted, cobwebs all over, bushes and grass around the house and dust in every place. She felt lonely. It was life lost. She was leading the most difficult life; full of curses and misfortunes, bad luck always lurking around her. She went to her neighbour the next day and asked for food. She was not lucky as the lady had absolute nothing for food. After several days, she felt pangs of hunger threatening her life. She decided to walk to far places; looking for food and in search for the doctor. She carried a few clothes and one pair of torn shoes. Along the way, she could came across good Samaritans who could save her with some food. She was determined to walk but her leg always slowed her down, forcing her to spend most of the time resting under tree-shades. She slept anywhere without caring if her life was in danger or not. Life had lost meaning to that extent.

She came to a small town and found it conducive for her to settle. She went door to door asking for jobs but was not successful. She could walk each day seeking for jobs but used to spend nights under shops' roofs on verandas. She spent few weeks without job and food became a major issue. She decided to be visiting dust-bins outside shops in the evening like what mad-people and street-children were doing. The cold and some heavy rains that fell on her most of the nights had some negative effects on her leg and general health. After three weeks, eating from pits and bins along the streets, her leg could not allow her to walk anymore. It became swollen and very painful. She could hardly leave the cave where she had finally made her home; behind the shops near a river in a small bush. No one could take care of her nor take her to hospital. No friend around, no relative, no enemy, no place to call home, no hope, no direction, no past nor future and no anything. There she was only groaning in pain and writhing in anguish. The leg was now decaying due to lack of proper care but she could find no help.

One evening, two street-men were passing on their daily trot when they heard sobbing from the bush. They went to see what was happening and found Muthoni in the cave. They talked to her for some minutes and left her a piece of bread. When they left, they were only discussing her beauty. They informed several other street-men who were their friends. These friends left their "home" and headed there in the middle of the night. They found Muthoni helpless, which was their joy. They witnessed her beauty. Then they rapped her in turns having sealed her mouth with a dirty, dusty and torn coat. The exercise took several hours but the pain on her leg was unbearable. She tried to resist in vain. She had no enough strength to fight back. The men left her still with the coat covering her mouth and nose, smashed her arching leg and ran away. Blood was gushing from her private parts and she bled to death just before dawn. That morning, the two street-men came to the cave but were shocked to find such a beautiful lady stiff and cold; lying in a pool of thick, black blood. She was gone. They left and did not say anything to anyone for fear of being caught as murderers. After two days, the rotten body's odour sent a signal to residents that there was something wrong in the bush. They went and found the "unknown lady" dead. Police were informed; they arrived the same day and took the body to the mortuary.

Since no one knew who she was, the body remained in morgue for two years. Then the government took all the unclaimed bodies and buried them in one grave, in a forest. Muthoni was among them. She was gone without any relative's knowledge and without any offspring. The bright girl, the hope for many, the beautiful and most loved girl in the village, the light and star for the world, was now in the forest, never to rise again, nor to be remembered.

THE MADNESS

---◆·◆·◆---

MWEGA WAS THE KIND OF BOYS MANY PARENTS ADMIRED. THE boy was brought up as usual. He was always playing together with his friends, both in school and at home. His parents took him to church at a very early age. He was taught many things in church. At Sunday school he interacted with many children and came to learn dozens of verses. He was excellent in memorizing verses and was retentive too. He enjoyed songs they were taught and could sing some of them in school and at home. His parents were very fond of him as they always wanted to hear him sing unto them. They could ask him to sing some of the songs as he was waiting for his mother to prepare supper. In school, the teachers also liked him. They always wanted to listen to some of these sweet and 'heart-touching' songs. Some even asked him to sing before they could begin their lessons. Not songs alone, no, he also knew numerous verses; the fruits of being a church member. He grew up knowing more and more of these songs and Bible verses until he was no longer part of Sunday-School team. He was now of age to join the grown-ups called youths. The youths were taught more complex things in church. Songs were longer than those of kids. Verses were longer too and full of messages. He was able to cope well with them.

Back in school, he was able to balance both academics and co-curricular activities. He did well in primary school and was able to join secondary school. The school was not far from his home; it was just a stone throw away. He seemed to be like a half-genius student. He had no difficulty in his studies. He also continued attending church services on Sundays. His parents were happy with his ways and hardly did they complain about his behaviour and temperament in general. He continued to learn a lot in church and in school too. They said he was the kind of person who was able to make the right decisions and was always under minimum supervision.

In secondary school, there were many teachers who loved him because he never slept or even dozed during their lessons. The history teacher was his role model in school. The teacher, Mr Munene, was always punctual for his lessons, ever in suits, ever smiling, never got angry with any student, and was always audible in class. He was ever encouraging his students to study hard for the sake of a brighter future. "My sons and daughters, study hard. Life is very short. Life is not about waiting for things to just happen, it's all about making choices, having goals and working hard towards achieving them. Never rely on what you do not know. Hard work pays as the white man says. Therefore, work hard and never let an opportunity go unutilized. The white man says that opportunity knocks on each man's door once." Those were his words each day he got into class, before he even introduced the topic of the day. Mwega had a good memory and could recite the exact words to his fellow students during break-times. Even when they were taking lunch, he could remind them of Mr Munene's words. He wrote the words at the back of his history book and in his diary. In fact, he used to call it Mr Munene's poem. Some students used to make fun of the 'poem' just to signal Mwega to recite the words. His efforts made many students to know the poem. Mr Munene came to know that most of the students could recite the words he used to tell them and was informed it was through Mwega's efforts that most came to recite them.

He wanted to know as to why Mwega made many students know his words off-head. One day, he called Mwega privately and asked him, "How comes that you know my words and have taught others to master them." Mwega smiled and answered, "I like everything you do. You are my role-model and always want to hear your words. The way you dress is very impressing and you are audible in class." Munene was pleased with Mwega and sent him away smiling. One afternoon, Munene came to class as usual. He introduced his poem and all the students recited it accurately. Then they laughed at the end of the exercise. He was really impressed and promised to buy Mwega a prize. He said to the class, "I love it. Mwega, well done, well done, keep it up! You have made my students make a step in life. Those words of my poem shall ring in their minds forever. You are very influential and shall be a great man. You shall go beyond your expectations.

Just keep the fire burning and keep the spirit active and alive." All the students turned to Mwega and gave him a big smile that left him joyful the whole day. "Who can guess today's topic? It is a new topic and you can guess whatever topic you know that we haven't yet tackled." Munene asked his class. The students tried a lot of guess work for two minutes but none got it right. He asked them to have their books and pens ready for the lesson's notes.

He then turned to his notes and introduced the new topic. "Before we go into details, I want to give you a highlight. Today's topic is 'THE EVOLUTION'." He wrote it on the board before he went on with his brief description. "Write that topic and listen to me carefully." The students wrote the topic faster than he expected. It seemed that all of them were eager and ready to know what the topic meant, not like before where he had only few students who were keen and curious to learn. He continued with his explanations, "This topic refers to gradual change. In involves slow improvement and mostly to better quality. It was an idea that was first explained by Dr Charles Darwin from another nation. This man gave his thought to others and we have been teaching about it since long time ago. He explains that man has evolved from other creatures. He has passed through the monkey stage. He is changing with time. Man was not the way he is from the beginning. The life began from simple form, started changing and becoming complex and more complex in each set of millenniums and has gone through stages such as those of monkeys. Today he is at the stage you are. Therefore, the topic talks about these stages, especially those that resemble monkey's family. It is a very interesting topic to those who have interest and want to learn more. To those who thirst for knowledge, be keen and learn as much as you can."

There was total silence in that classroom and one could think the room was a grave. Students looked at each other and at their teacher. Most could not believe it while others were just smiling to each other. The teacher waited for some minutes for any reaction or contribution from the students and was not shocked to hear the students opposing it. One of the students, class-monitor, stood up and challenged Munene. "What the hell are you telling us? Are you greater than God Himself? Are you saved with the blood of Jesus Christ of Nazareth, who is the Son of God Himself? Jesus was the son of David but came from heaven. Do you think you can challenge them in any way? We were eagerly waiting for today's topic but you have spoilt the broth. I think we should not continue with this topic because it has no meaning. In the beginning, God Himself decided to create man in His own image and He was with Christ Jesus and the Holy Ghost. The Bible is very clear on this and if you want to have more understanding, then we can get a Bible and read together. Go to the book of Genesis and John. You shall have more understanding and I think from that point, you won't teach us this topic. I had a great respect for you but you have proved me wrong. We won't allow you to teach us this topic. Evolution my foot!" The students were left with their mouths wide open. They could not believe the words that were flowing from the student's mouth.

Before the teacher could react, another student stood up without permission and added his voice. "You have tortured my spirit and attacked my faith. I think I can no longer be your student. My spirit is now incorrigibly damaged. What shall you do to help me recover, now that you have hurt me beyond being bereaved? Will God forgive you? Please my dear teacher, just kneel down on the floor and repent. Don't take time because it might be too late to receive forgiveness. God has been merciful to you; he has kept you alive and you should not mock Him. He is greater than anything and is above all. Please, I just want to forgive you because He has set an example to us on forgiveness. I want to see you on the floor and on your knees or belly asking for God's mercy. He is plenty of mercy and is willing to forgive. We will offer a prayer as a group and try to seek His face for the sake of His grace. I wish I were dead not to hear what you have said this afternoon. It is a sin to mock the Lord. When Jesus decided to come and save mankind, He had seen how far we were from God's grace. He felt pity for all of us and saw it wise to help the poor human race. It is good to evaluate ourselves each day and assess our sincerity in the face of the Lord. By doing this continuously, we are able to see ourselves clearly and this would lead us to ask Him for mercy. His mercy flows like water but should not be taken in vain. It seems that you have been residing in darkness yet there is light that is shining; please come to light- Jesus is this light I am talking about. Therefore, I am appealing to you as my role-model to repent now, not tomorrow."

There were another couple of minutes of great silence. The teacher smiled but before he could open his mouth for a word, another student raised her voice. "You think you are wise? As a teacher talking non-sense is more than sin. You have demeaned our God and Saviour and it's better if you were in grave. All that you have said is pure bullshit, trash and your mind is empty. Just repent and you shall live." Another student interjected in anger, "The white man said that, an idle mind is the devil's workshop. I think you have nothing to do and that is why you are giving the devil the chance to misuse you. Christ Jesus came to deliver all of us from the devil's chains for us to serve God our Father and Creator. Please, take time to study the Bible and the devil in you shall just flee out of your life. In fact, do you have a family? Are you married? It could be that you are not yet married and that is why you are having a lot of idle time. Or is that what you discuss with your wife in the evening when you leave school? If you had a family of your own, you would not be having time to listen to the devil and you would be busy raising your children. Please, stop this nonsense and have faith in God." The class-monitor interjected, "Do you go to church sir? Do you have a Bible in your house? Who is your pastor sir? Which church do you attend to? Just answer the few questions and maybe that will help us understand the emptiness in your mind."

"If you open the Bible in the book of Romans, you will find God saying that man professed himself to be wise but he became a fool in the process. I think your foolishness is beyond measure! Do you have a relationship with the devil? Or is your wife a devil or the devil's agent? My friend Mr Munene, God still loves you but you should know that bad company ruins or corrupts good morals. I tend to think that you were a good child when your mother brought you up but you have heaped fools around yourself and that is why your morals are spilling out like garbage. Where do you come from? Show me your friends and I will tell you who you are." The tallest student concluded. Before the class could stop laughing, another student raised his voice to be heard by all. "Your Honour Mr Munene, I want to believe that you have an idea on what the Bible says. Jesus gave us a clear way of understanding our fellow men. He said in Mathew 12:34, that '…For out of the abundance of the heart the mouth speaks'. We have come a long way and these words have helped us to avoid the devil's snare. The rubbish you have just spilt out of your mouth speaks a lot about you. You have just released waste and I now believe that your heart is just full of gibberish to the brim. Let me tell you this for free, my friend, just call several pastors to pray for you to help in your cleansing."

The student next to the class-monitor gave his contribution too. "Do you take drugs? Does it mean that you have been on drugs since you were young? My teacher, I would like to advise you like a close friend. When you take drugs that a doctor has not prescribed to you, we say you are abusing drugs and that can cause a serious problem. Please avoid drugs! If your friends are influencing you to take hard drugs, just avoid such friends. Where do you get these drugs from? Because I don't think the government has legalised the use of cocaine, mandrax and heroin. Bang is also prohibited and you should not involve yourself with such dirty things. Make your ways straight and God shall be pleased with you and shall pour His blessings on you and your family; that is when you get married because a married man cannot tell us such trash as you have done today." The students broke into laughter before another one added her voice. "Munene, have you ever suffered from mental disorder? Have your parents ever taken you for mental-challenge check-up? Is there anyone in your family whom you know suffers from madness? I think that it's not your fault but I blame the insanity that maybe you inherited from your lineage. Whom are you named after? Maybe that person was mad and could be possible that you now represent him and his madness. Therefore, Mr Munene, mad men and women are chained in hospitals because they can cause more damage than what we can imagine, if they are left on their own. Go and get married and I think that will help control your insanity!" Another loud laughter filled the class-room.

Mwega who had been silent for all that time raised his hand to offer his thoughts. The teacher pointed him as a sign of allowing him to go ahead. But before he positioned himself to speak, another student shouted at the top of his voice. "Where do you come from, Mr Munene the teacher? I think the place you have come from should be blamed for all this. Sometimes people come from places with so many witches and they end up as victims of their witchcraft. I think that is what has happened to you. Just go and inquire from your neighbours so that they can help investigate those behind your downfall." There was another voice from the corner of the class. "My talented and most learned teacher Munene, never crack dirty jokes when we are on serious matters. Go and learn how to differentiate between issues and non-issues. Never major on non-issues while minoring on issues. Vice-versa is always acceptable. But why did you decide to make such a joke? If you want to make dirty jokes, just get married and share such jokes with your family and not us. We have a lot to do and have no time for such garbage. But because you have mocked the Lord our God, know that you have inherited a curse and we cannot be your students anymore. You started the term so well but your much knowledge has corrupted your mind to the point of becoming mad. Go to hell!" The bell rung before the student finished attacking his teacher. By this time, Mwega had not gotten a chance to utter a single word. The teacher left the room but before he could disappear out of the door, one of the students threw his book with all his might at the teacher. But he was lucky. The book hit the door-frame and dropped to the floor with a thud. The teacher bent his body slightly to avoid being hit and rushed out. He hurried off to the office wondering whether he had 'thrown a stone in a beehive in broad daylight'. He was shocked to see how his students reacted like hooligans.

The news reached the principal's office the same day. There was a serious discussion in the office. Mr Munene informed the other staff that he would never take the students through the subject for the rest of his life. He asked the principal to assign him other subjects but not the History. Another teacher was allocated the subject in the meantime, Mrs Wanja. She accepted the task but asked the principal to intervene by first addressing the students because she would not be ready to face embarrassment. The next morning, the principal and his deputy went to class to meet the students. He criticised and reprimanded them for behaving like goons rather than like learned and disciplined students, meant to serve as exemplary to many people. The deputy too scolded them and gave them a stern warning. At that point, the students came to realize that actually, Munene was serious and what he was explaining to them the previous afternoon was in syllabus. They kept quiet and listened carefully. They were hoping that the principal would not take further actions against them. There was no worse punishment than sending a student home for some weeks due to indiscipline cases. That is what they feared most. The same evening of the incidence, Mwega started to think hard about what Munene had introduced to them. He knew in his heart that Munene was not joking when he said that man actually evolved from simple life forms. He longed to be close to Munene for more discussions about the same topic. His mind opened up to receive more light on that idea.

During the next lesson, Mrs Wanja appeared and introduced herself to the class politely. They received her warmly and promised to cooperate. She introduced the topic as Munene had done and gave them hand-outs to help understand the notes better. The students got more light on that idea from Charles Darwin. There was silence during the whole lesson and the students asked few questions for clarification. She explained to them how many facts have proved that man is actually evolving and Africa is the cradle for man. They were amazed to hear the facts and asked her to give them more explanations and facts. They also proposed to visit museums to witness the skulls in exhibition. Before she left the class, Mwega challenged her with a question. "Teacher, which is the truth now, is it the Bible or Charles Darwin? I am asking this because the Bible teaches us that God created man in His own image and placed him on earth to multiply, and that we have a common origin. Now Charles Darwin's theory and idea is talking about evolving from simple life forms through the ape-family's stage, and I see we almost resemble the apes. Who is telling the truth, God or Charles Darwin?"

The class was as quiet as a grave. All of the students looked at the teacher like a statue, waiting for her response. "Mwega, the question and concern are genuine. In fact, most people get confused in the process but I always recommend that you as a student should have an open mind. You accept what the two teach you and evaluate each carefully throughout your life. We cannot tell you that God is lying and we cannot say that Darwin is right. Just let the ideas from both sources sink into your mind and try to gather facts here and there as you enjoy life. Then finally, make a decision and stand with it. If you find you have a question in the process of considering the two, just ask the right people and you shall finally come to a conclusion. I would discourage you to refute any of them without good basis. Just strive to garner substantial evidence and whatever makes more sense than the other, stand with that and hold fast to it. A person is not wise if they banish ideas anyhow. Be wise and know how to make a way out of thickets. They say that what you know today could be a lie and what you accept tomorrow could be the truth. What if you are a fool and fail to accept what comes tomorrow yet it's the truth? That would mean you are holding and would continue to hold on a fallacy. Strive to resist misleading yourself at whatever cost. You knowing the truth are likened to a soldier who has the full armour in war. Do you want to be a soldier in battle ground without any fighting tool, even a sword? Whenever you discard the truth and continue holding on to a lie, I would compare you to a person who has swallowed burning coal and is claiming to be unhurt. It is like killing yourself and you are telling us that you are not dead. Is this possible? Therefore, avoid that way and exercise your witty in all matters."

"We usually have the inborn wisdom and the wisdom that comes from knowledge. Have the inborn wisdom and you shall see things that many cannot see. You will always remain few steps ahead of majority. One thing you should always have in your mind when making decision is that, never follow majority. Most of the times, majority are always wrong. Never follow their path simply because the old and young are travelling therein. For example, if your parents are holding on the sharpest edge of a knife, then that does not mean that you should always hold a knife by the sharpest edge. It also doesn't mean that they are not being hurt. It could mean that they are not wise enough to know that they can try to hold on another part of the same knife. Again, it could mean that your parents are blind and cannot see the handle of the knife. It could also mean that they found their ancestors holding knives by the sharp edges. Now, would you be wise if you also hold knives by the sharp edge? Is it logic to teach your children that knives are held by the sharpest edges, whether they cut fingers or not?"

"Consider our ancestors who used to live in caves. If we did not accept new ideas, then we would not be having houses, but would still be suffering in caves; under rain, cold, hot sun-rays, in danger of wild animals and so on. Would you tell me that a cave is better than a house? Of course not! What I am saying is this; don't be rigid in your mind. Be flexible and accommodative. Let new ideas come and be compared with what you have. If they gain weight over those that you know, then discard the old ones and accept the new ones, waiting for yet another one. Vice versa is also true. Listen to all, both young and old, then make your own decisions. Whenever you are in a dilemma, know that there is a way out of the dilemma. What I would add to your knowledge is that, one of the two is correct or both are wrong; either the Bible is wrong or the theory or both are wrong. Both cannot be right and contradict each other. Are we together my friends? So, strive to get the truth and you shall live happily. The truth is like the sharpest triple-edged sword. Such a sword can cause the most damage in war. Getting it would mean that you would be living happily without wasting your efforts on unnecessary issues and activities. Your mind is always at peace. The tranquillity that comes from it is great. Therefore, find out the truth between the two. If you find both wrong, throw them aside and go searching for new truth." The students sighed out of amazement. They could not believe what they were hearing from the teacher. The came to know that they actually knew nothing; they admitted that the lesson was the most fruitful since they joined secondary school. The lesson ended with the final words, "If you have more questions, see me in office or when we meet in class next week. Have a great evening." She walked out and the students gathered into small groups and continued with more discussions. They had gotten some light shining in darkness that they would never forget.

Mwega had the words of Wanja sinking in his mind deeper than any other words he had ever heard. Since he was born, he came to realize that there was a lot he had to learn in this world. He went home that evening thinking deeply and seriously, than before. He had a conversation in his heart and mind, "Is it true? Is the Bible wrong or right? Is Charles Darwin wrong or right? Who's wrong between the two? Have I believed a lie or the absolute truth? Was the theory revealed to Darwin by God? Or was it his thought as an academician? There are so many questions in my mind than the answers I have. I think the teacher was and is and shall always be right, that we could be holding on to a lie unknowingly. But the Bible shall never tell a lie. The Bible is the absolute truth and hence cannot be wrong. Since our teacher said that the two sources cannot be right at the same time, and that it's one of them that is right or both are wrong, then definitely the Bible is right and the theory is out of place. But then, the new question is, why should he strive to write to the world about it and was not ashamed about it? Why should his efforts be wasted if the document is not true? I think, if he is right, then God is not right, sorry, I am saying it wrongly, God forgive me for lying to myself that you are wrong."

The thoughts were interrupted by a call from his mother who was in kitchen. He rushed there and was asked to get her some water from the tank. He did it faster than was his custom. His mother congratulated him for his quick response. He later returned to his room and the thoughts went on, "But it's true that we resemble the apes or monkeys. Even some of our colleagues look clearly like apes; we can even confuse them with monkeys whenever they hide their necks downwards. Where did the man get the information from? Was he a genius of the century? No, no, no, this man was wrong and God is right. God shall never lie to us and shall never allow a man to mislead other men; whether rains come or winds, never! But, where did the Bible come from? Is it from man or from God Himself, or even from God through man? I think it's only God Himself who can answer the question. No one else can. But I think God is very clear in His word. It says clearly that God created man and other things that we see in the Genesis. In fact, it still adds that He created what we see and what we don't see. Therefore, the Bible is correct. But could Darwin challenge God on His face yet he is mortal? I am missing something here."

"But everyone believes so except very few men in the world who believe other things. Why should I waste my time thinking about the truth yet all of my people are fully equipped with the words in Bible? I think the way is very straight forward to even the blind. Ooh, no, no, no, the teacher was very open when she said that we shall never follow majority because they could be wrong. But if I discover that Darwin was right, I shall judge God and punish Him in broad daylight. I shall not forgive Him at all. Wait and see! Now, who was Charles Darwin? Was he a man like me? No, I think he was different and had some information that I lack and I need it today. If he was alive, I would approach him for more information. Maybe I could understand him better and faster. In conclusion, I would tell myself that God is right and the Bible is the ultimate truth. Darwin is mortal and a liar. May he die again and again because he almost misled me! He wanted me to lose track and be far from God. God is right and shall remain so forever. God forgive me for trying to judge you wrongly, I had lost my senses. Let us work together and have more believers in your word, the Bible." At that point, he was called to take his supper in the table-room. He went and took it in a hurry, then went to his room and started doing his homework. He did it within a very short time as the exercise was not difficult. He then fell asleep; he slept like a log as his mind was fully exhausted from processing countless questions in microseconds.

He continued with his studies in school and was very brilliant. But still, he did not forget what the teacher taught them; man evolved. The following week, the teacher came and taught the last part of evolution. There were no questions this time. But before she stepped out of the door, Mwega raised his hand and called her, "Madam, I need some few facts to help me connect some statements in my head. Now, you have taught us about the man, Darwin Charles. But the question is, where did the Bible come from? It is called the word of God and I am not able to question or challenge Him. But I need to know where the Bible came from, please help." The teacher smiled and asked him, "First of all, did you think about the theory?" "Yes madam, I thought about it the whole of last week and even this week up to today. I was even trying to ask myself if it's the Bible that is wrong or Darwin. Later, I decided to learn first about its origin. The theory's origin is already known since it was from Darwin himself." She smiled again and said to him, "Talk to me later privately. I need to discuss with you and not with the whole class as most would not be interested as you are." With those words, Wanja left for another class and the students were left applauding Mwega for such critical questions; in fact, they gave him a standing ovation.

The next day, Mwega approached Wanja for few words with her. She was very pleased with him for being so curious and inquisitive. "My son, I know you are spending sleepless nights trying to figure out the truth. I know you have countless queries in mind and most things don't add up in your inner being. I know you a like a man who is trying to find a specific drop of water in an ocean. But don't worry about all this. As long as you are willing, you shall know the truth. Remember what men usually say, that where there is a will, there is a way. So, a way shall appear and you shall travel therein. Keep the will alive and you shall find the treasure." "So, where did the Bible come from? I need to understand more because little knowledge is dangerous." "Ok, all I know is that you should continue searching for the truth and origin of these things. If I tell you my opinion, I may misguide you, which is even worse. I want you to reason till you exhaust your mind. You have a lot of knowledge and the answer lies within your vicinity. Just relax and think, remember and reason; that's all I can tell you." "Ok, madam. I am going to do so but if things turn into darkness, I shall come back to get your opinion, be it guiding or misguiding." She smiled and promised to give him her suggestions and opinions if the year ended without even some little light. He left to join his friends who were taking tea. She also left the office for a nature walk, which was her custom as long as she did not have much to do in the office.

Several weeks later, the school closed and Mwega went to spend his time with his grandmother. His mother did not see a big deal with this move though it wasn't his norm. He continued with the many questions in his mind and trying to find a hint to answer them. "Is Darwin a man or was he sent from heaven? Does God know that Darwin left us with a theory that can cause chaos if not well understood? Does He approve his work? If God is right and Darwin is right too, what does that mean? Whom should we believe then? Oooh, no, no, no, the teacher said it that the two cannot be right and be at variance at the same time. Or maybe the teacher is wrong and that the two can be right and are not actually contradicting. No, but they contradict each other when one says we were created while the other one preaches that we evolved. So the teacher is very right and deserves honour for being so wise. I have an idea, I should revisit the Bible, go through it and see if there is a hint that it came from God Himself. I shall afterwards think more about the Darwin's theory and I am sure I shall be able to make a comprehensive conclusion. Yes, that's what I am going to do. But men have approved Darwin's work and allowed it to be taught in schools; what does that mean, that men also understood his works?"

He rushed to the table-room and took several versions of Bible. He started from the introduction and went on reading till he was tired. He then retired to bed. In the middle of the night, he woke up and continued reading and trying to figure out all the clues that could help him come up with a conclusion. Almost dawn, he fell asleep and left the Bibles on the table. He went on with the process of sleeping, waking up, and reading, sleeping, waking up, and reading, whether daytime or at night. He went through all the versions he had. He was lucky as there was almost no work in her grandmother's home. Therefore, he had ample time to do his research without disturbances. He was able to highlight most of the key points and messages in the whole book with ease and in six weeks.

In the process, he was asking himself more and new questions. Later, he thought about going through the class-work to see what the teacher had taught them about evolvement of man. But before he could do it, stream of questions gushed in his mind. "Who wrote the Bible? I have seen some verses saying 'I Paul the servant of …' and other books being addressed to specific individuals. Could that be God doing so? In fact, most books are narrating life history of individuals of which I doubt if it's God doing it. Paul has talked too much and even saying he is speaking on his own while in some areas he is saying to be speaking from the Spirit. Which is which? This could mean that it is either men who were writing this thing on their own or God wrote it through men. Ooh, yes, the CRE I was taught was saying the Bible is the word of God written by men who were inspired by God's Spirit. Ooh, I remember!"

"So, the Bible I see was written by men and not God. So, did He actually inspire them? That is another query that needs to be answered before we go far. I think he did not inspire them. Yes, in the introductory part, I saw the writer saying they translated the original texts from one language to my native language. So, they have done the translation through several languages. Now, is it God who has been inspiring them to do so? Does it mean that God does not understand other languages or to be specific, He does not understand my language, hence needs men to help Him in translating it to my language? When they change even His name to that name they say is Lord and LORD, what does it mean? Does it mean that God Himself inspired them to hind His identity from us? Why should He do it? He does not want to be known yet He loves me and the rest? I think it's the Bible that is contradicting itself at the same time. I think the writer is confused! Aaah, no, no, no, God forgive me because you are not confused. Sorry for that mistake. But did you actually inspire anyone? If so, why is it that men are speaking on their authority and again with God's approval or inspiration? Look at what Paul is saying in 1st Corinthians chapter 7 verses 6, "But I speak this by permission and not of commandment." Again in the same book and chapter but verses 26, "I suppose therefore that this is good for the present distress, I say, that it is good for a man so to be." And verses 28, "But if thou marry, thou hast not sinned; and if a virgin marry, she hath not sinned. Nevertheless, such shall have trouble in the flesh; but I spare you." Who is speaking here in all these verses? Is it Paul or God? Paul is saying "I spare you", who is he then? Paul is saying "I suppose", what are these? Is he giving us his opinions and thoughts or God's word and command? And you tell me that God inspired men to write it? No, not God but man is doing his own works of fabrication. The Bible is confused! The writer is out of their senses. Everything is misplaced."

"Now, how can this God love me so much and call me His son, and even promise me to live with Him forever and does not want me to know His original name, save LORD and Lord, Father and other titles? Does it mean He is trying to conceal something to me? If He knows me by my names, why not me know Him by His name too?"

"All I know is that translation from one language to another mostly leads to loss of the original meaning and message. If you do translation from one language to another, then from the new one to another and so on, finally you get something totally different. Try to interpret some information to another person and see how you deliver erroneous message most of the time. One thing I am now sure of is that the Bible was never written by God Himself. That is now clear to me. Now, they say that the Bible was inspired by God through His Spirit and that one must have the Spirit to help him or her understand the scriptures. The question is, if I must have the Spirit to understand it, then, why do we need pastors yet we have our own Bibles and the pastor cannot interpret the same to me? So, as long as I have a Bible, then I do not need a preacher, yet the same Bible tells us that God has such men to preach. What is not happening? Ok, let me not question His words. Now, if He gave His word to some men who were inspired by His Spirit and wrote the words in one language, was He having one language in the whole world? If not so, then why did He address one people and is telling me how He loves me? If He loves me as the Bible claims, then He should have inspired some from my tribe to write to my people at the same time He was doing it to the rest. It's like telling me that you love us when we are hungry, then you cook some food for some people and after they are full in their stomachs, then you tell the men in full stomachs to make some more for us. Does it make sense really? What if I die from hunger as I wait for them to cook for us? I think the person who said that He inspired the writing of the Bible was wrong and their intension was malicious. Yes, tis true because the Bible says we are all His people, He created us and loves us so much. But we see Him treating others better than the rest. Then He is not righteous. Sorry, God is righteous and right. Sorry for that. My heart and mind are misleading me, but God forgive me now."

"But how can He kill such a large number of Amalekites, Amorites, Moabites, Philistines and Ammonites, among others, in the name of protecting and defending one group, the Israelites? And He loves all in equal measures as the Bible claims! Are you sure that He created them too, yet He allowed them to be killed like animals? Look at what He is calling His servant and a man with His heart, David. In Chronicles 19:18, he killed seven thousand charioteers and forty thousand foot soldiers and their commander. If His man is such a ruthless killer, why not say He too is a chief murderer? I think He is a terrible murderer and has taught His servants like David to emulate His ways. They are like demons and no one would like to be associated with such devils. Go to 2nd Samuel chapter 8 and verses 1 onwards. See for yourself how mad he is and how thirsty for blood he can be. See David attacking Philistines, defeating Moabites and forcing them to do his will and taking their property to become his. Is he a thief and a well-trained thug? He is delighting in evil! I think even his wealth was based on shedding blood and looting and not a blessing. Look at verses 10 and 11; he is receiving some gifts which I can term them as bribe, and he is dedicating them to the Lord. You mean he was attacking communities, fought them, defeated and subdued them, forced them to be slaves, and received bribes from those spared and later dedicated the loot to the Lord. So, all are one thing and collaborate in this? And one would like me to join them and claim such a god to be my God, to be asking Him for help yet He is busy taking what is not His. I refuse to join a gang of hooligans and goons! In 1st Samuel chapter 15 verses 1 onwards, He is instructing Saul through Samuel to go and attack Amalekites, utterly destroy all that they had, killing everything and all; in fact, He wants even the infants to be cleared together with animals. What a demon! This God is worse than vampires and Satan Himself."

"In Judges Chapter 3, we find this God busy instigating Ammon and Amalekite against Israel, His own people according to His own claims. He is busy forcing them to be slaves to Eglon king of Moab for eighteen years. This is another confusion and irony. He was defending them before but now He is busy confounding them. He is confused like the Bible itself. He doesn't know what He wants in life. I can liken Him to our politicians who make peace with those who are serving their interests and later turn against them whenever they fail to help them achieve their agendas. In fact, there is no difference between Him and politicians who practice dirty politics in my country; they instigate one tribe against the other for political gain, and to the tribes that support them, they enjoy peace and protection. If one of these friendly tribes goes against them again, they lose the prosperity they had and suffer wars from all over the tribes that are around them. This is a way of ensuring that you remain a slave forever. That is what God is doing and I feel pity to Israelites who fail to discern all this craftiness. Even Jesus Himself declared in Mathew 10:34 that He did not come to bring peace on earth but a sword. I think He came to extend the same wickedness and iniquity to us as David was doing in the name of his Lord. But all this is as a result of man writing his own works and claiming to be from God. I think it is the Bible (man's word) that is false and that God is not represented therein. God is true and has nothing to do with what we are claiming to be from Him."

"In fact, there are some verses that are showing Him boasting of killing them and even reminding Israelites of how He eliminated them to clear their way to Canaan. In Joshua Chapter 24, He is narrating to Israelites through Joshua all the wickedness He had done to Egyptians through plagues, clearing Amorites out of their land, driving groups out of their places, giving Israelites land they did not deserve through robbing and coning others, and other evils that cannot be mentioned. He is actually rejoicing in His own iniquity. Does that imply that He delights in evil-doing? Or that is what He means when He says He loves us? There is a lot of contradiction and confusion in the Bible itself. I think the Bible cannot be inspired by God, His Spirit or anything like that. This is just like any other text book that is subject to correction and criticism, hence not from God. This is not God's word. How can it be His Book or His word? Impossible! There are so many deaths mentioned in the Bible that are said to be orchestrated by God Himself. For example, David was driven by His Spirit to kill Goliath. David was also helped by the same God to kill many more people and even wiping groups of people from the face of the earth, yet, one of His commandments is that thou shall not kill. Is that not confusion and contradiction? Is that the Lord who is love? Why kill in the first place? Even me, I don't kill my enemies or those who wrong me in any way. So were these men His enemies? If so, then I am better than Him because I don't kill any of my enemies. I think that God is good but the Bible is not His word. He has nothing to do with it. If He insists that it is His book, then He is mistaken and needs guidance and counselling. That can help Him a lot. It can teach Him how to treat those who wrong Him and how to love all men equally and not with partiality."

"Look at how He is discriminative! He is never interested in all people since time immemorial yet the Bible is busy lying to us that He loves all equally and is infallible. If He loves equally, then why does He hate some groups and seclude them in His affairs? Like in Deuteronomy 23 verses 3, "An Ammonite or Moabite shall not enter the assembly of the Lord; even to the tenth generation none of his descendants shall enter the assembly of the Lord." In all this, does He show us His eternal mercies and love together with grace? I think He is showing us His filth and corruption. Ooh, He is unforgiving and should be ignored. He is very clear in Mathew 12:31-32- "Therefore I say to you, every sin and blasphemy will be forgiven men, but the blasphemy against the Spirit will not be forgiven men. Anyone who speaks a word against the Son of Man, it will be forgiven him; but whoever speaks against the Holy Spirit, it will not be forgiven him, either in this age or in the age to come." He has made it clear that there are things you can do that He cannot try to forgive. If I forgive everything, why does He not emulate my example? He is actually preaching tea when He is greedy taking beer; how can He tell me to forgive any wrongs to my fellow humans when He is not forgiving all wrongs too? He is a hypocrite and should be avoided like a disease."

"If it was His word and book, them how comes some people doze in church yet they are not children? Just like we doze in class during lessons, these parents doze too during preaching; which means that it is the same as any other book, there is no difference. I think if it was God's word, no one would be bored with its teachings; God would be keeping all people awake to learn a lot about Himself. Yes, tis true. That should be the case. This is not from God. In fact, many people are still missing the book; there are places where people have not yet received the Bible and yet God loves them. It should not be so; He would have thrown a Bible to such people as early as He did to other people. But that can also mean love, maybe He does not want them to know their sins this early, He still wants them to enjoy sins and life of vanity. Ouch, God forgive me for trying to advise you. It seems that the person who gave us the Bible was tainting God's image, he or she was out to ruin God's reputation. Or does God inspire such confusion?"

"Ooh, yes, it's not from God. In fact, God does not have anything to do with this book. It is men's book and God doesn't know whether it exists or not. He has no idea, unless we inform Him. No, no, no, I am lost, God knows everything and is omnipresent and the only wise hence does not need our advice. I ask for forgiveness from God. Yeah, yeah, yeah, the Bible is a man's fabrication! We have so many religions in this world and who can prove that theirs is the true religion? Who can do that? Who can prove to us that their book came from heaven or God inspired them to write it down for the rest of mankind? We have Islamic, Buddhism, Christianity, Taoism, among others, and even Atheism. You mean all these have their books received from heaven as they claim? Yes, all cannot be right and contradict each other at the same time. Now I have found more evidence, that we don't have books from heaven and that God has never inspired anyone to write His word to men. All these are men's books and man-made. Who can refute that? No, no not one. If God had a book of His choice, then He would have ensured that all religions had one book; the book He had inspired to men. Otherwise, the whole thing is a fallacy! Or does He still love all equally but hide His book from them? He loves them so much that He just wants to wait and see them get lost in Hell-fire? Yes, that is love according to the Bible- God's book and word. Or maybe His love is different from what we know and understand. Then we need to understand love from His perspective. Aaah, but He has not hidden His book from other religions because all can purchase these Bibles from anywhere in the world. So, anyone can still access the Bible, hence God has made it possible for all to have it. But how shall they accept it yet even their books are inspired by the same God or are directly from Him? Who can convince them that what they possess is a lie and that the Bible carries the truth? It's not possible to do it as He has not spoken to anyone."

"In fact, He has not made it accessible to all because it is not free at all. You mean we are such fools; we buy the Bible yet it's from God? Or

God is doing business with us? Does He have a company that helps Him gather world riches? This book is never free, in fact, you visit shops and it has price-label on it. So, this is just like any other book, in terms of price and business? I think that this is just like any other business. Again, I see in the book of Revelation, He talks about torturing those that don't belong to His flock. Torturing! Torturing! How can you torture a human being? Is this the kind of God we are dealing with? God who delights in suffering of men? No, I am mistaken in believing that the Bible is from God. You mean you can torture men? No one can torture a human being because in the sight of torture, one's mind and heart are 'touched' to a point of regretting. One changes their mind and forgives; but the Revelation is talking about torturing without mercy, regret or even forgiving! What God is this who is worse than men? Then men are better by far, they are more humane than this God!"

"Leave alone such filth, look at what the Bible says and compare it with the reality. The Bible is telling me how God is caring, merciful, loving, patience and others yet human beings have been suffering without measure; whether you are saved or not. What a hell! People are suffering due to wars and insecurity, diseases, stress, famine and drought, family issues, thuggery, kidnapping, untimely and unwanted deaths, accidents and other issues. People suffer beyond the reasonable punishment. Could He be behind all these things and at the same time have the characteristics portrayed in the Bible? Aaah, yes, He is not the one but sin. Sin is doing it all. If men had no sin, then they would not be suffering. But love covers it all! His mercy, love, patience, kindness and other qualities should overcome it all. Or sin is stronger than Him. If that is the case, then we should turn to sin for help in times of need because it is stronger and powerful than Him. Or who controls who, does God control sin or sin controls Him? But how can you make and force all suffer, even those who do not know about this Bible and sin? We all lead a very hard life; whether saved or unsaved, whether Christian or not and doesn't matter you age, race or tribe. In fact, even kids or infants suffer the same fate like an adult. How can a child lack food and suffer from diseases to a point of death and then you say it's because of sins; sins the kids don't even know? Is that God? Then it must be just a book written with a sole purpose of portraying God's character negatively; because a reasoning man cannot be deceived therein. It is meant to deceive men, should be done away with! All this means that He never wrote it and never inspired the writings. Let no man deceive you."

"What about this Jesus that is insulting and reviling people anyhow? He is not disciplined at all and has no respect to men. Or does it mean that when you are above others you don't need to respect them? You do whatever pleases you? Mathew 12:33, "Brood of vipers! How can you, being evil, speak good things?..." He is calling people vipers? Telling them they are evil? No, no, I refuse that. He cannot take authority in his hands and go unpunished, never. Even in verses 45 He is saying that the generation is wicked. Who is He to judge these men? Aaaaaiiii! That is wrong!"

The school was almost to resume as there were only two weeks remaining. He had almost exhausted his mind and the Bible. He had some light of what he wanted; to dilute some darkness that was surrounding him. He continued thinking hard and trying to gather fact here and there to help make a final decision. He dedicated the whole holiday to discovering more and reasoning. "Wow, nice one, even those who write the Bible indicate that they revise it each time they are writing. Ooh, in fact, they say they find words that are not clear and hence replace or write them in brackets. Some are even accompanied by explanations at the bottom of the pages. Is that God who was not clear while writing or inspiring it? Hahahaaaa, what God is this that is confused? That is why we have so many versions of the same Bible; Revised Standard Version, American Bible, New International Version, Good News Bible, Gideon's Bible, Jerome Bible, King James Bible, Youth Bible and many more. In fact, they are named after persons and clearly indicate that they belong to such men. Consider King James Bible, who can say it's not his book? The name suggests and affirms that that Bible belongs to James and not God. See Gideon's Bible too. The Revised Standard Version concludes it all that the book is as a result of normal revision. Or they want to tell us that the Lord wrote the first version but later amended it; revised, edited, formatted and gave them a new version? Or the same God inspired wrong texts but with time He is trying to edit the wrong texts to the corrects ones? New International Version is suggesting that, there was an old version, whether international or local. Why not give us the old version instead? Even America has not been left behind, they too possess a version. What is not happening? And want to tell me that each word therein was God's word and that I should take it the way it is without question, even when it doesn't bring any sense? I think these things are making more non-sense than sense."

"Furthermore, all of them are not identical; each has a variation from the other. Some tell us that they omit the name Jehovah and replace it with the name LORD because it is very holy. So men should not know anything holy? And yet, the same God want to manifest Himself to men whom He loves beyond measure. Some say that they have Jehovah or Yahweh. Now, which is which? If either is correct, where did the other come from? Is it as a result of translation or God Himself gave them the two versions of name? Some say it is YHWH, who made it Yahweh then and if that was in Hebrew and Jehovah is in Latin and English, then these are different things. Even in some languages, the Bible has the holy name replaced with the old communities' names of their deities. So if the community called their deity Enkai, that is what you find in their Bible version; this Jehovah or Yahweh is replaced with Enkai all the time. So, the question is, was the Bible talking about Enkai, Jehovah, Yahweh, LORD or Lord? Or it depends on the community; such that if you come from the Akamba people, then the Bible was written by your former deity Mulungu, if you come from Luhya, Nyasaye gave you the Bible, if from Luo, then Were was in charge of inspiring the Bible, if from the Agikuyu, Ngai dictated and inspired men to write it and handed over to your community and so on?"

"If that was the case, then the Bible is not holy, is not from God and is confused and misleading. This is because the same Bible tells us that our ancestors worshipped Demons hence the translation of the Holy name into communities' deities' names is erroneous and misguiding. It is another deception. In 1st Corinthians 20:20, we see the message clear, "But I say that the things which the Gentiles sacrifice, they sacrifice to devils, and not to God: and I would not that ye have fellowship with devils." In other verses, it had classified us as Gentiles as long as we were not part of Israelites. And Paul was sent to preach to us as Gentiles. So, we are sure it was referring to us as Gentiles who were sacrificing to devils. The same God cannot tell you that you were worshipping Demons, then ask you to change from old ways of worship and turn to Him, and at the same time let you believe that the Bible was handed over to your tribe by those Demons. What I have in mind is that; if you come from the Agikuyu community, then the Bible classifies your deity Ngai as a demon, because you were worshipping Ngai before the Bible came. That Bible is asking you to turn to the true God who is the Lord of Israelites, YHWH/ Yahweh and Jehovah. Now, when you read the Kikuyu Bible you find names Ngai all over the verses. Does it mean that your demon Ngai has now given you the Bible, yet it is from Yahweh the true God? Who has given you that Bible and who is asking you to turn from who to who? In whichever community you come from, that is the confusion and trend but often we fail to reason and open our eyes wide to help discern the trap. Thanks to my teacher for teaching me the wisdom she has; that we could be clinging on to a lie thinking tis the truth. I wish Mrs Wanja could live long to impart the wisdom to many generations. There is no sense at all simply because all this is man's work. Is that the way God works? Pathetic! How can they be different, even a single word, yet they are from the same source and unaltered? This is a proof of how man has contaminated the message therein and given mankind something different. This is not from God and cannot be from God, unless if I am more organised and orderly than Him. I think this is a business company whose men are not ready to toil for daily bread."

"I think there is deception here. And my ancestors had a religion, who and what told and convinced them that their former religion was misplaced and wrong and that the Christianity they received is the right one, worthy of replacing the old ways of worship? If they worshipped their Master in one way or the other, who and what convinced them to discard their former ways and adopt the new one? Maybe that is why there is so much suffering? Maybe we discarded what was right and embraced what was wrong, a lie and erroneous things? Who made them believe that they moved from worse to better and not vice versa? Something is not adding up and it does not make any sense. Maybe the one they worshipped before got angry when they disregarded them and decided to punish them with such sufferings? This could be possible. We need to re-evaluate the new religion called Christianity and see whether we went wrong when we took it upon our shoulders and threw the former one into the dust-bins. Did that God talk to our old men personally and told them that their former ways and religion were dirty and hence He was offering a better and clean one? We need to find answers. The Bible is not from God, not His word, never inspired it and has no basis to help one accept it, especially if one is thinking and the mind is open and sober. One would discard it from afar."

"Again, how true is all this work in Bible? Aaah, they say that we just believe even if there are no facts and even when it is unreasonable. You just believe it the way it is, like a fool. It is taken by faith and nothing else, believing without seeing. This is where the trap lies! This is what is meant to force you to become a victim of its lie. And they expect me to believe it? Never! But they have been able to deceive many, imagine the millions who believe and take the Bible as the word of God! Many are heading in that direction without questioning it simply because it is taken by faith. What a tragedy and deception! I think the person who gave us this book wanted to give people some hope of life after death to stop them asking questions on what happens to you after you die. It has nothing else to offer. In fact, how comes that all the miracles I read from the Bible are only in the Bible and not in real life and in current generation? How comes that nowadays we don't have people resurrecting? Is it a different God, who was doing those miracles, from today's God? I have read so many miracles like raising the dead, curing the sick, feeding many, walking on water and so on. If He did all these and promised that we would do greater miracles than He did, how comes we don't see these things these days? Ooh, they say that we shall perform these miracles if and only if we believe. Does it mean that no one in this world believes? You mean that all of these billions of people I see each day are non-believers? No one has found favour in God's sight to have the power to perform the miracles? What a fallacy! Not even a single pastor, a villager, an elder or a youth, a woman or a man and not even a single sane person has believed in God? These things are pure lies. The truth is that there are many believers and many who have faith in God but the painful and bitter truth is that they believe in a lie called Bible, period!"

"Many have continued to believe in man's work, words, books and lies, thinking that they are believing in God's words and books. I thank my teacher, Wanja, for shedding the right light in my life's path. She has helped me greater than anyone else in this world so far; that most of the time we hold and cling on what is wrong, thinking that it is the solemn truth. People need to be given true wisdom and insight. We don't have long life to waste it on lies. We need the truth for the sake of making our lives better each day. And it is only a fool who would continue dwelling in lies after receiving the truth. I wish all of us would be thinking to the maximum each time we have something at our disposal. Aaah, I have remembered being taught that there are additional books accepted by the universal church, Catholic. Where did these books come from? Are they also from God Himself or did He inspire them to be written to His church? If there were some discussions on what to include in the normal Bible, how can we tell that those left to Catholic alone are not the ones that God wrote to men? There is a problem here. But who made the final decision that those sixty-six books we have today are the only ones that God intended to reach us? Who wrote the additional books accepted by Catholic like Maccabees, Judith etc? Who was able to differentiate those given by God Himself and those not given by Him? To make the matter worse, all mention God and Spirit."

"I think that all of us are the same and have the same fate. There is no difference between those who own the Bible and those who don't. We suffer the same, have the same short life; face the same challenges and calamities. You cannot differentiate between those who are worshipping God according to the Bible and those who worship in their own devised ways. In fact, those who have taken this business of selling Bibles and other church books continue to be richer each day from the revenue and profits they get. This is man's work! But I am glad that I have discovered these things before I waste my life on such a prevarication. If at all people learnt the truth and embraced it, they would be far much ahead in life. They would be determined to solve their daily problems. But now, according to this Bible, they are told to concentrate on the kingdom to come and the rest would be left to God. They have found themselves leaving any challenge to God, making the society weak and helpless. That should not be the case; people claiming that any problem is caused by God because He has good plans on us! What is that for sure? How can challenges and calamities befall you and you fail to think and fight to solve them, claiming that God would take them away at the right time and has good plans after that, on you and your generations?"

"I think we are lost fully. But one cannot realize these things if they continue to believe lies and dwell in non-sense. A person is sick but is not willing to go to hospital to meet experts for help, simply because they are clinging on what they have been made to believe; that God has allowed the disease for the sake of glorifying His name in you, and that He wants to embarrass your enemies? Which enemies is He trying to embarrass? Even when a disease invades you or an accident occurs and you suffer greatly and you finally die, He is still glorifying His name in you? What is wrong with us? Furthermore, if He is trying to embarrass your enemies, is He a God of such works and revenge? We as men value forgiving and working together without variance, then you are telling me He is embarrassing enemies. Where are the enemies from? If He loves you so much to the point of promising you everlasting life, why not help you in solving life problems that 'eat you alive' and make everyone to be your friend? People leave problems unsolved in the name of God solving them at the right time. People dying from hunger and drought; in the name of God glorifying Himself in your suffering! What God is this again, that delights in my challenges and anguish? I would like to meet Him for just few seconds. But I think God is Good, only that people are trying to malign His nature. They are trying to give the thinking person a negative image about His true nature and character. It's man's work that has brought all these sufferings."

"Look at the developed countries. They literally solve their problems and don't turn to anyone for help. They don't tell their citizens to pray to God so that He may take their famine and droughts, diseases and other calamities away, as He has promised in the Bible. They don't tell the citizens to study Bible hard and pray according to the Bible so that God would not cause insecurity, famine, earthquakes, floods etc. They believe in their efforts and making the lives of their citizens better. They come together and use their wisdom and brains to make way where there is no way. In our country, we are told to be good Christians and should always pray to God to help solve our issues. We are told to pray that He may intervene even when challenges are man-made. Our leaders cause mayhem and we are told to gather in churches and other avenues to have joint prayers for the sake of seeking this God's face to restore peace. This is not the right way! But there is still room for change as long as the truth cannot be hidden forever; it still surfaces itself in time of need and to those worth receiving and propagating it."

"This Bible is misplaced and erroneous, has no basis and only meant for fools. Turn to this name Jesus. How many Jesus do we find in the Bible? How many for sure? Several people sharing the same name 'Jesus' yet it was a name given from heaven. No, no, only an idiot can believe the Bible and take it seriously. All these books talk about Jesus Christ, Jesus Son of Man, Jesus Son of God, Jesus of Nazareth, Jesus Son of David and so on. Why are they trying to specify the Jesus they are talking about? Simple, because there are several Jesus in the Bible! And remember that the name Jesus was unique, Holy and from Heaven. Look at Luke 1:31, "And behold, thou shalt conceive in thy womb, and bring forth a son, and shalt call His name Jesus." Look at Acts 4:10-12, "Let it be known to you all, and to all the people of Israel, that by the name of Jesus Christ of Nazareth, whom you crucified, whom God raised from the dead, by Him this man stands here before you whole. ... Neither is there salvation in any other name under heaven given among men, whereby we must be saved." In these verses, first, we find the reference of the name of 'Jesus' as from Nazareth (which means there is possibility of having other Jesus from other regions). Secondly, there is clarification that the name is given under heaven and we are saved by that name or in that name (meaning there is no other name that can save except Jesus). Again we see that it was a name from the angel who is ordering Mary to call the child Jesus when he is born (meaning it is from heaven as it is angel who is bringing it). In general, there is the name Jesus, tis from heaven and we are only saved by it and in it, and the name is not unique."

"Let's turn to Colossians 4:11, "And Jesus who is called Justus. These are my only fellow workers for the kingdom of heaven who are of circumcision; they have proved to be a comfort to me." See for yourself that this is another Jesus who is working in the ministry of Jesus Christ. Turn to Mathew 27:16-17, "At that time they had a notorious prisoner, called Jesus Barabbas. So after they had gathered, Pilate said to them, 'Whom do you want me to release for you, Jesus Barabbas or Jesus who is called the Messiah?'" Here, we have encountered a new Jesus; in fact, this one is a thug, murderer and notorious prisoner. Such a guy is sharing name with this 'holy Jesus'; a name from heaven. We have seen several Jesus in the Bible and I am sure that there were many of them but these versions of Bibles are concealing most of them. There is another clarification that the Jesus who was accused before Pilate was called the Messiah. Such clarification was clear to a thinking person that the name Jesus was never unique and was on earth before this Jesus Christ came. The question is;

which name saves men, which Jesus is saving men? When we pray, which Jesus should we mention? We are told that that is the only name that saves and we should always pray in His name (…we pray this in Jesus' name, amen.), which Jesus is this? Is it Justus, the notorious thug or what? This is a mess and I can't waste my time with such non-sense. Shaitani ishindwe! (Satan be confounded). These different Bible versions have revealed a lot to me. They have brightened my life and all. I have realized the craftiness therein. The Bible is a book that should be abolished and criminalized in the world and hell, as well as in heaven."

After the holiday, his mind 'cooled down' and started concentrating on class work and school life. He was a high performing student who was feared greatly by his close competitors. He could outdo any of them with ease, even when he was not able to concentrate fully on academics. He was the only one who was questioning the teachers with a lot of wit, showed a lot of interest and curiosity in all subjects while his competitors were only interested in few subjects. They were not even asking questions in class and hence their performance was low. He had another advantage over them; he could concentrate with one thing at a time and was fully resilient. He believed in doing one thing at a time, which was wisdom of its own kind. He was not the kind of persons who could give easy time to any unprepared teacher. Teachers feared taking subjects they were not well-conversant with and were rushing for those they were well- acquainted with. They were afraid of the questions that would arise from Mwega. Anyway, this was encouraging to them too as they were assured that there was one who could understand what they taught.

Later that term, Mwega approached Mrs Wanja for some talks with her. He was ready to explain to her few things about his progress in determining the truth. "Good morning Madam? I have spent my holiday well and have gained a lot in the process of thinking, reasoning and studying thoroughly. So far, what would you say about the Bible and the theory of Darwin Charles?" "Hahahaaaa, you mean you have been struggling with these things? Before I advise you more or before I give you my opinion, tell me what you have found so far." He composed himself before he aired his findings. "Ok, let me brief you on what I found during that holiday. I went through the whole Bible trying to see any clues that could help me assess the authenticity of that book. After a lot of work and sleepless nights, I concluded that the Bible is not from God; He has not written to anybody, He has not inspired anyone to write it down and He has nothing to do with the book. In fact, I found that God is not represented in that book. The book is full of confusion and is fully contradictory. It has no meaning to even animals, leave alone mankind. It does not represent reality and should not be regarded by anyone. People believe a lie and should open their minds up to receive the truth."

He paused to signal her that he was through with the briefings. The teacher smiled and asked, "Did you discover all this by yourself or did anyone help you by giving you advice and opinions." "No, no, no Madam, I got all this by myself. I never even consulted. I only took your advice seriously that we could be dwelling in lies while thinking we are in the light. So, I thought first that I was in darkness and wanted to get the light. I even sacrificed myself and my time and other resources, simply because I wanted to liberate myself. I went to my room with several versions of Bible, went through all of them, comparing one with another and so on." "Ok, thank you. That is quite commendable and I would encourage you to keep the spirit up. Now, did you test the theory? Remember I said that both can be wrong or one is genuine while the other one is misplaced. Both shall never be true and hence you still need to work a little bit more. If you have not tested the other one, then you cannot make a final decision." "Ok Madam, but do you have any clue on where I can get facts to help me in evaluating the theory?" "Ok, so far I would encourage you to study the history books, see the evidence they are providing and continue searching for more. Never give up when searching for truth. Truth is like a tool; a tool that can be used in lifetime. It cannot become useless with time but shall be of use forever. Once you know the truth, life becomes easy because you shall never waste your efforts and resources in dealing with a falsehood. A falsehood makes life difficult and brings confusion to one's mind. The mind shall never be allowed to become unstable. It is like a computer that should never be confused with a program that is ambiguous. Once the mind is decided, it is stable and strong. It can do anything even the impossible in life. It is very powerful when it has the truth. So, never give up when searching for this tool." "Ok, I shall do that, I won't get tired. The spirit is willing and ready. Thank you so much for your guidance and encouragement." "Ok, enjoy your day and all the best in your research. Good bye."

After the term, he asked his teachers to help him with several history books. He took his notes and headed back to his grandmother's home. He did not waste many days idling around. It was only the day he arrived that went into waste. The next day, he opened the history notes and text books. He studied them carefully and keenly, mulling on every detail. He cogitated for all the days he was on holiday. After going through the history books, ideas started flowing in his mind. "So it is this simple? Darwin is explaining how we change gradually with time, how scientists have found remains in the ground of humans who were exactly like apes. These remains are actually evidence of this change that we undergo. He has given enough evidence; especially from Africa, together with other archaeologists. Even people like Leakey Mary have found so many remains! Human remains as well as tools, both wooden and stony ones, together with iron ones, and caves and houses as shelter have been discovered. What wonderful news! In fact, they don't quote miracles, believe or faith. They are giving solid evidence mixed with logic, which they are even referring us to go and witness. This man must have known what he was doing. I know he must have found it unbelievable when the Bible and religions said it was to be accepted by faith. He must have cast doubt when he was not satisfied by the explanations that the religions were offering. Therefore, he decided to search for truth and hence secured his hearts stability and tranquillity. He was really a great man, someone who does not contradict himself in any way like what the Bible is doing."

"Aaah, even Biology talks about the theory of survival for the fittest. In this theory and fact, there lies a lot of truth. That those that are not fit in an ecosystem perish while those that can adapt are fit and survive. They continue adapting and changing to stand the harsh and unconducive challenges. Eventually, they emerge stronger and better in that environment. Those that survive and adapt gain some changes that help them live comfortably even in poor conditions. I think that these are the changes that Darwin refereed to; that with time, there is a gradual change which is evolution. Wonderful! There is even more truth; that if a member of the body is not in use, it becomes rudiment. On the other hand, if it is in use, it develops fully and even gets some traits that help it adapt and function even better. Even our experiments are supporting these facts. For example; if you decide not to use the right hand when you are right-handed, the right hand becomes weak and shrinks with time. On the other hand, the left hand becomes very strong and broader, the fingers are very thick and it functions like the right hand. If you again start using both hands as before, the right hand regains its former state; it becomes thicker and stronger as before, to adapt to the work done. These are simple truths and facts that don't require faith and miracles. They don't even require rocket science to understand and observe. Everything is straight forward, even to the blind."

"If things were not changing and evolving, then, where did we come from? There are different races in this world and if God created one race and there is no evolution, where did the other races come from? If He created one race (maybe that of Europeans as many claim that Jesus was a white man), and yet we are several races in this world, where did the other races come from? Did He do another creation later or what? We must be evolving as Darwin was elaborating to us and that is why we have many races and tribes within each race. We must be changing gradually to bring forth these different varieties of men."

"Hahahaaaa, even better, the current human beings, we say that 'the beautiful ones are not yet born'. This is the reality that we all witness, that we have for example beautiful girls being born, and with time, more beautiful ones are born and so on. I am sure that those who were born like fifty years ago were not comparable with today's girls. These of today are extremely beautiful and fifty years from now, more and more beautiful ones shall be born. What is causing this change? This must be evolution, that with time, genes adapt to the environment and produce better offspring. We must be evolving for sure. I heard one student ask me how it can be that we don't find any evidence of evolution among the living. But we have evidence. Look at how we vary in terms of beauty and shape. Some among us are like typical monkeys when looked at a glance and closely. Others are intermediate while most are very beautiful and far from the face of monkeys. There are those that you cannot embrace because they are as ugly as monkeys, still among us, while there are those that look like imaginary creatures, as beautiful as flowers, and one would want to have them and embrace them forever, still among us. There is still variation among us, which is a fact that we are evolving and I believe that after like a million years to come, we shall be having very different creatures in place of men."

"Again, look at what Geography teaches us. It offers explanations on how the formation of things like mountains, valleys, ranges, rain and others occur. For example, mountains; the hot molten rocks find a path to the earth's surface and gush out like water from a tap. Later it cools and leaves a heap of these materials, becoming a mountain. We have witnessed and still witness all this because some mountains still produce this magma and the mountain continues to 'grow'; these are the still active mountains. Others are dormant and inactive. And the Bible is lying to us that these mountains were created by God from the beginning. Look at how the rain forms and waters the earth's surface. Winds come and carry moisture to greater heights, later the moisture cools and gains enough weight to fall as water. Heavy rains cause soil erosion and gullies. These gullies could be large enough to become valleys. Also, the magma flows from the point of fault outwards, and between several such flows, we have a valley. Things are very simple and observable. Things are explained in science on how they occur and form, and we witness them with time; yet the Bible is very quick to tell us that this God made them so, and we only need to believe it and take them by faith. Science does not tell you to go and have faith, believe without seeing, no, it presents solid facts and evidence. No doubts at all. Think about how the lightning and thunders occur; there are clear explanations from Physics, and no doubts. While things are being explained and facts presented, the Bible is busy explaining faith, miracles and lies. It must be man's work and fabrication."

"In fact, God as shown in the Bible is a liar and has no power to control anything; He is not merciful, loving, patient, and long-suffering and so on; He is helpless more than men. I remember how heavy rains descend and cause great sufferings and destruction through floods; all the plants and constructions that men toil to achieve for so long are swept in days by these floods. Many lose their lives and all the good soils are swept from the land. On the other hand, rains disappear for so long, causing drought and famine; the plants die and people harvest nothing even after toiling and sacrificing a lot towards these crops. Livestock die, men succumb to hunger and famine while plants die when men are longing for rain. In both cases (whether it is raining or sun-shining), men, animals and crops suffer without mercy. And you tell me that God is controlling these rains and sun? The Bible has given us the wrong picture about the whole thing. Which God would delight and glorify His name in such circumstances? What does He gain when men lose and long for help in vain? That can only be an enemy of the mankind. Man is struggling to solve problems and another force called God is dragging their efforts backwards towards mess."

"Look at how so many Christians cry unto this God; full of hope and faith, determination and living spirit, with all psyche and quoting the promises in the Bible, when offering their prayers and songs of praises and adoration, only to be disappointed and ashamed. They offer thousands of prayers in a day but only receive nothing, and when they get something after so long waiting, they claim that this God has heard their prayers and answered them. They have even gone to the extent of fabricating non-sense, that God has three answers; yes, no and wait. This is what they use to comfort themselves with when things fall apart. They are never answered but claim that this God has said no or wait because it was not right in His sight or its time is not yet full, nonsense! If He was caring and loving, why doesn't he speak to you face to face and tell you His stand on whatever you ask; if at all He was the one who promised these things in the Bible? How many times have I offered prayers since I was born and none I got a definite answer? And when I struggle to get something, idiots hover around me, telling me how God has blessed me and covered me in Jesus' blood. Telling me how God has chosen me as His instrument of glory! Telling me how God has decided to confound my enemies. This is pure nonsense!"

"Some people seek the powers of the witches and such people. A person is bewitched and suffers for the rest of their lives. You see a person's efforts being sabotaged through witchcraft and their lives become useless. Later, these persons die in pain and what do we hear from the religious men and women? That God has done His will and has glorified His name. Which human being would be happy over such things? Not even one, leave alone the God represented in the Bible as wise, loving and such trash. We need to wake up from our sleep; we need to see around us to help make better decisions. We don't need a book that is sabotaging our ability, talents and wisdom, in the name of Holy Book from God Himself. I have realized that actually, Charles Darwin wanted and was willing to open the clogged minds of men, he was after enlightening us so that we could see beyond the bush, which is the Bible. He must be the living genius of his time. In fact, we better have him as our deity rather than that God of the Bible. He is far much better than what the Bible offers. He is busy offering sense and logic to us when the Bible is busy giving us garbage and darkness."

After finalizing on his research, the school was one week away from opening date. He composed himself to cascade his thoughts for the sake of briefing Wanja when they were to meet in school. He looked very joyous throughout the week until his grandfather, in the middle of the week, asked him what the reason could be. He gave him a summary on his findings. The grandfather was shocked and called his grandmother in the table-room. The grandfather asked him to repeat what he had explained to him in the presence of his grandmother. He hesitated but was threatened. He immediately explained to the two in fear. The two screamed to the top of their voices after hearing such a 'kid' demeaning God and uplifting and honouring man. Villagers came at a neck-breaking speed to answer the call from the family. The ululations were so loud that many thought they had been attacked while others thought there was a thug who had rapped the grandmother, which was at high-rise in the village in those days. They were fully armed with swords, knives, spears, arrows and bows. They really wanted to eliminate the culprit by lynching him in broad daylight. The grandfather could not stop howling. Villagers got to the room and found the three persons. The two old parents were screaming the same words concurrently, "Uuuuuuiiii, he is mad, uuuuuuiiii, he is mad!" People got confused when they heard all this with the two pointing at Mwega who was standing at the corner of the room. He was shivering. His whole body was trembling to the point of being unable to alter even a single word.

The grandfather told all the villagers to listen to what Mwega was to narrate in the presence of all. They kept quiet and waited eagerly to what Mwega had to offer that had made his grandparents howl and break into tears. He ordered Mwega to say what he had said to them in front of the whole village. He shed tears and murmured words that no one could hear. He was forced to be audible and that is when he decided to present his thoughts to the villagers. He explained to them in a clear voice and in more details than he had done it before. The villagers got confused while some wanted to lynch him in the same room in front of the grandparents.

They declared him insane and lost. They cursed him in accord and sent two men to call his parents. The two left the room, running like young boys. They considered the message urgent and also wanted the parents to be witnesses before Mwega was executed. The crowd was extremely angry and thirsty to shed 'the guilty blood'. They could not believe how such a mere young man could disgrace God who has the power over everything in this world and in heaven. They also blamed him for his reckless statements and blasphemy; when he exalted man, Darwin, above God. They reached a consensus to tie him on the door-post because it was too risky to have a mad man free. A mad man could harm anyone without notice.

Within a very short time, the parents arrived, sweating profusely. They had been briefed by the men, who called them, on the whole thing. Their anger was beyond measure. The father was the first one to speak, "You bastard, how dare you to attract a curse from heaven to our family? Who has bewitched you and died? What are you telling these people? Are you greater than your parents, grandparents, ancestors, spirits and God Himself? You should die today and not tomorrow. The disgrace you have brought to us is beyond measure. You can no longer live with us. You are mad and your mind is already rotted. Let's kill him now!" Many lifted their swords high in the air ready to thrash and dismember him like grass. But before they could land their tools on him, one old man stopped them, "Stop it! Listen to me my people. Pay attention to what I have to say. Let us not shed blood of our son, whether he is mad or not, whether innocent or guilty, whether blasphemous or not, and whether he is cursed or blessed, lest we curse ourselves in the process. We are men of peace and we have been avoiding curses in many ways. Remember how we killed a young man who had rapped his daughter and the consequences we got afterwards. No one has forgotten all these as it is only twenty years down the line. Remember how our land was cursed and was no longer productive, how diseases devoured our men and children, the drought that resulted and left thousands residing in graves and such terrible calamities as we had not witnessed before." Before he went on, everyone withdrew their swords and faced down on the floor. They became more keen and alert.

He continued, "We cannot afford to go back to such a mess. We tried to offer sacrifices but all was in vain. It was one big blow that has left us weak for so many years. I think he only expressed his mind and that is not a good ground to help us do away with him. In any community, we must have few persons who are different from the rest. When we are pushing to the right, there are those few pushing to the left, when we sleep, few are awake, when we bless, few curse, when we are hungry, few are full, and consequently, when we call upon God, few don't waste their time on that. But we have never done away with such few people by killing them. Sometimes we chase them out of the community if their acts hurt others. Let us allow the independence of the mind. Look at what a judge does; people are brought in his court, he listens to all and has never sentenced an innocent man on the ground of his ideas and stand. Again, he has never set a guilty person free on the grounds of their mind, ideas and stand. Look at our government; it accommodates all, wise and unwise, religious and unreligious, without considering race, tribe origin, status and so on. The president when elected to office has never surrounded himself with his tribe only, or his region, or his fellow men; no, he combines Muslims with Christians, atheists are also in his offices, men from different tribes, races, marital status, social status and many other factors. We cannot be identical at all, never."

"I would be against any form of killing, be it justified or not, be it wrong or right, that is not the solution to those who don't walk with us. I would prefer we take him to a mental hospital and the doctor can help confirm his madness, then we send him away from our community. There are pros in testing whether a person is mentally retarded or fit to live freely among other men. Why don't we go that way?" All shouted, "Yes, let's do as you have said. Your wisdom has saved him from grave." Few men untied Mwega from the door-post and led him to the hospital. All men followed them from a distance up to the hospital gate. They waited from without the gate while the two men took him inside. They explained to the doctor all that had happened and he promised to remain with Mwega for few hours of thorough testing. He then asked them to leave and go back to the hospital, the next day, for the results. They left and spread gossips all over the region, beyond their village, on what the 'mad Mwega' had explained to them that day. They were discussing him in anger and bitterness. Their parents were accused too by the village elders for bringing up a mad child secretly until he was a grown up. They informed them that they would have sliced them to death too had they done so to Mwega.

They were found guilty of concealing such vital information to the elders. They tried to defend themselves but all was in vain. They were told that no one could bring a normal child up and he or she turns insane when already a grown up.

In the hospital, Mwega explained to the doctor all about his ideas, thoughts, and findings. The doctor examined him thoroughly again and again but found Mwega almost a genius rather than a mad man. He wrote a report on his findings and handed Mwega over to another doctor. The second doctor did his testing and also listened to him about what had caused the accusations of madness. He found Mwega normal, sane and recommended him as one of those with a mind almost to that of a genius. The two reports were combined and a comprehensive report was prepared. The next day, all the villagers went to the hospital and those from the neighbouring villages accompanied them too. The two doctors who worked on Mwega called them for a brief meeting. They explained to them in details on how Mwega was like a genius and that he was one of those people that the government and companies were interested in employing. They promised the villagers that they would ensure that Mwega studied medicine, and they would scramble for his skills in the referral hospitals. They also said that after his studies in medicine, they would recommend him to be the president's personal doctor. They assured them that he would make it in life, irrespective of what he would study in school. They later dismissed them and went back to attend to the patients.

The villagers were not happy but the parents were overwhelmed by the doctors' reports. They praised their child for being a genius and proving it to all. When they went back home, the elders convened a short meeting to discuss over the matter. They concluded that Mwega had colluded with the doctors to avoid their curses. They agreed to curse and evict the whole of his family out of their region, never to come back, if the parents did not send Mwega away. The word reached the family and they decided to help Mwega. At the beginning of the following week, the school opened and Mwega met Wanja. He explained briefly on what had taken place during the whole of that holiday. She was overwhelmed by his efforts but promised to discuss with him later about the whole issue. When they met the next day, they went into solitude and discussed a lot. They never disclosed their discussions and it has never been known what they concluded up to date.

The following week, he approached Mr Munene and had a word with him. He informed him of his calamities back at home, and he offered to home him for many years, till he was successful in life to be on his own compound. The joy that ensured from Munene's offer was so great that Mwega shed tears of joy.

He later informed his parents who helped him move with Mr Munene. They went and Mwega met Munene's sons who welcomed him warmly in their home. They became great friends and used to call Mwega 'Genius' rather than by his name, just as a joke and nickname. Mwega was able to concentrate on his class work for the rest of his years in school. He was ever portraying traits of a genius in every aspect. After form four in secondary school, he passed the examinations so well and with ease that the news spread to the villages and beyond. The elders from his village could not believe what they were hearing about the 'mad man' they sent out of their village. They were ashamed and some became enemies to each other over the issue of evicting a genius out of their vicinity. The doctors also heard the news and went to advise him on the course he was suited best to study in university. They sent a letter to the president requesting him to cater for his school fee and all expenses. The president did not hesitate as he knew that, when the ministry of health in conjunction with the doctors asked him to pay Mwega's expenses, they were up to nurturing the best doctor ever to become his personal doctor. He paid his fee and all expenses in advance and promised to help him more and more in furthering his studies until he became what he wanted to be in life. He also promised to help his family throughout their lives.

Later on, the parents got the promises of the president fulfilled. They were relocated and had a big house built for them on an extremely vast piece of land. They received livestock in plenty, workers and security personnel, few cars and a petro-station in their compound, and their bank accounts never got 'dry'. They enjoyed life as kings; courtesy of the 'mad man' they had 'brought up secretly'. Mwega studied hard in college and even discovered a cure of a deadly disease that had been a ménage to the citizens; both small and great, rich and poor. The news spread all over the world and even foreign countries gave him awards for his discovery. He achieved all this while still a student. He entered the Guinness world book of records as the first student to discover a curative drug. After his success in school, he was immediately absorbed as one of the experts in health sector, being in the department of the president's health. He showcased his prowess in maintaining the president's health and was made the chief doctor in that department and in the whole country. They all recognized him as a distinguished doctor in the world; he was able to detect diseases and infirmities that other doctors could not, including those that had experience for over forty years. He was again added in the Guinness world book of records for being the youngest doctor to become the chief doctor in any nation, and for becoming the youngest billionaire through employment. He became great and the last time the village elders heard about him, he was being recommended to be the next president in their nation after the current president had retired. The village elders could not believe it. They cursed themselves and two of them were reported to have committed suicide after too much guilt overcame them for chasing 'the mad man' out of their village.

Printed in the United States
By Bookmasters